TERRORISM, HOT SPOTS AND CONFLICT-RELATED ISSUES

TERRORISTS, ENEMY COMBATANT DETAINEES AND THE JUDICIAL SYSTEM

TERRORISM, HOT SPOTS AND CONFLICT-RELATED ISSUES

Additional books in this series can be found on Nova's website
under the Series tab.

Additional E-books in this series can be found on Nova's website
under the E-books tab.

TERRORISM, HOT SPOTS AND CONFLICT-RELATED ISSUES

TERRORISTS, ENEMY COMBATANT DETAINEES AND THE JUDICIAL SYSTEM

JIAN SUN
AND
MIGUEL MASIPAG
EDITORS

Nova Science Publishers, Inc.
New York

For permission to use material from this book please contact us:
Telephone 631-231-7269; Fax 631-231-8175
Web Site: http://www.novapublishers.com

Library of Congress Cataloging-in-Publication Data

Terrorists, enemy combatant detainees and the judicial system / editors, Jian Sun and Miguel Masipag.
p. cm.
Includes index.
CRS report for Congress prepared for members and committees of Congress.
ISBN 978-1-61470-391-4 (hardcover)
1. Terrorism--Prevention--Law and legislation--United States. 2. Detention of persons--United States. 3. Terrorists--Legal status, laws, etc.--United States. 4. Combatants and noncombatants (International law) I. Sun, Jian. II. Masipag, Miguel.
KF9430.T475 2011
344.7305'32517--dc23
2011024323

Published by Nova Science Publishers, Inc. † New York

CONTENTS

PREFACE

As part of the conflict with Al Qaeda and the Taliban, the United States has captured and detained numerous persons believed to have been part of or associated with enemy forces. Over the years, federal courts have considered a multitude of petitions by or on behalf of suspected belligerents challenging aspects of U.S. detention policy. Although the Supreme Court has issued definitive rulings concerning several legal issues raised in the conflict with Al Qaeda and the Taliban, many others remain unresolved, with some the subject of ongoing litigation. This book discusses major judicial opinions concerning suspected enemy belligerents detained in the conflict with Al Qaeda and the Taliban and addresses all Supreme Court decisions concerning enemy combatants and notable circuit court opinions concerning issues of ongoing relevance to the U.S. detention policy.

Chapter 1- As part of the conflict with Al Qaeda and the Taliban, the United States has captured and detained numerous persons believed to have been part of or associated with enemy forces. Over the years, federal courts have considered a multitude of petitions by or on behalf of suspected belligerents challenging aspects of U.S. detention policy. Although the Supreme Court has issued definitive rulings concerning several legal issues raised in the conflict with Al Qaeda and the Taliban, many others remain unresolved, with some the subject of ongoing litigation.

Chapter 2- After the Supreme Court held that federal courts have jurisdiction under the federal *habeas corpus* statute to hear legal challenges on behalf of persons detained at the U.S. Naval Station in Guantanamo Bay, Cuba, in connection with the conflict against Al Qaeda and associated groups (*Rasul v. Bush*), the Pentagon established administrative hearings, called "Combatant Status Review Tribunals" (CSRTs), to allow the detainees to contest their status as enemy combatants, and informed them of their right to pursue *habeas* relief in federal court. Lawyers subsequently filed dozens of petitions on behalf of the detainees in the District Court for the District of Columbia, where district court judges reached inconsistent conclusions as to whether the detainees have any enforceable rights to challenge their treatment and detention.

Chapter 3- The sections use a common definition for the term "material support or resources:" any service or tangible or intangible property. The Supreme Court recently held that the forms of material support in the challenge before it were not unconstitutionally vague nor was their proscription inconsistent with the First Amendment's freedom of speech and freedom of association requirements. Violations of either section are punishable by imprisonment for not more than 15 years. Although neither section creates a civil cause of action for victims, treble damages and attorneys fees may be available for some victims under 18 U.S.C. 2333. Section 2339B has two extraterritorial jurisdiction provisions. One is general (there is extraterritorial jurisdiction over an offense under this section) and the other descriptive (there is extraterritorial jurisdiction over an offender under this section if the offender is a U.S. national, etc.). Section 2339A has no such provisions, but is likely applicable at a minimum when an offender or victim is a U.S. national; the offense has an impact in the United States; the offense is committed against U.S. national interests; or the offense is universally condemned.

Chapter 4- Federal authorities can and have prosecuted terrorist attacks on commercial airlines under a wide variety of federal statutes. Some of those statutes outlaw crimes committed aboard a commercial airliner; some, crimes committed against the aircraft itself; others, crimes involving the use of firearms or explosives; still others, crimes committed for terrorist purposes. Within each category, the law reaches co-conspirators and other accomplices. Moreover, although most apply when committed within the United States, many apply to terrorist attacks overseas, particularly but necessarily, when the victims are Americans or U.S. airlines.

Chapter 5- The Fifth Amendment to the United States Constitution provides in part that "No person ... shall be compelled in any criminal case to be a witness against himself, nor be deprived of life, liberty, or property, without due process of law." In *Miranda v. Arizona*, the Supreme Court declared that statements of an accused, given during a custodial interrogation, could not be introduced in evidence in criminal proceedings against him, unless he were first advised of his rights and waived them. In *Dickerson v. United States*, the Court held that the *Miranda* exclusionary rule was constitutionally grounded and could not be replaced by a statutory provision making all voluntary confessions admissible. In *New York v. Quarles*, the Court recognized a "limited" "public safety" exception to *Miranda*, but has not defined the exception further. The lower federal courts have construed the exception narrowly in cases involving unwarned statements concerning the location of a weapon possibly at hand at the time of an arrest.

In: Terrorists, Enemy Combatant Detainees …
Editors: Jian Sun and Miguel Masipag ISBN: 978-1-61470-391-4

Chapter 1

JUDICIAL ACTIVITY CONCERNING ENEMY COMBATANT DETAINEES: MAJOR COURT RULINGS*

Jennifer K. Elsea and Michael John Garcia

SUMMARY

As part of the conflict with Al Qaeda and the Taliban, the United States has captured and detained numerous persons believed to have been part of or associated with enemy forces. Over the years, federal courts have considered a multitude of petitions by or on behalf of suspected belligerents challenging aspects of U.S. detention policy. Although the Supreme Court has issued definitive rulings concerning several legal issues raised in the conflict with Al Qaeda and the Taliban, many others remain unresolved, with some the subject of ongoing litigation.

This report discusses major judicial opinions concerning suspected enemy belligerents detained in the conflict with Al Qaeda and the Taliban. The report addresses all Supreme Court decisions concerning enemy combatants. It also discusses notable circuit court opinions addressing issues of ongoing relevance to U.S. detention policy. The report also summarizes a few notable decisions by federal district courts, which have addressed whether the executive may lawfully detain only persons who are "part of" Al Qaeda, the Taliban, and affiliated groups, or also those who provide a sufficient degree of support to such entities in their hostilities against the United States and its allies; adopted a functional approach for assessing whether a person is "part of" Al Qaeda; decided that a preponderance of evidence standard is appropriate for detainee habeas cases, but suggested that a lower standard might be constitutionally permissible, and instructed courts to assess the cumulative weight of evidence rather than each piece of evidence in isolation; determined that Guantanamo detainees have a limited right to challenge their proposed transfer to the custody of a foreign government, but denied courts the authority to order detainees released into the United States; and held that the constitutional writ of habeas does not presently extend to noncitizen detainees held at U.S.-operated facilities in Afghanistan. Finally, the report discusses several criminal cases involving persons who were either involved in the 9/11 attacks (Zacarias Moussaoui) or were captured abroad by

* This is an edited, reformatted and augmented version of a Congressional Research Service publication, CRS Report for Congress R41156, from www.crs.gov, dated March 29, 2011.

U.S. forces or allies during operations against Al Qaeda, the Taliban, and associated entities (John Walker Lindh and Ahmed Ghailani).

INTRODUCTION

As part of the conflict with the Taliban and Al Qaeda, the United States has captured and detained numerous persons believed to have been part of or associated with enemy forces. Over the years, federal courts have considered a multitude of petitions by or on behalf of suspected belligerents challenging aspects of U.S. detention policy. The Supreme Court has issued definitive rulings concerning several legal issues raised in the conflict with Al Qaeda and the Taliban, including executive authority under the 2001 Authorization to Use Military Force (AUMF; P.L. 107-40) to detain properly designated enemy belligerents captured on the Afghan battlefield; the application of at least some provisions of the 1949 Geneva Conventions to the conflict with Al Qaeda; and the ability of detainees held in the United States or at the U.S. Naval Station in Guantanamo Bay, Cuba, to challenge the legality of their detention in habeas corpus proceedings. However, many other issues remain the subject of ongoing litigation, including the full scope of the executive's detention authority; the degree to which noncitizens held at Guantanamo and other locations outside the United States are entitled to protections under the Constitution; the authority of federal habeas courts to compel the release of detainees determined to be unlawfully held into the United States if the executive cannot effectuate their release to another country; and the ability of detainees to receive advance notice and challenge their proposed transfer to a foreign country.

This report briefly summarizes major judicial opinions concerning suspected enemy belligerents[1] detained in the conflict with Al Qaeda and the Taliban. It discusses all Supreme Court decisions concerning enemy combatants. It also addresses notable circuit court opinions addressing issues of ongoing relevance to U.S. detention policy. The report also discusses a few notable decisions by federal district courts, including criminal cases involving persons who were either involved in the 9/11 attacks or were captured abroad by U.S. forces or allies during operations against Al Qaeda and the Taliban.

SUPREME COURT DECISIONS

Since 2004, the Supreme Court has made several rulings concerning enemy combatants. These have addressed, *inter alia*, the executive's authority to detain enemy belligerents under the 2001 AUMF; the legality of military commissions established by presidential order to try suspected belligerents for violations of the law of war; and detainees' access to federal courts.

Hamdi v. Rumsfeld, 542 U.S. 507 (2004)[2]

The *Hamdi* case addressed the President's authority to detain "enemy combatants" as part of the conflict authorized by the AUMF, and whether a detained individual could seek independent review of the legality of his detention. Four separate opinions were written, with none receiving support of a majority of the justices. However, a majority of the Court recognized that, as a necessary incident to the 2001 AUMF, the President is authorized to detain persons captured while fighting U.S. forces in Afghanistan (including U.S. citizens), and potentially hold such persons for the duration of the conflict to prevent their return to hostilities.[3] A divided Court found that persons deemed "enemy combatants" have the right to challenge the legality of their detention before a judge or other "neutral decision-maker," with a majority clearly recognizing the existence of such a right in the case of a detained U.S. citizen.[4] In a plurality opinion joined by three other Justices, Justice O'Connor wrote that a citizen detained as an enemy combatant must receive notice of the factual basis for his classification and a fair opportunity to rebut the government's factual assertions before a neutral decision-maker, and has a right to counsel in connection with such a hearing. The plurality suggested, however, that the exigencies of the circumstances of a detainee's capture may allow for a tailoring of enemy combatant proceedings "to alleviate their uncommon potential to burden the Executive at a time of ongoing military conflict," possibly allowing hearsay evidence and "a presumption in favor of the Government's evidence," as long as a fair opportunity to rebut such evidence is provided.[5]

Rumsfeld v. Padilla, 542 U.S. 426 (2004)[6]

The *Padilla* case, decided on the same day as *Hamdi*, concerned a habeas challenge by Jose Padilla, a U.S. citizen being held on U.S. soil as an "enemy combatant." Unlike Hamdi, however, Padilla was captured on U.S. soil, where he was declared an "enemy combatant" and militarily detained for his alleged involvement in an Al Qaeda plot to detonate a "dirty bomb." In a 5-4 ruling, the Court remanded the case without deciding the merits on the ground that Padilla's habeas petition had not been filed in the proper venue. In doing so, the majority did not reach the merits of Padilla's claim that any authority the President might have under the AUMF to detain "enemy combatants" did not extend to persons captured on American soil and away from the Afghan battlefield. Four Justices would have found jurisdiction based on the "exceptional circumstances" of the case and affirmed the holding below that detention is prohibited under the Non-Detention Act, 18 U.S.C. § 4001(a) (prohibiting the detention of U.S. citizens unless authorized by an act of Congress). Padilla filed a new petition in the Fourth Circuit, and the appellate court considered the legality of his detention in *Padilla v. Haft*, discussed *infra*.

Rasul v. Bush, 542 U.S. 466 (2004)[7]

In *Rasul v. Bush*, the Court held in a 6-3 ruling that the federal habeas *corpus* statute, 28 U.S.C. § 2241, provided federal courts with jurisdiction to consider habeas corpus petitions by or on behalf of persons detained at the U.S. Naval Station in Guantanamo Bay, Cuba. Having found that Guantanamo detainees were entitled by statute to seek habeas review of their detention, the Court did not reach the issue of whether the constitutional writ of habeas also extended to noncitizens held at Guantanamo. Congress subsequently attempted to limit the reach of the federal habeas statute to Guantanamo detainees through the enactment of the Detainee Treatment Act of 2005 (DTA)[8] and the Military Commissions Act of 2006 (MCA).[9]

Hamdan v. Rumsfeld, 548 U.S. 557 (2006)[10]

In *Hamdan v. Rumsfeld*, the Supreme Court reviewed the validity of military tribunals established pursuant to presidential order to try suspected terrorists for violations of the law of war. The petitioner Hamdan was charged with conspiracy to commit a violation of the law of war. Prior to reaching the merits of the case, the *Hamdan* Court first had to determine whether the DTA stripped it of jurisdiction to review habeas corpus challenges by or on behalf of Guantanamo detainees whose petitions had already been filed prior to enactment of the DTA. In a 5-3 opinion, the Court held that the DTA did not apply to such petitions. Turning to the merits of the case, the majority held that the convened tribunals did not comply with the Uniform Code of Military Justice (UCMJ) or the law of war, as incorporated in the UCMJ and embodied in the 1949 Geneva Conventions, which the Court held applicable to the armed conflict with Al Qaeda. The Court held that, at a minimum, Common Article 3 of the Geneva Conventions applies to persons captured in the conflict with Al Qaeda, according to them a minimum baseline of protections, including protection from the "passing of sentences and the carrying out of executions without previous judgment pronounced by a regularly constituted court, affording all the judicial guarantees which are recognized as indispensable by civilized peoples." The Court held that military commissions were not "regularly constituted" because they deviated too far from the rules that apply to courts-martial, without a satisfactory explanation of the need for departing from such rules. In particular, the Court noted that the commission rules allowing the exclusion of the defendant from attending portions of his trial or hearing some of the evidence against him deviated substantially from court-martial procedures.

A four-justice plurality of the Court also recognized that for an act to be triable under the common law of war, the precedent for it being treated as an offense must be "plain and unambiguous."[11] After examining the history of military commission practice in the United States and internationally, the plurality further concluded that conspiracy to violate the law of war was not in itself a crime under the common law of war or the UCMJ.

Boumediene v. Bush, 553 U.S. 723 (2008)[12]

In the aftermath of the *Hamdan* decision, Congress enacted the Military Commissions Act of 2006 (MCA), which, *inter alia*, expressly eliminated court jurisdiction over all pending and future causes of action other than the limited review permitted under the DTA. In the 2008 case of *Boumediene v. Bush*, the Court ruled in a 5-4 opinion that the constitutional privilege of habeas extends to Guantanamo detainees. In doing so, the Court stated that the Constitution's extraterritorial application turns on "objective factors and practical concerns."[13] The Court deemed at least three factors to be relevant in assessing the extraterritorial scope of the constitutional writ of habeas: (1) the citizenship and status of the detainee and the adequacy of the status determination process; (2) the nature of the site where the person is seized and detained; and (3) practical obstacles inherent in resolving the prisoner's entitlement to the writ.

The Court also found that MCA § 7, which limited judicial review of executive determinations of the *Boumediene* petitioners' enemy combatant status to that authorized by the DTA, did not provide an adequate habeas substitute and therefore acted as an unconstitutional suspension of the writ of habeas corpus. The majority listed a number of potential constitutional infirmities in the DTA review process, including the absence of provisions (1) empowering a reviewing court to order the release of a detainee found to be unlawfully held; (2) permitting petitioners to challenge the President's authority to detain them indefinitely; (3) enabling a presiding court to review or correct administrative findings of fact which formed the legal basis for an individual's detention; and (4) permitting the detainee to present exculpatory evidence discovered after the conclusion of administrative proceedings.

Although the *Boumediene* Court held that the constitutional writ of habeas extends to noncitizens held at Guantanamo, it did not opine as to the scope of habeas review available to detainees, the remedy available for those persons found to be unlawfully held by the United States, and the extent to which other constitutional provisions extend to noncitizens held at Guantanamo and elsewhere.

Gates v. Bismullah, 128 S.Ct. 2960 (2008) (Mem.)

Prior to the Supreme Court's decision in *Boumediene*, the D.C. Circuit Court of Appeals considered a number of challenges brought under the DTA in which detainees contested determinations by Combatant Status Review Tribunals (CSRTs) that they were properly detained as enemy combatants. In 2008, the government petitioned the Supreme Court to review two rulings by the D.C. Circuit regarding the scope of judicial review of CSRT determinations.[14] The Supreme Court granted certiorari and vacated the appellate court's decisions, remanding for reconsideration in light of the Supreme Court's decision in *Boumediene*. Upon remand, the D.C. Circuit reinstated without explanation its decisions, presumably because it did not find the *Boumediene* ruling to conflict with its decisions in these cases.

al-Marri v. Spagone, 129 S.Ct. 1545 (2009)

In December 2008, the Supreme Court granted certiorari to review an *en banc* ruling by the Fourth Circuit Court of Appeals regarding petitioner al-Marri, a lawful alien resident who had been arrested in the United States and thereafter detained as an enemy combatant. At the time, the Court's decision to review the Fourth Circuit's ruling was thought to have potentially set the stage for a definitive pronouncement regarding the President's authority to militarily detain terrorist suspects apprehended away from the Afghan battlefield. However, before the Court could consider the merits of the case, the government requested that the Court authorize al-Marri's release from military custody and transfer to civilian authorities to face criminal charges. The Court granted the government's request, vacated the appellate court's earlier judgment, and transferred the case back to the lower court with orders to dismiss it as moot. The appellate court's ruling is discussed in more detail below.

Kiyemba v. Obama, 130 S.Ct. 1235 (2010)

In October 2009, the Supreme Court agreed to review a ruling by a three-judge panel of the D.C. Circuit Court of Appeals in the case of *Kiyemba v. Obama*, discussed *infra*. The *Kiyemba* case involved several Guantanamo detainees who, despite no longer being considered enemy combatants and having been cleared for release, had not been transferred from Guantanamo on account of the government being unable to effectuate their release to a foreign country. The *Kiyemba* petitioners sought reversal of a D.C. Circuit ruling finding that a federal habeas court lacked the authority to compel the executive to release the detainees into the United States. Following the Supreme Court's grant of certiorari, however, several *Kiyemba* petitioners were resettled in foreign countries, and the United States was able to find countries willing to settle the remaining petitioners, although five petitioners rejected these countries' offers for resettlement. On March 1, 2010, the Supreme Court vacated the appellate court's opinion and remanded the case in light of these developments. Because the Supreme Court had granted certiorari on the understanding that no remedy was available for the petitioners other than release into the United States, it returned the case to the D.C. Circuit to review the ramifications of the new circumstances. Discussion of subsequent action taken by the D.C. Circuit is found below.

RULINGS BY THE D.C. CIRCUIT COURT OF APPEALS

Most judicial activity concerning U.S. detention policy in the conflict with Al Qaeda has occurred within the D.C. Circuit. Following the Supreme Court's ruling in *Boumediene* that the constitutional writ of habeas corpus extends to detainees held at Guantanamo, over 200 habeas petitions were filed by detainees in the U.S. District Court for the District of Columbia. District courts considering habeas claims have sometimes reached differing conclusions regarding the scope of the executive's detention authority; the admissibility of hearsay evidence and involuntary statements by made detainees; the appropriate methodology for assessing the sufficiency and reliability of evidence proffered by the government to justify the legality of a habeas petitioner's detention; and the remedy available for those persons whom a habeas court determines to have been unlawfully detained.[15] Some of these rulings have subsequently been reviewed by the D.C. Circuit Court of Appeals. Since 2009, the appellate court has issued rulings concluding that, among other things:

- the executive may lawfully detain persons who are "part of" Al Qaeda, the Taliban, and affiliated groups, and possibly also persons who provide a sufficient degree of support to such entities in their hostilities against the United States and its allies (*Al-Bihani v. Obama*);
- a functional approach is appropriate when assessing whether a person is "part of" Al Qaeda, meaning that judges should consider the significance of a person's activities in relation to the organization, rather than requiring formal proof of membership, such as evidence the petitioner received orders from the organization's hierarchy (*Awad v. Obama*, *Bensayah v. Obama*, *Salahi v. Obama*);

- the government may satisfy its evidentiary burden in support of a person's detention when its factual claims are supported by a preponderance of evidence (*Al-Bihani v. Obama*, *Al Odah v. United States*), but a lower standard might be constitutionally permissible (*Al-Adahi v. Obama*);
- it is proper for a habeas court to assess the cumulative weight and effect of proffered evidence according to a "conditional probability analysis" when determining whether the government has demonstrated factual grounds for detaining a habeas petitioner (*Al-Adahi v. Obama*, *Salahi v. Obama*);
- the writ of habeas affords Guantanamo detainees with a limited right to challenge their proposed transfer to the custody of a foreign government (*Kiyemba II*);
- habeas courts lack authority, absent an authorizing statute, to compel the executive to release non-citizen detainees into the United States, even if such persons have been determined by the court to be unlawfully detained (*Kiyemba I* and *III*); and
- the constitutional writ of habeas does not presently extend to noncitizen detainees held at U.S.-operated facilities in Afghanistan (*Maqaleh v. Gates*).

In some of these cases, affected detainees have requested Supreme Court review. A few of these requests have been denied, but other requests remain pending on the docket awaiting grant or denial of certiorari.

The following section discusses major rulings made by the D.C. Circuit Court of Appeals regarding persons designated as enemy combatants that involve matters of continuing relevance to U.S. detention policy. It does not discuss those rulings that were subsequently overruled by the Supreme Court on the merits.

Scope of Executive's Detention Authority and Related Evidentiary Burdens

The D.C. Circuit has issued several opinions relating to the scope of the executive's authority to detain persons as part of the conflict with Al Qaeda, the Taliban, and affiliated organizations. These opinions have also addressed the issues related to the sufficiency and reliability of evidence proffered by the government in support of its factual claims.

Al-Bihani V. Obama, 590 F.3d 866, En Banc Rehearing Denied, 619 F.3d 1 (D.C. Cir. 2010)

In January 2010, a three-judge panel of the D.C. Circuit Court of Appeals issued a ruling concerning the scope of the government's detention authority under the AUMF in the case of *Al-Bihani v. Obama*. In an opinion supported in full by two members of the panel,[16] the appellate court recognized that, at a minimum, the President was authorized to detain persons who were subject to the jurisdiction of military commissions established pursuant to the Military Commissions Acts of 2006 and 2009; namely, any person who was "part of forces associated with Al Qaeda or the Taliban," along with "those who purposefully and materially support such forces in hostilities against U.S. Coalition partners."[17] While the panel concluded that either purposeful and material support for an AUMF-targeted organization in hostilities against the United States or membership in such an organization may be independently sufficient to justify detention, the court declined "to explore the outer bounds of what constitutes sufficient support or indicia of membership to meet the detention standard." It did, however, note that this standard would permit the detention of a "civilian contractor" who "purposefully and materially supported" an AUMFtargeted organization through "traditional food operations essential to a fighting force and the carrying of arms."[18] Notwithstanding the government's reliance on the law of war to interpret the scope of the AUMF and arguably in conflict with Supreme Court discussion of the issue in *Hamdi*, the panel rejected the idea that the international law of war has any relevance to the courts' interpretation of the scope of the detention power conferred by the AUMF.

The panel also held that the procedural protections afforded in habeas cases involving wartime detainees do not need to mirror those provided to persons in the traditional criminal law context, where evidence must demonstrate guilt beyond reasonable doubt. The government need only support its authority to detain using a "preponderance of evidence" standard.[19] The panel also held that habeas courts assessing the validity of a petitioner's detention may properly consider hearsay evidence proffered by the government.

The D.C. Circuit Court of Appeals thereafter denied a petition for an *en banc* rehearing of the *AlBihani* case. However, a concurring opinion joined by a majority of the active appellate court judges characterized certain aspects of the panel's decision, concerning the application of international law of war principles in interpreting the AUMF, to be non-binding dicta.[20] It did not address whether any portions of the *Al-Bihani* ruling concerning the lawfulness of detaining persons on account of membership or support for Al Qaeda, the Taliban, or associated forces also constituted non-binding dicta. While it has been recognized in subsequent circuit rulings that *AlBihani* establishes, at a minimum, that the executive may lawfully detain persons who are "part of" organizations targeted under the AUMF, there is some ambiguity as to whether its conclusion that persons may also be lawfully detained on account of providing support to such entities is binding precedent or merely dicta.[21] In subsequent habeas litigation involving Guantanamo detainees, the Obama Administration has not argued that a particular habeas petitioner is not "part of" Al Qaeda or the Taliban, but nonetheless may be lawfully detained on account of providing support to such groups. Instead, its legal justification for holding persons on account of wartime activity has been on the grounds that such persons were "part of" Al Qaeda, the Taliban, or associated forces at time of capture.

A petition has been filed with the Supreme Court seeking review of the circuit decision, but the Court has yet to rule on whether to grant certiorari.

Al-Adahi v. Obama, 613 F.3d 1102 (D.C. Cir. 2010), Cert. Denied, 131 S. Ct. 1001 (2011)

In *Al-Adahi*, a three-judge panel of the D.C. Circuit endorsed the use of "conditional probability analysis" by habeas courts when considering the sufficiency and reliability of evidence proffered by the government in support of its claim that a person is lawfully detained under the AUMF. The case involved review of a district court decision granting a habeas petition by a Guantanamo detainee who the government claimed was "part of" Al Qaeda, following its determination that the government had failed to demonstrate its claim by a preponderance of evidence.

On appeal, the D.C. Circuit panel assumed *arguendo* that the government was required to show by a preponderance of evidence that the petitioner was lawfully detained under the AUMF, but suggested that reliance on this standard may not be constitutionally required. It next turned to the district court's analysis of evidence proffered by the government in support of its detention of petitioner, and concluded that the lower court "clearly erred in its treatment of the evidence" and its application of the preponderance of evidence standard. Examining the record, the circuit panel held that the lower court erred by separately considering the sufficiency of each item of evidence proffered by the government, and finding that the government failed to meet its evidentiary burden because no individual piece of evidence provided sufficient grounds to justify the petitioner's detention. The circuit panel was also critical of the lower court for failing to make any findings regarding the petitioner's "implausible" and inconsistent explanations for some of his activities, stating that it is a "well-settled principle that false exculpatory statements are evidence—often strong evidence—of guilt."

According to the circuit panel, "conditional probability analysis" is appropriate for assessing whether a person's detention under the AUMF is supported by the preponderance of the evidence. Using this framework, a habeas court must consider the cumulative weight and effect of proffered evidence when assessing whether the government has satisfied its evidentiary burden. In describing conditional probability analysis and its implications for the assessment of the evidence in the case before it, the *Al-Adahi* panel wrote:

> "Many mundane mistakes in reasoning can be traced to a shaky grasp of the notion of conditional probability." JOHN ALLEN PAULOS, INNUMERACY: MATHEMATICAL ILLITERACY AND ITS CONSEQUENCES 63 (1988). The key consideration is that although some events are independent (coin flips, for example), other events are dependent: "the occurrence of one of them makes the occurrence of the other more or less likely...." JOHN ALLEN PAULOS, BEYOND NUMERACY: RUMINATIONS OF A NUMBERS MAN 189 (1991). Dr. Paulos gives this example: "the probability that a person chosen at random from the phone book is over 250 pounds is quite small. However, if it's known that the person chosen is over six feet four inches tall, then the conditional probability that he or she also weighs more than 250 pounds is considerably higher." INNUMERACY 63.
>
> Those who do not take into account conditional probability are prone to making mistakes in judging evidence. They may think that if a particular fact does not itself prove the ultimate proposition (e.g., whether the detainee was part of al-Qaida), the fact may be tossed aside and the next fact may be evaluated as if the first did not exist. This is precisely how the district court proceeded in this case: Al-Adahi's ties to bin Laden "cannot prove" he was part of Al-Qaida and this evidence therefore "must not distract the Court." ... The fact that AlAdahi stayed in an al-Qaida guesthouse "is not in itself sufficient to justify detention." AlAdahi's attendance at an al-Qaida training camp "is not sufficient to carry the Government's burden of showing that he was a part" of al-Qaida. And so on. The government is right: the district court wrongly "required each piece of the government's evidence to bear weight without regard to all (or indeed any) other evidence in the case. This was a fundamental mistake that infected the court's entire analysis."[22]

Employing this standard, the circuit panel examined the evidentiary record (including false exculpatory statements made by the petitioner during interrogation),[23] and concluded that the government had satisfied its evidentiary burden of proving that the petitioner was subject to detention on account of membership in Al Qaeda. The circuit panel also concluded that some of the individual pieces of evidence proffered by the government—including evidence showing that the petitioner had voluntarily stayed at an Al Qaeda guesthouse and had received and executed orders from Al Qaeda members while at a weapons training camp—constituted sufficient grounds to justify his detention.

On January 18, 2011, the Supreme Court denied a petition of certiorari to review the *Al-Adahi* ruling.

Awad v. Obama, 608 F.3d 1 (D.C. Cir. 2010)

This case involved the review of a district court's denial of habeas relief to a Guantanamo detainee whom the government alleged to have been "part of" Al Qaeda at the time of capture. The petitioner, a Yemeni national, admitted to U.S. interrogators that he had travelled to Afghanistan to receive weapons training and fight U.S. forces. He was subsequently injured in an air raid, which resulted in the amputation of one of his legs. When Al Qaeda took over a portion of a hospital where petitioner was being treated, he allegedly joined Al Qaeda fighters barricaded there when coalition forces attempted to re-take the hospital, but was surrendered by Al Qaeda fighters due to his injury.

In upholding the district court's denial of habeas relief, the circuit panel rejected several legal and factual challenges raised by petitioner. As an initial matter, the *Awad* panel reaffirmed the propriety of using conditional probability analysis, previously relied upon by the D.C. Circuit in *Al-Adahi*, to assess petitioner's evidentiary challenges; accordingly, it would not "weigh each piece of evidence in isolation, but [would] consider all of the evidence taken as a whole." The circuit panel then proceeded to consider petitioner's argument that some of the evidence that had been proffered against him, including Al Qaeda documents and out-of-court statements by another detainee who was present at the hospital where petitioner was apprehended, were unreliable hearsay. The panel noted past jurisprudence recognizing that "hearsay evidence is admissible in this type of habeas proceeding if the hearsay is reliable," and concluded that the proffered evidence was sufficiently reliable to have been considered by the lower court.

The court then turned to petitioner's legal challenges. The panel rejected petitioner's argument the government was required to justify its claims that he was lawfully detainable through clear and convincing evidence, and found that the less rigorous "preponderance of evidence" standard that had been relied upon by the district court was constitutionally permissible. The circuit panel also dismissed petitioner's argument that his habeas petition could only be denied if a specific finding of fact was made that petitioner would pose a threat to the United States and its allies if released. The panel characterized the circuit court's prior decision in *Al-Bihani* as foreclosing this argument, and it went on to state that:

> the United States's authority to detain an enemy combatant is not dependent on whether an individual would pose a threat ... if released but rather upon the continuation of hostilities.... Whether a detainee would pose a threat to U.S. interests if released is not at issue in habeas corpus proceedings in federal courts concerning aliens detained under the authority conferred by the AUMF.

Finally, the panel rejected petitioner's argument that, in order for the government to justify his detention under the AUMF, it would have to demonstrate that he was part of Al Qaeda's "command structure." The panel held that petitioner's actions in joining Al Qaeda fighters behind a barricade were sufficient grounds to conclude he was "part of" Al Qaeda. It also suggested other situations where the government would not need to prove that a detainee was subject to Al Qaeda's "command structure" in order to justify its conclusion that he was "part of" Al Qaeda, such as when a person was captured in Afghanistan as part of a group that was shooting at U.S. forces and identified himself upon capture as an Al Qaeda member.

A petition to the Supreme Court for review was filed in November 2010, but the Court has yet to decide whether to hear the case.

Al Odah v. United States, 611 F.3d 8 (D.C. Cir. 2010)

In June 2010, a three-judge panel of the D.C. Circuit Court of Appeals upheld a district court's denial of a habeas petition brought on behalf of a person who had been detained at Guantanamo since 2002 due to his allegedly being part of Al Qaeda and Taliban forces. The petitioner challenged the procedures used by the district court when admitting evidence, and also the sufficiency of the evidence upon which its judgment on the merits was based. The circuit panel rejected these challenges as being foreclosed by controlling legal precedent. Specifically, the panel rejected the petitioner's argument that the government was required to support its factual claims in support of the legality of the petitioner's detention through "clear and convincing evidence." The panel recognized that based on binding precedent within the circuit, it is "well-settled law that a preponderance of the evidence standard is constitutional in considering a habeas petition from an individual detained pursuant to authority granted by the AUMF." The panel further rejected petitioner's argument that the admission of hearsay was statutorily restricted by the Federal Rules of Evidence and federal habeas statute. The court found this argument unpersuasive, citing both to the Supreme Court's ruling in *Hamdi* and the appellate court's prior jurisprudence as recognizing that district courts may admit reliable hearsay evidence when considering a habeas petition by an individual detained under the AUMF. The panel also rejected the petitioner's challenges to the individual pieces of evidence proffered by the government in support of his detention.

A petition seeking review of the circuit panel's ruling was filed with the Supreme Court in September 2010, but the Court has yet to decide whether to grant a writ of certiorari in the case.

Bensayah v. Obama, 610 F.3d 718 (D.C. Cir. 2010)

This case involved the review of a district court denial of habeas relief to an Algerian citizen who had been arrested by Bosnian authorities in 2001 and was subsequently transferred to U.S. custody for detention at Guantanamo. The government claimed that although the petitioner had not directly taken part in combat activities against the United States, he had intended to travel to Afghanistan to fight U.S. forces and had facilitated the travel of others to do the same. The executive branch initially argued that it had legal authority to hold the detainee, pursuant to the authority vested by the AUMF and the President's "inherent authority" as Commander-in-Chief, on account of the detainee's alleged membership in and support for Al Qaeda. In 2008, a federal district court judge denied the detainee's habeas petition.[24] The court found that the government had sufficient grounds to detain the petitioner for providing support to Al Qaeda, but declined to decide whether there were also sufficient grounds to detain the petitioner for being "part of" the organization. On appeal, the executive eschewed reliance on certain evidence that it earlier relied upon to demonstrate that petitioner acted as a travel facilitator for Al Qaeda, and also modified its argument in support of petitioner's detention—abandoning its argument that the petitioner was subject to detention on account of providing support to Al Qaeda, and instead arguing that he was subject to detention on account of being "part of" the organization. The government also relied solely on the authority granted by the AUMF to justify its detention authority, rather than any independent authority deriving from the Commander-in-Chief Clause. The reviewing circuit panel reversed and remanded the case back to the district court, finding that evidence relied upon by the lower court to conclude that the petitioner had supported Al Qaeda was insufficient to show that he was "part of" the organization.

Portions of the appellate panel's opinion discussing the sufficiency and reliability of the evidence proffered by the government were largely redacted. However, the published opinion provided further clarification regarding the D.C. Circuit's view of the detention authority conferred by the AUMF. The *Bensayah* panel recognized that the D.C. Circuit had previously made clear that "the AUMF authorizes the Executive to detain, at the least, any individual who is functionally part of al Qaeda." According to the panel, because Al Qaeda's organizational structure is generally unknown and thought to be amorphous, a determination as to whether an individual is "part of" the organization "must be made on a case-by-case basis by using a functional rather than a formal approach and by focusing upon the actions of the individual in relation to the organization." Although the panel concluded that evidence demonstrating that a person operated within Al Qaeda's command structure was sufficient to show that he was "part of" the organization, it suggested that there "may be other indicia that a particular individual is sufficiently involved with the organization to be deemed part of it." Nonetheless, the panel indicated that the "purely independent conduct of a freelancer" is not sufficient grounds to deem him to be functionally part of Al Qaeda.

Salahi v. Obama, 625 F.3d 745 (D.C. Cir. 2010)

This case involved review of a district court order granting habeas relief to a Guantanamo detainee captured in 2001 in Mauritania. Although the petitioner had not fought against the United States, the government alleged that he was lawfully detained on the grounds that he was "part of" Al Qaeda. Most of the evidence proffered by the government in support of its allegations concerned activities by the petitioner which occurred years before the 9/11 attacks. In habeas proceedings before the lower court, the government presented evidence that petitioner swore an oath of loyalty to Al Qaeda in 1991 and provided support to the organization at various points thereafter, including by recruiting members, hosting organization leaders, and providing the organization with financial support. For his part, the petitioner claimed that he severed ties with Al Qaeda in the early 1990s. The district court ruled that the government failed to satisfy its evidentiary burden in proving that the petitioner was "part of" Al Qaeda at the time of capture, and ordered the detainee to be released. In doing so, it rejected the government's argument that once the petitioner swore an oath of allegiance to Al Qaeda, he bore the burden of demonstrating that he had later withdrawn from the organization.

On appeal, a three-judge panel vacated the lower court's decision, finding that intervening case law—namely, the circuit court's opinions in the *Al-Adahi*, *Awad*, and *Bensayah* cases discussed above—cast doubt on the lower court's approach to determining whether petitioner was "part of" Al Qaeda. In particular, the *Salahi* panel found that the lower court had improperly required the government to prove that the petitioner had received and executed orders from Al Qaeda in order to demonstrate his membership in the organization. Subsequent circuit jurisprudence established that membership could be demonstrated not only from evidence that a person was part of Al Qaeda's "command structure," but also from activities which revealed a person to be functionally part of the organization. The panel recognized, however, that in cases like the one involving petitioner, who had not engaged in combat activities against the United States, "the government's failure to prove that an individual was acting under orders from al-Qaida may be *relevant* to the question of whether the individual was 'part of' the organization when captured."[25]

Although the government requested that the *Salahi* panel direct the district court to deny the habeas petition, it declined to do so, finding that it was appropriate to remand the case so the lower court could conduct further proceedings consistent with circuit jurisprudence that developed after its initial ruling. The panel found that because the lower court lacked guidance from subsequent circuit jurisprudence, it had primarily looked for evidence as to whether petitioner participated in Al Qaeda's command structure, but "did not make definitive findings regarding certain key facts necessary for us to determine as a matter of law whether Salahi was in fact 'part of' al-Qaida when captured."

In remanding the case to the lower court for further factual findings, the *Salahi* panel reiterated the admonition made by the circuit court in *Al-Adahi* that courts considering habeas petitions by Guantanamo detainees must consider the assorted evidence relating to the government's claims collectively rather than in isolation. While the panel stated that the lower court appeared to have generally followed this approach, it suggested that its consideration of certain evidence "may have been unduly atomized." Notably, the panel suggested that when the lower court determined that the petitioner's limited relationships with Al Qaeda operatives might have been too insubstantial to independently serve as a basis for deeming the petitioner "part of" Al Qaeda, those connections made it more probable that the petitioner was a member of the organization and were thus relevant to an assessment as to whether he had been lawfully detained. The panel also suggested that examining the petitioner's oath to Al Qaeda in isolation from his subsequent "sporadic support" may have resulted in the lower court failing to consider the possibility that this support demonstrated the petitioner's continued adherence to his oath of loyalty.

In reaching its ruling, the appellate court did not squarely address the government's argument that the petitioner's oath to Al Qaeda in the early 1990s established an evidentiary burden upon him to demonstrate that he had subsequently withdrawn from the organization. The appellate court also declined to consider the government's argument that the district court had accorded insufficient weight to certain inculpatory statements that were made by petitioner in interrogations subsequent to a period of time when he had been, by the government's admission, subject to mistreatment, because the panel viewed this issue to be irrelevant to the legal questions addressed by its opinion.

Transfer and Release of Detainees

The D.C. Circuit has also considered a number of cases involving issues related to the transfer or release of Guantanamo detainees. Some of these cases concern the remedy available to persons whom a reviewing court has determined to be unlawfully held, but who cannot be resettled or repatriated to a foreign country in the near future due to legal or practical obstacles.[26] Other cases involve challenges by detainees to their impending transfer to a specific foreign country, where detainees claim that they would be tortured or unlawfully detained by the government of the receiving country. The D.C. Circuit has considered these issues most prominently in three cases entitled *Kiyemba v. Obama*, which are discussed below.

Kiyemba v. Obama, 555 F.3d 1022 (D.C. Cir. 2009) ("Kiyemba I"), Vacated, 130 S.Ct. 1235 (2010), Reinstated as Amended, 605 F.3d 1046 (D.C. Cir. 2010) ("Kiyemba III")

In October 2008, a federal district court ordered the release into the United States of several Guantanamo detainees who were no longer considered enemy combatants but who could not be returned to their home country (China) because of the likelihood they would be subjected to torture there, finding that the political branches' plenary authority in the immigration context did not contravene the petitioners' entitlement to an effective remedy to their unauthorized detention.[27] However, the D.C. Circuit panel stayed the district court's order pending appellate review,[28] and subsequently reversed the district court's decision in the case of *Kiyemba v. Obama* ("*Kiyemba I*"), decided in February 2009. The majority held that although the constitutional writ of habeas enables Guantanamo detainees to challenge the legality of their detention, habeas courts lack authority (absent the enactment of an authorizing statute) to compel the transfer of a non-citizen detainee into the United States, even if that detainee is found to be unlawfully held and the government has been unable to effectuate his release to a foreign county. The *Kiyemba I* panel's decision was primarily based on long-standing jurisprudence in the immigration context which recognizes that the political branches have plenary authority over whether arriving aliens may enter the United States. The majority of the panel also found that Guantanamo detainees were not protected by the Due Process Clause of the Constitution, as they are non-citizens held outside the U.S. and lack significant ties to the country.

As discussed *supra*, the Supreme Court granted certiorari to review the *Kiyemba* ruling, and subsequently vacated the appellate court's opinion and remanded the case in light of the fact that several countries had thereafter agreed to resettle the petitioners. In May 2010, the D.C. Circuit panel reinstated its earlier opinion, as modified to take into account subsequent congressional enactments limiting the use of funds to release any Guantanamo detainee into the United States (the panel's reinstatement is commonly referred to as "*Kiyemba III*," to distinguish it from the Circuit panel's initial ruling and an intervening case also entitled *Kiyemba v. Obama*). The detainees at issue in *Kiyemba III* have filed a petition for writ of certiorari with the Supreme Court, seeking review of the circuit court's ruling.

Kiyemba v. Obama, 561 F.3d 509 (D.C. Cir. 2009) ("Kiyemba II"), Cert. Denied, 130 S.Ct. 1880 (2010)

In another case entitled *Kiyemba v. Obama* (commonly referred to as "*Kiyemba II*"), a D.C. Circuit panel considered habeas petitions by detainees who were no longer considered enemy combatants, and who sought to prevent their transfer to any country where they would likely face further detention or torture. The *Kiyemba II* panel rejected the government's argument that the MCA stripped the court of jurisdiction to hear claims related to the petitioners' proposed transfer. The panel interpreted *Boumediene* as invalidating the MCA's court-stripping provisions with respect "to all *habeas* claims brought by Guantanamo detainees, not simply with respect to so-called 'core' *habeas* claims" relating to the legality of the petitioners' detention. However, the panel held that an executive branch determination that a detainee will not be tortured if transferred to a particular country is binding on the court, and a habeas court may not second-guess this assessment. The circuit panel also reversed a district court ruling that required the government to provide 30 days' notice to detainees' counsel before any proposed transfer. As a result of this ruling, the detainees' ability to challenge their proposed transfer from Guantanamo may be quite limited. On March 22, 2010, the Supreme Court denied a petition for writ of certiorari to review the appellate court's ruling.

The *Kiyemba II* decision has been relied upon by the D.C. Circuit in subsequent rulings concerning detainees' right to challenge the executive's determination that they would not face torture if transferred to a particular country and receive advance notice of their proposed transfer. Some of these cases are the subject of ongoing litigation. Petitions for Supreme Court review have been filed by detainees seeking review of a few circuit court decisions, but the Court has yet to rule on these petitions.[29]

Other Notable Rulings

Besides the rulings discussed above, the appellate court for the D.C. Circuit has also issued opinions on several other distinct issues related to U.S. detention policy. These rulings have involved issues including, *inter alia*, the continuing application of the judicial review procedures established under DTA following the Supreme Court's ruling in *Boumediene v. Bush*; the ability of former Guantanamo detainees to bring civil suit against U.S. officials based on the detainees' allegedly wrongful treatment while in U.S. custody; and the application of the constitutional writ of habeas to persons held by the United States in foreign locations other than Guantanamo.

Parhat v. Gates, 532 F.3d 834 (D.C. Cir. 2008)

In June 2008, a three-judge panel of the D.C. Circuit ruled in the case of *Parhat v. Gates* that the petitioner had been improperly deemed an "enemy combatant" by a Combatant Status Review Tribunal (CSRT), the first ruling of its kind by a federal court. The ruling, which occurred prior to the Supreme Court's decision in *Boumediene*, was made under the judicial review process that had been established by the DTA. Although the D.C. Circuit has since held that the DTA review process is no longer in effect, the *Parhat* decision continues to be cited within the D.C. Circuit for its holding that evidence presented by the government must be in a form that permits a reviewing court to assess its reliability.[30]

The petitioner in *Parhat*, an ethnic Chinese Uighur captured in Pakistan in December 2001, was found by a CSRT to be subject to detention on account of his affiliation with a Uighur independence group known as the East Turkistan Islamic Movement (ETIM), which was purportedly "associated" with Al Qaeda and the Taliban and engaged in hostilities against the United States and its coalition partners (the petitioner denied membership in the ETIM). The *Parhat* panel found that the evidence presented by the government to support its claims regarding the ETIM was insufficient to support the CSRT's determination that Parhat was an enemy combatant. Most significantly, the court found that the principal evidence presented by the government regarding the ETIM being associated with Al Qaeda and the Taliban and engaged in hostilities against the United States and its coalition allies—four government intelligence documents describing ETIM activities and the group's relationship with Al Qaeda and the Taliban—did not "provide any of the underlying reporting upon which the documents' bottom-line assertions are founded, nor any assessment of the reliability of that reporting."[31] As a result, the Circuit Court found that neither the CSRT nor the reviewing court itself were capable of assessing the reliability of the assertions made by the documents. Accordingly "those bare assertions cannot sustain the determination that Parhat is an enemy combatant,"[32] and the CSRT's designation was therefore improper. The circuit court stressed that it was not suggesting that hearsay evidence could never reliably be used to determine whether a person was an enemy combatant, or that the government must always submit the basis for its factual assertions to enable an assessment of its claims. However, evidence "must be presented in a form, or with sufficient additional information, that permits the [CSRT] and court to assess its reliability."[33]

The *Parhat* panel also denied without prejudice a government motion to protect from public disclosure any nonclassified information raised in the litigation that the executive branch had labeled "law enforcement sensitive," along with names and identifying information of U.S. personnel mentioned in the record. While the panel acknowledged that information falling under both of these categories warranted protection from public disclosure, it characterized the government's argument for nondisclosure as being supported only upon "a generic explanation of the need for protection, providing no rationale specific to the information actually at issue in this case." In particular, the panel faulted the government motion for failing either to "give the court a basis for withholding" a specific category of information, or a basis upon which the court could "determine whether the information it has designated properly falls within the categories it has described."

Bismullah v. Gates, 551 F.3d 1068 (D.C. Cir. 2009)[34]

This case concerned the continuing availability of DTA review procedures in light of the Supreme Court's ruling in *Boumediene v. Bush* that the constitutional privilege of habeas corpus extends to non-citizen detainees held at Guantanamo. As discussed *supra*, following the Supreme Court's ruling in *Gates v. Bismullah*, the D.C. Circuit reinstated two earlier rulings concerning the scope of judicial review of CSRT determinations available under the DTA. The government subsequently petitioned for a rehearing of the case, arguing that the Supreme Court's ruling in *Boumediene* effectively nullified the review system established by the DTA, as Congress had not intended for detainees to have two judicial forums in which to challenge their detention. The D.C. Circuit granted the government's motion for rehearing, and in *Bismullah v. Gates*, a three-judge panel held that, in light of the Supreme Court's ruling in *Boumediene* restoring detainees' ability to seek habeas review of the legality of their detention, the appellate court no longer had jurisdiction over petitions for review filed pursuant to the DTA.

Rasul v. Myers, 563 F.3d 527 (D.C. Cir. 2009) (Per Curiam), Cert. Denied, 130 S.Ct. 1013 (2009)

Four British nationals formerly detained at Guantanamo sued the Secretary of Defense and various military officers for damages, alleging that their treatment while in U.S. military custody violated their rights under the Fifth and Eighth Amendments to the Constitution, the Geneva Conventions, and other provisions of law. The district court dismissed the *Bivens*[35] claims on the basis of qualified immunity, holding that the officers could not reasonably be expected to have anticipated that the plaintiffs, as aliens held overseas, would be entitled to rights under the U.S. Constitution.[36] The D.C. Circuit twice affirmed,[37] interpreting *Boumediene* (on remand) as "disclaim[ing] any intention to disturb existing law governing the extraterritorial reach of any constitutional provisions, other than the Suspension Clause,"[38] which, in the circuit court's view, appears to mean that those detained at Guantanamo have no rights under the Constitution (other than the right to petition for habeas corpus). It rested its holding, however, on its analysis of qualified immunity under *Bivens*, agreeing with the lower court that even if the Constitution does provide some protections to the plaintiffs, the defendants were protected by qualified immunity. Even were this not so clear, the D.C. Circuit noted a "special factor" precludes extending a *Bivens* remedy to plaintiffs; namely, the "[t]he danger of obstructing U.S. national security policy."[39]

Having found that the claims for damages were barred by the Federal Tort Claims Act, the circuit court did not address whether *Boumediene*'s holding invalidating section 7 of the MCA encompassed only the portion of the provision that stripped courts of jurisdiction over habeas claims, or whether the language eliminating other causes of action against the government had also been invalidated.[40] District court judges have uniformly held that the language eliminating causes of action other than habeas corpus survived *Boumediene*.[41]

Maqaleh v. Gates, 605 F.3d 84 (D.C. Cir. 2010)

This case concerned the application of the constitutional writ of habeas corpus to non-citizens detained by the United States in Afghanistan. In 2009, a federal district court ruled that constitutional writ of habeas may extend to non-Afghan detainees held in a U.S.-operated facility in Bagram, Afghanistan, when those detainees had been captured outside of Afghanistan but were transferred to Bagram for long-term detention as enemy combatants. The district court held that the circumstances surrounding the detention of the petitioners in *Maqaleh* were "virtually identical to the detainees in *Boumediene*—they are [non-U.S.] citizens who were ... apprehended in foreign lands far from the United States and brought to yet another country for detention."[42]

A three-judge panel of the D.C. Circuit Court of Appeals reversed, and held that the constitutional writ of habeas did not extend to non-citizens detained in the Afghan theater of war. In making this determination, the circuit court applied factors listed by the Supreme Court in *Boumediene* as being relevant to analysis of the writ's extraterritorial application, namely: (1) the citizenship and status of the detainee and the adequacy of the status determination process; (2) the nature of the site where the person is seized and detained; and (3) practical obstacles inherent in resolving the prisoner's entitlement to the writ. According to the circuit panel, consideration of the first factor weighed in favor of extending the writ of habeas to the petitioners, because the status determination process employed in Afghanistan to determine whether persons were subject to detention afforded fewer procedural protections than the process used at Guantanamo.[43] However, the circuit panel found that the application of the other two enumerated factors conclusively weighed against extending the constitutional writ of habeas to non-citizens held at Bagram. In particular, the circuit panel found that the degree and likely duration of U.S. control over Bagram were more limited than U.S. control over Guantanamo. The panel also found that significant practical obstacles would be inherent in attempting to resolve the habeas claims of Bagram detainees, including the petitioners' location in an active theater of war. The court considered it pertinent that the Unites States held persons at Bagram pursuant to a cooperative agreement with the Afghan government, and suggested that extending constitutional protections to Bagram detainees could be disruptive to the U.S.-Afghan relationship.

Although the *Maqaleh* panel held that the constitutional writ of habeas did not extend to persons in petitioners' situation, it suggested that its analysis might be different if evidence were presented that the executive branch opted to transfer detainees into a theater of war to evade judicial review. Relying on this statement, the *Maqaleh* petitioners sought a rehearing of their habeas claims. In February 2011, a lower district court permitted the petitioners to amend their habeas complaint to take into account new evidence that purportedly undercut the reasoning of the *Maqaleh* panel. Litigation in the case is ongoing.

RULINGS BY THE FOURTH CIRCUIT COURT OF APPEALS

Although most judicial activity concerning U.S. detention policy has occurred in the D.C. Circuit, two notable cases have been decided in the Fourth Circuit Court of Appeals. Both cases concerned the military detention of a resident alien within the United States following the executive's determination that the person was an unlawful enemy combatant. In each case, the individual was ultimately transferred to civilian custody, and thereafter tried and convicted for terrorism-related activity. Nonetheless, it is possible that the circuit court's analysis of the scope of executive detention authority may inform subsequent judicial rulings on the matter.

Padilla v. Hanft, 423 F.3d 386 (4th Cir. 2005)

After the Supreme Court vacated an earlier ruling in his favor by the Second Circuit (see above), Jose Padilla filed a new petition in the District Court for the District of South Carolina. The district court granted Padilla's motion for summary judgment and ordered the government to release him from military detention, while suggesting Padilla could be kept in civilian custody if charged with a crime or determined to be a material witness.[44] Padilla's attorneys had based their argument on the dissenting opinion of four Supreme Court Justices, who would have found Padilla's detention barred by the Non-Detention Act, 18 U.S.C. § 4001(a), and the language in *Hamdi* seemingly limiting the scope of detention authority under the AUMF to combatants captured in Afghanistan. The government argued that Padilla's detention is covered under the *Hamdi* decision's interpretation of the AUMF as an act of Congress authorizing his detention because he is alleged to have attended an Al Qaeda training camp in Afghanistan before traveling to Pakistan and then to the United States.[45] The judge disagreed with the government, finding that more express authority from Congress would be necessary and that the AUMF contains no such authority. Accordingly, the court found Padilla's detention barred by 18 U.S.C. § 4001(a). The court also disagreed that the President has inherent authority as Commander-in-Chief of the Armed Forces to determine wartime measures.[46]

The Fourth Circuit Court of Appeals reversed, finding that Padilla, although captured in the United States, could be detained pursuant to the AUMF because he had been, prior to returning to the United States, "'armed and present in a combat zone' in Afghanistan as part of Taliban forces during the conflict there with the United States."[47] As the Supreme Court again considered whether to grant review, the government charged Padilla with conspiracy based on evidence unrelated to the original "dirty bomb" plot allegations and petitioned for leave to transfer him from military custody to a federal prison for civilian trial.[48] The Court granted the government permission to transfer Padilla[49] and later denied certiorari.[50] Padilla was found guilty and sentenced to 17 years and three months' imprisonment, the trial court having rejected his motion to dismiss charges against him due to his alleged mistreatment at the hands of the military.[51]

al-Marri v. Pucciarelli, 534 F.3d 213 (4th Cir. 2008) (Per Curiam)[52]

In *al-Marri*, the Fourth Circuit sitting *en banc* considered whether the AUMF and the law of war permit the detention of a resident alien alleged to have engaged in activities within the United States in support of Al Qaeda, but who had not been part of the conflict in Afghanistan. Four of the nine judges would have held that even if the allegations were true, al-Marri did not fit within the legal category of "enemy combatant" within the meaning of *Hamdi*, and that the government could continue to hold him only if it charged him with a crime, commenced deportation proceedings, or obtained a material witness warrant in connection with grand jury proceedings (as a majority of the original three-judge panel had found). A plurality of the fractured *en banc* court, however, found that the AUMF and the law of war give the President the power to detain persons who enter the United States as "sleeper agents" on behalf of Al Qaeda for the purpose of committing hostile and war-like acts such as those carried out on 9/11 (although the judges did not arrive at a common definition of "enemy combatant"). The case was remanded to the district court for further consideration of the evidence to determine whether the government had established that al-Marri was a sleeper agent.

The *en banc* panel also considered the evidentiary burden that the government would be required to fulfill to detain al-Marri as an enemy combatant. In his controlling opinion, Judge Traxler wrote that the lower court had erred in applying the relaxed evidentiary standards of *Hamdi* to persons captured in the United States. While the *Hamdi* plurality suggested that hearsay evidence might be sufficient to support detention of a person apprehended in combat zone, Judge Traxler wrote that *Hamdi* does not establish a "cookie-cutter procedure appropriate for every alleged enemy-combatant, regardless of the circumstances of the alleged combatant's seizure or the actual burdens the government might face in defending the *habeas* petition in the normal way."[53] However, he recognized that some relaxation of normal procedural safeguards may be warranted if the government demonstrates the need for this relaxation on account of national security interests and an undue burden that would result if it was compelled to produce more reliable evidence.

After the Supreme Court granted review, the government brought charges against al-Marri in federal court and asked the Court to dismiss the case as moot and to vacate the decision below, which the Court agreed to do, leaving the applicability of the AUMF to persons captured in the United States uncertain. Al-Marri pled guilty to conspiring to provide material support to terrorists and was sentenced to eight and a half years in prison.

CRIMINAL CASES

Although numerous cases have been brought in federal civilian court involving persons who allegedly engaged in terrorist activity, relatively few involve persons who were captured abroad by U.S. forces during operations against either Al Qaeda or the Taliban, and only one case has been tried in civilian court involving a person involved in the September 11, 2001, terrorist attacks. This section discusses notable rulings made in criminal cases involving Zacharias Moussaoui, who was tried and convicted for his role in the September 11, 2001, terrorist attacks, but was never officially designated as an "enemy combatant"; John Walker Lindh, thus far the only person captured abroad and tried and convicted in federal civilian court for belligerent activities occurring on the Afghan battlefield; and Ahmed Khalfan Ghailani, a suspect in the 1998 African Embassy bombings who was incarcerated at Guantanamo and charged at a military commission, but was later transferred to the Southern District of New York for trial on terrorism charges. Ghailani is the only Guantanamo prisoner to have been transferred for civilian trial in the United States.

Moussaoui Litigation

Zacharias Moussaoui, a French citizen, was arrested by immigration authorities for overstaying his visa after he raised suspicions at a Minnesota flight school where he was enrolled. Less than a month after he was taken into custody, a group of Al Qaeda terrorists carried out the September 11, 2001, attacks, and Moussaoui was charged in connection with the conspiracy to commit those attacks. On January 7, 2002, after Moussaoui's arraignment, the Department of Justice (DOJ) imposed Special Administrative Measures (SAMs) to prevent his communication with other terrorists. Moussaoui was permitted unmonitored attorney/client and consular communications and mail, and monitored communications with others. The court also issued a protective order under the Classified Information Procedures Act (CIPA; 18 U.S.C. app. 3, § 3), which permitted defense counsel to access classified information, but did not permit Moussaoui to receive such information unless the government consented or the judge determined that it was necessary to protect his right to prepare a defense.

After a competency hearing in which the judge explained that the lack of personal access to classified information could impede Moussaoui's ability to defend himself without counsel appropriately cleared for access to such information, the judge permitted the defendant to proceed *pro se*, and appointed the public defenders who had been assigned to the case to act as standby counsel. After Moussaoui refused to cooperate with his appointed lawyers, the judge replaced some of them, but ultimately concluded that Moussaoui was unlikely to approve any court-appointed attorneys, and also held that he was not entitled to unmonitored access to "advisory counsel" of his choice. Despite Moussaoui's rejection of virtually all efforts by standby counsel to assist him, the lawyers continued to file motions on his behalf, including motions seeking relief from the SAMs or to revoke his *pro se* status on the grounds that he was not in a position to take advantage of exculpatory information in the government's possession. Moussaoui attempted to plead guilty in July 2002, but was unwilling to admit to the facts necessary to support the plea and withdrew it.

Moussaoui then sought access to several persons held overseas by the government as enemy combatants who might provide information that would be useful to his defense by testifying that Moussaoui was not involved in the September 11 attacks. (The government had advanced theories that Moussaoui was the intended "20th hijacker" or pilot of a fifth plane intended to target the White House, whose participation in the actual attack was thwarted due to his incarceration, and that Moussaoui's refusal to provide agents information about the plot that might have prevented the attacks from taking place contributed to the deaths of the several thousand victims, a factor relevant to death penalty eligibility. Moussaoui claimed to be part of a plan for subsequent terrorist operations and to have had no knowledge regarding the September 11 plot.) The government offered to provide redacted summaries of reports presumably based on intelligence interrogations of the enemy combatant witnesses,[54] but the judge rejected the proffered substitutions as possibly unreliable and inadequate to protect Moussaoui's Sixth Amendment right to compulsory process.

The government appealed the district court's order requiring the government to make three of the requested enemy combatant witnesses available for deposition to be conducted by remote video. The United States Court of Appeals for the Fourth Circuit affirmed the district court's holding that that the enemy combatants in question could be reached through judicial process (directed at their custodians) for the purpose of providing testimony and that their testimony would be relevant to the case, but reversed the order for depositions and the sanctions the court had imposed for the government's refusal to comply.[55] The appellate court held that substitutions for depositions could be prepared that would provide substantially the same ability to prepare a defense, although it agreed with some of the objections the district court had articulated regarding the government's proposed substitutions. The majority viewed the intelligence reports as possessing adequate indicia of reliability because they were produced through methods designed to produce accurate analyses of foreign intelligence.[56] Consequently, the court remanded the case to the district court with instructions to prepare substitutions for the deposition testimony by a process involving collaboration with the parties,[57] noting that adequate jury instructions would be necessary in some cases to permit the jury to assess the reliability of the evidence.

In the meantime, the district court revoked Moussaoui's *pro se* privilege for his continued submission of improper filings, some of which contained veiled or overt threats, political statements with no relevance to the case, attempts at communicating to persons overseas, and insulting language, despite repeated warnings that such conduct would result in sanctions. After the Supreme Court denied certiorari with respect to the appellate court's ruling on his right to depose enemy combatant witnesses in the custody of the United States, Moussaoui again decided, over his counsel's objections, to plead guilty as an apparent tactic to avoid the death penalty. After a hearing in which Moussaoui demonstrated to the court's satisfaction that he understood a guilty plea would result in forfeiting his right to appeal based on any violation of his constitutional rights that might have occurred prior to the plea, the court accepted his plea. Moussaoui admitted to the government's allegations, including some he had previously denied, and signed the statement of facts supporting the guilty plea, adding the designation of "20th Hijacker" below his signature. During the sentencing phase, Moussaoui claimed that his mission on September 11 was to have been piloting a commercial airliner into the White House, although statements by enemy combatant witnesses introduced by the government contradicted that claim, along with some other allegations Moussaoui had admitted as true. In the bifurcated sentencing proceeding, the jury found Moussaoui to be eligible to receive the death penalty but declined to impose it, sentencing him instead to life in prison.

Just days after receiving his sentence, Moussaoui filed a motion to withdraw his guilty plea, claiming that his understanding of the American legal system had been "completely flawed" and asking for a new trial "[b]ecause I now see that it is possible that I can receive a fair trial ... even with Americans as jurors and that I can have the opportunity to prove that I did not have any knowledge of and was not a member of the plot to hijack planes and crash them into buildings on September 11, 2001."[58] He then appealed the court's denial of his motion for a new trial, arguing among other things that his plea was not voluntary as a matter of law because of district court rulings that violated his constitutional rights, and that it was not knowing because he did not have access to classified information in the government's possession that contradicted the government's theory of the case. Finding that his guilty plea was entered with full knowledge and understanding of its ramifications and that his objections to constitutional claims were waived, the circuit court affirmed. The circuit court reviewed the procedural history regarding Moussaoui's access to classified information because these claims were relevant to the adequacy of the plea and were therefore not waived for purposes of appeal, but reiterated its earlier view that adequate substitutions under CIPA would have protected Moussaoui's rights had the CIPA process not been cut short by the guilty plea. Moreover, it noted that CIPA information had been made available during the sentencing phase for establishing death-eligibility factors, and that not only did Moussaoui make no effort to withdraw his plea upon receiving the information, but he contradicted the supposedly exculpatory statements at trial. Finally, the circuit court rejected Moussaoui's contention that plain error had resulted in the jury's false belief that the only sentencing options available to them were the death penalty or life imprisonment without possibility of parole, in violation of his right to have his sentence decided by the jury, on the basis that Moussaoui had requested the jury be instructed that the sentencing options were limited as part of an apparently successful strategy to avoid the death penalty.

United States v. Lindh, 227 F. Supp. 2d 565 (E.D. Va. 2004)

John Walker Lindh, a U.S. citizen, was captured in Afghanistan and charged with 10 counts of supplying services to the Taliban under various statutes. He moved to have the charges dismissed, arguing, *inter alia* that he was entitled to combatant immunity as part of the Taliban. While the judge refused to accept the government's argument that the President's designation of Lindh as an "unlawful combatant" was not subject to second-guessing by the court, he nevertheless concluded that the Taliban is not entitled to combatant immunity under international law and rejected the defense.[59]

Lindh was also unsuccessful in his bid to avoid the government's request for a protective order covering unclassified but sensitive information as well as classified information that the government had concluded was subject to discovery by the defendant.[60] At issue was whether the defendant could adequately prepare a defense given the government's proposal to restrict certain information from the government's redacted reports of relevant interviews with detainees held at Guantanamo. Rule 16(d) of the Federal Rules for Criminal Procedure permits the court to restrict discovery with respect to any information for good cause, including cases where the government claims the protection of such information is vital to the national security. The court found good cause to issue a protective order to prohibit the public dissemination of the detainee interview reports, which would serve to prevent Al Qaeda members from learning "the status of, the methods used in, and the information obtained from the ongoing investigation of the detainees."[61] Lindh objected to the order on the basis that it would burden his ability to prepare for trial by requiring the pre-screening of investigators and expert witnesses before he would be permitted to disclose unclassified information to them, which he argued could reveal his defense strategy to the prosecution. The judge found the needs of both parties could be accommodated by amending the proposed order to require investigators or expert witnesses for the defense to sign a memorandum of understanding, under oath, promising not to disclose information provided under the order, rather than requiring pre-screening. Lindh also objected to the proposed protective order because he believed it would impair his ability to use the media to influence public opinion, as he contended the government had done. Noting that the "[d]efendant has no constitutional right to use the media to influence public opinion concerning his case so as to gain an advantage at trial" under either the Sixth Amendment right to a public trial or the public's First Amendment right to a free press,[62] the judge rejected the argument, but cautioned that information that turned out to be relevant and material to the trial as the case progressed might eventually require unsealing to further those rights.[63]

Prior to the beginning of the merits phase of the trial, Lindh struck a plea deal with prosecutors, admitting to one count of carrying an explosive during the commission of a felony, and was sentenced to 20 years' imprisonment.

United States v. Ghailani, No. S10 98 Crim. 1023 (S.D.N.Y.)

Alleged Al Qaeda member Ahmed Khalfan Ghailani was indicted in 1998 and charged with conspiracy to kill Americans abroad in connection with the bombing the United States Embassies in Nairobi, Kenya, and Dar es Salaam, Tanzania. He was arrested in Pakistan in 2004 and turned over to U.S. custody to be held and interrogated at an undisclosed site abroad by Central Intelligence Agency (CIA) officials. In 2006, he was transferred to DOD custody and held as an enemy combatant at Guantanamo. He was charged before a military commission for his role in one of the embassy bombings, but the charges were later withdrawn so that he could be transferred to the Southern District of New York to be tried on the earlier indictment. The transfer occurred in May 2009. Ghailani has since been convicted and sentenced to life imprisonment for his part in the conspiracy.

The case has resulted in a number of rulings on constitutional issues that are likely to be pertinent to the debate as to whether to try similar crimes in federal court or before military commissions, including such issues as the right to effective assistance of counsel, the right to a speedy trial, the privilege against self-incrimination and the right to counsel in custodial interrogation, and the consequences of a jury trial. How these issues might be resolved in a military commission or by reviewing courts remains to be seen. A military commission would also have had to resolve the issue of whether crimes committed prior to the 9/11 attacks can properly be charged as war crimes, a highly charged question for which arguments can be made either way, but which appears to be lacking in precedent.

After his transfer to New York, Ghailani moved for an injunction or other relief against the Secretary of Defense to prevent the reassignment of the military defense attorneys who had been detailed to serve as his defense counsel before the military commission. Ghailani urged the court to order the government to permit the two officers to act as his appointed counsel in federal court, arguing that depriving him of the assistance of the counsel he had grown to trust amounted to a violation of his Sixth Amendment right to the effective assistance of counsel. The government urged the court to decline to adjudicate the motion or grant relief based on the political question doctrine, arguing that the assignment of military officers to particular duties is the prerogative of the executive branch alone. The judge did not think the political question doctrine prevented his consideration of the matter, since he was not considering the propriety of the reassignment as much as he was assessing the impact of the decision on the defendant's rights, but ultimately denied the motion, holding that an indigent defendant's right to appointed representation does not mean the right to continuous representation by counsel of his choice.[64]

Ghailani also filed a motion for dismissal of his indictment based on his claim that the government violated his Sixth Amendment right to a speedy trial. In connection with this motion, Ghailani sought discovery of documents in the government's possession that demonstrate the government delayed his prosecution from 2004 until his transfer to New York for reasons other than national security. Rule 16 of the Federal Rules for Criminal Procedure permits discovery of items "within the government's custody, possession, or control" that are material to the case, excluding documents that were prepared by government attorneys or agents that constitute work product connected to the prosecution. The judge excluded one document specifically requested by the defendant as attorney work product, but approved a more general request for information relating to the reasons behind the timing of Ghailani's transfer for trial based on a Supreme Court ruling that makes the "reason for delay" one part of the test for determining whether charges must be dismissed for failure to provide a speedy trial.[65] The judge defined the scope of "in the government's possession, custody, or control" as reaching beyond the officials of the U.S. Attorney's Office who had worked on the case to include higher-level DOJ officials who were not intimately involved in the case but were involved in the decision about where to prosecute Ghailani. This requirement will not unduly burden the prosecution with unreasonable discovery requirements, according to the court, because the embassy bombing crime had "commanded the attention of the highest levels" of the government long before Ghailani was in American custody. Under these circumstances, high-level officials involved in the important decisions involving Ghailani's treatment can be included within the meaning of "government" in Rule 16.[66] Accordingly, the judge issued an order requiring production of documents held by the DOJ that are material to the case and not otherwise privileged under the rule.

The court ultimately denied the speedy trial motion after applying the multi-factor balancing test established by the Supreme Court in *Barker v. Wingo*,[67] which takes into account the length of the delay, the reason for the delay, the defendant's assertion of the right, and the prejudice to the defendant.[68] The court held that the time Ghailani spent in CIA detention was justified by the need to interrogate him for intelligence purposes, a process that was incompatible with prosecution in federal court.[69] The time between Ghailani's transfer to Guantanamo in 2006 and his transfer to New York in 2009, however, was held insufficient to justify postponement of trial, because the need to prevent the defendant from returning to hostilities was not incompatible with federal prosecution.[70] The aborted military commission prosecution did not justify delay because the government had complete discretion as to where to prosecute the defendant.[71] However, although the Guantanamo portion of the delay was attributable to the government, it was assessed as a "neutral factor" because there was no evidence that its purpose had to do with a "quest for tactical advantage."[72] Because Ghailani was detainable as an "enemy combatant" with or without prosecution, the need to avoid excessive incarceration was not a relevant factor under *Barker* analysis, either. The court was not persuaded that Ghailani was prejudiced by the delay, and it held there was no violation of his Sixth Amendment rights.

Although Ghailani's overseas detention by the CIA did not preclude his prosecution, it did result in the exclusion of a government witness whose identity was uncovered during Ghailani's interrogation and whose cooperation with prosecutors was less than willing.[73] The government having stipulated that any statements Ghailani made to CIA interrogators were coerced, the judge held that the Fifth Amendment's privilege against self-incrimination would permit the government to introduce such witness testimony only if it had proven that the connection between Ghailani's coerced statements and the witness's testimony was sufficiently remote or attenuated to purge the taint of illegality, or if it could establish another basis upon which the testimony could be admitted. The government failed to establish the inevitability of its identification of the witness independent of the defendant's coerced statement, and it did not persuade the judge that the "core application" doctrine applicable to the exclusionary rule in the Fourth Amendment search and seizure context should hold sway in the Fifth Amendment context.[74] Consequently, the court held hearings to examine whether the witness's testimony was truly voluntary; the extent to which the coerced statements played a role in securing the witness's cooperation; and whether the lapse of time between the illegal government action and contact with the witness established a sufficient attenuation to avoid the exclusion of his testimony. The judge ultimately found each of these criteria weighed in favor of the defendant, but the facts leading to this determination remain classified.[75]

After a jury trial, Ghailani was found guilty of conspiracy to destroy buildings and property of the United States, but not guilty of 284 other counts—one count of murder or attempted murder for each of the Americans killed or injured in the attacks, one count each for the bombing the U.S. embassies in Dar es Salaam, Tanzania, and Nairobi, Kenya, and various other charges related to the bombings.[76] The jury concluded that Ghailani's participation in the property destruction conspiracy was a direct or proximate cause of the death of a person other than a conspirator. After rejecting the defendant's motion for acquittal or a new trial on the property conspiracy charge,[77] which the defense argued was necessary in light of the seemingly inconsistent verdict,[78] the judge sentenced Ghailani to life imprisonment based on the aggravating factor the jury found.

The results of Ghailani's trial have fueled the debate over whether military commissions or federal court trials are appropriate in terrorism cases. Some observers view the trial as a demonstration that federal trial courts using the ordinary tools of criminal justice are up to the task of meting out justice to terrorists, while others characterize the outcome as a "near acquittal" that demonstrates the superiority of military commissions. The judge's post-trial opinion denying the defendant's motion for acquittal sheds some light on what may seem to be a curious verdict. Ghailani's defense throughout the trial was that he had been unknowingly duped into carrying out what he thought were innocent acts, but which in hindsight turned out to be acts in furtherance of the bombing conspiracy. The charge of conspiracy to destroy property, however, did not require that the government prove beyond a reasonable doubt that Ghailani was aware of the exact objective and targets of the plot; it merely required proof that Ghailani understood that his activities would very likely result in the bombing of American facilities somewhere, for which the judge agreed there was abundant evidence. The jury was instructed that willful blindness on the part of the accused to the precise objective of the conspiracy would invalidate a defense based on the lack of requisite knowledge, and that conviction was therefore proper if the facts demonstrated that the defendant "was aware of a high probability of the fact in dispute and consciously avoided confirming that fact"[79] In contrast, the charge for participating in the Dar es Salaam embassy bombing required proof that "Ghailani knew that the embassy was a target and that he acted to further that goal."[80] Apparently the jury did not agree that the government's evidence adequately established these elements.

CONCLUSION

Although the political branches of government have been primarily responsible for shaping U.S. wartime detention policy in the conflict with Al Qaeda and the Taliban, the judiciary has also played a significant role in clarifying elements of the rights and privileges owed to detainees under the Constitution and existing federal statutes and treaties. These rulings may have longterm consequences for U.S. detention policy, both in the conflict with Al Qaeda and the Taliban and in future armed conflicts. Judicial decisions concerning the meaning and effect of existing statutes and treaties may compel the executive branch to modify its current practices to conform with judicial opinion. For example, judicial opinions concerning the scope of detention authority conferred by the AUMF may inform executive decisions as to whether grounds exist to detain an individual suspected of involvement with Al Qaeda or the Taliban. Judicial decisions concerning statutes applicable to criminal prosecutions in Article III courts or military tribunals may influence executive determinations as to the appropriate forum in which to try detainees for criminal offenses. Judicial rulings may also invite response from the legislative branch, including consideration of legislative proposals to modify existing authorities governing U.S. detention policy. They may also influence legislative activity in future armed conflicts. For example, Congress may look to judicial rulings interpreting the meaning and scope of the 2001 AUMF for guidance when drafting legislation authorizing the executive to use military force in some future conflict.

While the Supreme Court has issued definitive rulings concerning certain issues related to wartime detainees, many other issues related to the capture, treatment, and trial of suspected enemy belligerents are either the subject of ongoing litigation or have yet to be addressed by the judiciary. Some judges have expressed a desire for more guidance from Congress. Accordingly, the courts appear likely to play a significant role in shaping U.S. policies relating to enemy belligerents in the foreseeable future.

End Notes

[1] The Obama Administration has discontinued the use of the term "enemy combatant" to describe persons detained pursuant to the law of war or the Authorization to Use Military Force (AUMF). *See* Department of Justice (DOJ), "Department of Justice Withdraws 'Enemy Combatant' Definition for Guantanamo Detainees," press release, March 13, 2009, http://www.usdoj.gov/opa/pr/2009/March/09-ag-232.html (hereinafter "DOJ Press

Release"); In re Guantanamo Bay Detainee Litigation, Respondents' Memorandum Regarding the Government's Detention Authority Relative to Detainees Held At Guantanamo Bay, No. 08-0442, filed March 13, 2009 (D.D.C.) (hereinafter "Detention Authority Memorandum"). We use the terms "enemy combatant" or "enemy belligerent" broadly to describe persons who might be subject to detention or prosecution in connection with the conflict authorized by the AUMF as interpreted by the executive branch.

[2] For further discussion of *Hamdi*, see CRS Report RS21884, *The Supreme Court 2003 Term: Summary and Analysis of Opinions Related to Detainees in the War on Terrorism*, by Jennifer K. Elsea.

[3] Hamdi v. Rumsfeld, 542 U.S. 507, 518 (2004) (O'Connor, J., plurality opinion); *id.* at 588-589 (Thomas, J., dissenting).

[4] *Id.* at 518, 533 (O'Connor, J., plurality opinion, joined by Breyer, J., Kennedy, J., and Rehnquist, C.J.); 553 (Souter, J., concurring in part and dissenting in part, joined by Ginsburg, J.). Justices Scalia and Stevens supported a more limited view concerning the executive's authority to detain U.S. citizens, believing that detention without criminal charge was only permissible if Congress suspended the writ of habeas corpus. *Id.* at 554 (Scalia, J., dissenting, joined by Stevens, J.).

[5] *Id.* at 533-534 (O'Connor, J., plurality opinion).

[6] For further discussion of the *Padilla* decision, see CRS Report RS21884, *supra* footnote 2.

[7] For a more detailed summary of the *Rasul* opinion, see *id.*

[8] P.L. 109-148, Title X; P.L. 109-163, Title XIV.

[9] P.L. 109-366.

[10] For further discussion of the *Hamdan* opinion, see CRS Report RS22466, *Hamdan v. Rumsfeld: Military Commissions in the "Global War on Terrorism,"* by Jennifer K. Elsea.

[11] Hamdan v. Rumsfeld, 548 U.S. 557, 602 (2006) (Stevens, J., plurality opinion, joined by Souter, J., Ginsburg, J., and Breyer, J.).

[12] A more extensive discussion of *Boumediene* is found in CRS Report RL34536, *Boumediene v. Bush: Guantanamo Detainees' Right to Habeas Corpus*, by Michael John Garcia.

[13] Boumediene v. Bush, 553 U.S. 723, 764 (2008).

[14] The D.C. Circuit in July 2007 issued an order rejecting the government's motion to limit the scope of the court's review to the official record of the CSRT hearings. Bismullah v. Gates, 501 F.3d 178 (*Bismullah I*). The circuit court decided that in order to determine whether a preponderance of evidence supported the CSRT determinations, it must have access to all the information a CSRT is "authorized to obtain and consider, pursuant to the procedures specified by the Secretary of Defense." The court thereafter denied the government's request for rehearing, explaining its view that its previous order would not require a search for information that was not "reasonably available." Bismullah v. Gates, 503 F.3d 137(D.C. Cir. 2007) (*Bismullah II*).

[15] *See generally* Benjamin Wittes, Robert Chesney & Rabea Benhalim, *The Emerging Law of Detention: The Guantánamo Habeas Cases as Lawmaking*, Brookings Institute, Jan. 22, 2010, available at http://www.brookings.edu/papers/2010/0122_guantanamo_wittes_chesney.aspx (discussing different approaches taken by district courts in the handling of habeas petitions brought by Guantanamo detainees).

[16] A third member of the panel issued a separate opinion concurring with the majority's judgment. However, the opinion did not clearly endorse the majority's view as to the scope of the executive's detention authority. *See* Al-Bihani v. Obama, 590 F.3d 866, 883-885 (D.C. Cir. 2010) (Williams, J., concurring) (arguing that petitioner was detainable on account of being "part of" an AUMF-targeted organization, but not deciding whether a person could be detained on account of "support" for a targeted organization that he was not also a "part of").

[17] *Id.* at 872 (quoting 2006 MCA, P.L. 109-366, § 3, and 2009 MCA, P.L. 111-84, Div A, § 1802).

[18] *Id.* at 872-873. The panel found that even if petitioner was not a member of an AUMF-targeted organization, his service as a cook for a military brigade affiliated with Taliban and Al Qaeda forces, in addition to his accompaniment of the brigade during military operations, constituted sufficient grounds for his detention. *Id.*

[19] The preponderance standard is generally interpreted to require that the evidence presented by both sides taken together makes the facts in question more likely true than not. *See* 29 AM. JUR. 2d Evid. § 173.

[20] *Al-Bihani v. Obama*, 619 F.3d 1 (D.C. Cir. 2010) (Sentelle, C.J., concurring).

[21] *Compare, e.g.,* Hatim v. Gates, Civ. No. 10-5048, 2011 U.S. App. LEXIS 3171 (D.C. Cir., Feb. 15, 2011) (per curiam panel decision) (finding that district court ruling that military could only detain person who was "part of" Al Qaeda or the Taliban was "directly contrary to *Al-Bihani v. Obama*, which held that 'those who purposefully and materially support' al-Qaida or the Taliban could also be detained"); Alsabri v. Obama, Civ. No. 06-1767, 2011 U.S. Dist. LEXIS 17208 at *25 (D.D.C., Feb. 18, 2011) (Urbina, J.) ("This Circuit has

stated that the AUMF authorizes the government to detain two categories of persons: (1) individuals 'part of' forces associated with al-Qaida or the Taliban and (2) individuals who purposefully and materially support such forces in hostilities against the United States"); Almerfedi v. Obama, 725 F. Supp. 2d 18 (D.D.C., 2010) (Friedman, J.) (recognizing that *Al-Bihani* established that detention under the AUMF could be justified either on grounds that person was either a member of or provided substantial support to an AUMF-targeted organization); *with* Bensayah v. Obama, 610 F.3d 718, 725 (D.C. Cir. 2010) (describing circuit jurisprudence in the aftermath of *Al-Bihani* as having "made clear ... that the AUMF authorizes the Executive to detain, at the least, any individual who is functionally part of al Qaeda").

[22] Al-Adahi v. Obama, 613 F.3d 1102, 1105-1106 (D.C. Cir. 2010) (omitting some citations contained in original).

[23] In support of its finding that the government had demonstrated by a preponderance of evidence that the petitioner was a member of Al Qaeda, the circuit panel cited, *inter alia,* evidence relating to the petitioner's travel to Afghanistan in 2001, his subsequent meetings with Osama Bin Laden, his stay at an Al Qaeda guesthouse, his presence at an Al Qaeda-affiliated training camp, and his wearing of a watch at the time of capture that was of the same model as that used by Al Qaeda operatives.

[24] Boumediene v. Bush, 579 F. Supp. 2d 191 (D.D.C., 2008)

[25] Salahi v. Obama, 625 F.3d 745, 752 (D.C. Cir. 2010) (italics in original).

[26] For discussion of U.S. policy relating to the transfer or release of Guantanamo detainees to foreign countries, see CRS Report R40139, *Closing the Guantanamo Detention Center: Legal Issues*, by Michael John Garcia et al.

[27] In re Guantanamo Bay Detainee Litigation, 581 F. Supp. 2d 33 (D.D.C. 2008).

[28] Kiyemba v. Bush, No. 08-5424, 2008 WL 4898963, Order (D.C. Cir., October 20, 2008) (*per curiam*).

[29] Mohammed v. Obama, 2010 U.S. App. LEXIS 16023 , No. 10-5218 (D.C. Cir. Jul. 8, 2010), 131 S. Ct. 811 (granting motion to file petition for writ of certiorari under seal); Khadr v. Obama, 2010 U.S. App. LEXIS 9036, 2010 U.S. App. LEXIS 9036 (D.C. Cir. Apr. 29, 2010), petition for cert. filed, Dec. 2, 2010.

[30] Indeed, the D.C. Circuit in *Bismullah* implied that, despite its determination that the DTA review process was no longer available to detainees, the circuit court's ruling in *Parhat* remained in force. *Bismullah*, 551 F.3d 1068, 1075, n. 2 (D.C. Cir. 2009). *See also* Bensayah v. Obama, 610 F.3d 718, 725-726 (D.C. Cir. 2010) ("In *Parhat* we made clear that the reliability of evidence can be determined not only by looking at the evidence alone but, alternatively, by considering 'sufficient additional information ... permit[ting the fact finder] to assess its reliability.'"); Ameziane v. Obama, 620 F.3d 1 (D.C. Cir. 2010) (holding that district court had failed to properly apply *Parhat* in its consideration of government motion to designate certain information as "protected" under the governing protective order).

[31] Parhat v. Gates, 532 F.3d 834, 846-47 (D.C. Cir. 2008).

[32] *Id.* at 847.

[33] *Id.* at 849.

[34] A more detailed discussion of the *Bismullah* case is found in CRS Report RL33180, *Enemy Combatant Detainees: Habeas Corpus Challenges in Federal Court*, by Jennifer K. Elsea and Michael John Garcia.

[35] Bivens v. Six Unknown Agents of Fed. Bureau of Narcotics, 403 U.S. 388 (1971) (providing for cause of action in tort for violation of certain constitutional rights).

[36] Rasul v. Rumsfeld, 414 F. Supp. 2d 26 (D.D.C. 2006).

[37] Rasul v. Myers, 512 F.3d 644 (D.C. Cir. 2008) ("Rasul I") was vacated by the Supreme court and remanded for reconsideration in light of *Boumediene*. 129 S.Ct. 763 (2008) Rasul v. Myers, 563 F.3d 527 (D.C. Cir. 2009) ("Rasul II") reinstated the earlier opinion but limited its scope to rest the holding on qualified immunity without adjudicating the constitutional questions. The appellate court reversed a holding by the district court that would have enabled plaintiffs to pursue claims based on the Religious Freedom Restoration Act (RFRA), 42 U.S.C. §§ 2000bb *et seq*.

[38] *Rasul II*, 563 F.3d at 529.

[39] *Id.* at 532 & n.5.

[40] 28 U.S.C. § 2241(e)(2), provides that [n]o court ... shall have jurisdiction to hear or consider any other action against the United States or its agents relating to any aspect of the detention, transfer, treatment, trial, or conditions of confinement of an alien who is or was detained by the United States and has been determined by the United States to have been properly detained as an enemy combatant or is awaiting such determination.

[41] Al-Zahrani v. Rumsfeld, No. 09-0028, slip op. at 7 (D.D.C. 2010) (citing Al-Adahi v. Obama, 596 F. Supp. 2d 111, 119 (D.D.C. 2009); Khadr v. Bush, 587 F. Supp. 2d 225, 235-36 (D.D.C. 2009); *In re* Guantanamo Bay Detainee Litig., 577 F. Supp. 2d 312, 314 (D.D.C. 2008); *In re* Guantanamo Bay Detainee Litig., 570 F. Supp. 2d 13, 18 (D.D.C. 2008)). *See also* Kiyemba v. Obama, 561 F.3d 509, 512 n.1 (D.C. Cir. 2009) (in habeas case, noting that *Boumediene* "referred to § 7 without specifying a particular subsection of § 2241(e) but its

discussion of the Suspension Clause clearly indicates it was referring only to that part of § 7 codified at § 2241(e)(1)")).

[42] Maqaleh v. Gates, 604 F. Supp. 2d 205 (D.D.C. 2009).

[43] After the district court's initial ruling in *Maqaleh*, DOD announced modifications to the administrative process used to review the status of aliens held at Bagram, which would afford detainees greater procedural rights. The modified process does not contemplate judicial review of administrative determinations regarding the detention of persons at Bagram. *See* Letter from Phillip Carter, Dep. Asst. Sec. Defense for Detainee Policy, to Sen. Carl Levin, Chairman of Sen. Armed Serv. Comm., Jul. 14, 2009, available at http://www.scotusblog.com/wp/wp-content/uploads/2009/09/USBagram-brief-9-14-09.pdf. The circuit panel stated that its analysis was not informed by these new procedures, as those procedures were not in place when the case was appealed to the circuit court.

[44] Padilla v. Hanft, 389 F. Supp. 2d 678 (D.S.C. 2005).

[45] *See* Respondents' Answer to the Petition for a Writ of Habeas Corpus at 2, Padilla v. Hanft, C/A No. 02:04 2221-26AJ (D.S.C. filed 2004).

[46] 389 F. Supp. 2d at 690.

[47] 423 F.3d 386, 390-91 (4th Cir. 2005).

[48] The government initially asked the Fourth Circuit to approve Padilla's transfer and suggested it should vacate its opinion, but the judges preferred to defer to the Supreme Court to make that determination. In rejecting the government's application, Circuit Judge Luttig (who has since stepped down from the bench) issued a harsh opinion expressing disappointment at the government's decision abruptly to abandon its position that national security imperatives demanded Padilla's continued military detention: [A]s the government surely must understand, although the various facts it has asserted are not necessarily inconsistent or without basis, its actions have left not only the impression that Padilla may have been held for these years, even if justifiably, by mistake—an impression we would have thought the government could ill afford to leave extant. They have left the impression that the government may even have come to the belief that the principle in reliance upon which it has detained Padilla for this time, that the President possesses the authority to detain enemy combatants who enter into this country for the purpose of attacking America and its citizens from within, can, in the end, yield to expediency with little or no cost to its conduct of the war against terror—an impression we would have thought the government likewise could ill afford to leave extant. Padilla v. Hanft, 432 F.3d 582, 587 (4th Cir. 2005)(order).

[49] Padilla v. Hanft, 546 U.S. 1084 (2006).

[50] 547 U.S. 1062 (2006).

[51] United States v. Padilla, 2007 WL 1079090 (S.D.Fla. 2007) (unreported opinion). While one district court held Padilla can pursue civil damages against a former government official for his treatment in military detention, Padilla v. Yoo, 633 F. Supp. 2d 1005 (N.D.Cal. 2009), another has rejected a civil suit on the basis of qualified immunity for the government officials involved, Lebron v. Rumsfeld, 2011 WL 554061 (D.S.C. 2011)

[52] For further discussion of *al-Marri*, see CRS Report RL33180, *Enemy Combatant Detainees: Habeas Corpus Challenges in Federal Court*, by Jennifer K. Elsea and Michael John Garcia.

[53] al-Marri v. Pucciarelli, 534 F.3d 213, 221 (2008) (Traxler, J., concurring).

[54] The exact nature of the information and its acquisition by the government is obscured by the many redactions in the reported opinions.

[55] United States v. Moussaoui, 382 F.3d 453, 456-57 (4th Cir. 2004) ("*Moussaoui II*"). In "*Moussaoui I*," 333 F.3d 509, 517 (4th Cir. 2003), the circuit court dismissed the appeal of the discovery order as unripe and remanded for the government to propose substitutions for the witness testimony similar to those available under CIPA. (CIPA applies to the production of documents during discovery but does not address witnesses). The district court imposed sanctions on remand after the government refused to make the enemy combatant witnesses available for deposition. The judge rejected the parties' proposal for an order of dismissal, the ordinary sanction under CIPA in cases in which the government declines to provide classified information the court has determined is necessary for the defense. Instead, she dismissed the death notice on the grounds that the witnesses could provide testimony that might preclude a jury from finding Moussaoui eligible for the death penalty. Because the testimony could exonerate Moussaoui of involvement in the September 11 attacks, the district court prohibited the government "from making any argument, or offering any evidence, suggesting that the defendant had any involvement in, or knowledge of, the September 11 attacks." United States v. Moussaoui, 282 F. Supp. 2d 480, 327 (E.D. Va. 2003). Evidence that would have been excluded under the order included cockpit voice recordings, video footage showing the collapse of the World Trade Center Towers, and photographs of victims.

[56] 382 F.3d at 487 n. 31. Judge Gregory noted in dissent that such information may be reliable for intelligence purposes and yet omit relevant information that might be helpful to the defense because such information was not deemed to have any actionable foreign intelligence value. *Id.* at 488, n. 6.

[57] As noted by a dissenting judge of the appellate panel, the procedures crafted by the majority deviate from CIPA procedures by having the district judge, rather than the government, prepare the substitutions for the potential testimony, arguably making the district court judge an advocate in the proceedings. 382 F.3d. at 484-85 (Gregory, J., concurring in part and dissenting in part).

[58] Moussaoui v. Obama, 591 F.3d 263, 278 (4th Cir. 2010).

[59] United States v. Lindh, 212 F. Supp. 2d 541, 557-58 (E.D. Va. 2002). The judge also rejected Lindh's contention that media publicity had rendered a fair trial for him impossible, at least in that particular court, and that the International Economic Emergency Powers Act ("IEEPA") (50 U.S.C. § 1701 et seq.) regulations he was charged with violating were not valid.

[60] United States v. Lindh, 198 F. Supp. 2d 739 (E.D. Va. 2002).

[61] *Id.* at 742.

[62] *Id.* at 743.

[63] *Id.* at 744.

[64] United States v. Ghailani, No. S10 98 Crim. 1023, slip op. at 30, 2009 WL 3853799, at *11-12 (S.D.N.Y. Nov. 18, 2009) (citing Morris v. Slappy, 461 U.S. 1, 14 (1983); Wheat v. United States, 486 U.S. 153, 159 (1988)).

[65] United States v. Ghailani, No. S10 98 Crim. 1023, slip op. at 7-8, 2010 WL 653269, at *2-3 (S.D.N.Y. Jan. 21, 2010) (citing Barker v. Wingo, 407 U.S. 514 (1972)).

[66] *Id.*, slip op. at 12, 2010 WL 653269, at *4.

[67] Barker v. Wingo, Warden 407 U.S. 514, 519 (1972).

[68] *See id.* at 530. Courts have recognized at least three types of prejudice, including "'oppressive pretrial incarceration,' 'anxiety and concern of the accused,' and 'the possibility that the [accused's] defense will be impaired' by dimming memories and loss of exculpatory evidence." *See Doggett v. United States*, 505 U.S. 647, 654 (1992) (citing *Barker*, 407 U.S. at 532; *Smith v. Hooey*, 393 U.S. 374, 377-379 (1969); *United States v. Ewell*, 383 U.S. 116, 120 (1966).

[69] United States v. Ghailani, No. S10 98 Crim. 1023, 2010 WL 2756546, *12 (S.D.N.Y. 2010).

[70] *Id.* at *13-14. The court pointed out that the defendant had been "no more able to engage in hostilities against the United States while in the custody of the Bureau of Prisons pending trial on this indictment than he was at Guantanamo in the custody of the DoD. He could have been brought to this Court in 2006 or any subsequent date to face this 1998 indictment and, at the same time, prevented from engaging in hostilities against this country." *Id.* at 14.

[71] *Id.* at *15. The judge contrasted this factor against situations where delay is justified by ongoing state investigations and prosecutions.

[72] *Id.* at *17.

[73] United States v. Ghailani,—F.Supp.2d—, 2010 WL 4058043 (S.D.N.Y. 2010).

[74] United States v. Ghailani, 743 F. Supp. 2d 242 (S.D.N.Y. 2010) (order). Under the "core application" doctrine, the exclusionary rule should be limited to cases where it serves as a deterrent to unlawful police actions, which typically means barring the use of unlawfully seized evidence in the government's case in chief for the offense that precipitated the search, and that extension of the rule to cases where the remedial purpose is not served (such as cases in which a search is defective due to clerical error) must be justified by weighing the additional marginal deterrence against the cost to the public interest in pursuing the truth. *See* Arizona v. Evans, 514 U.S. 1 (1995). The government argued that the exclusion of any evidence obtained as a result of Ghailani's coerced statements would not serve any deterrent purpose because the interrogation was conducted as part of a CIA effort to gather intelligence necessary for national security purposes rather than part of a law enforcement operation., and that CIA interrogators did not contemplate nor were motivated by the prospect of a criminal investigation. Judge Kaplan rejected the government's rationale, noting that a Fourth Amendment violation occurs at the time of an unlawful search or seizure, while the Fifth Amendment's Self-Incrimination Clause is violated whenever a coerced statement or its fruit is introduced at trial. Accordingly, he reasoned that the direct protection of a constitutional right rather than the deterrence of future violations was at stake in the case before him, and that the rationale of the core application doctrine did not apply.

[75] United States v. Ghailani, Slip Copy, 2010 WL 4006381 (S.D.N.Y. 2010). A redacted opinion memorializing the decision is said to be forthcoming.

[76] For a complete list of charges, see Press Release, U.S. Justice Department, "Ahmed Ghailani Transferred from Guantanamo Bay to New York for Prosecution on Terror Charges," June 9, 2009, *available online* at http://www.justice.gov/opa/pr/2009/June/09-ag-563.html.

[77] United States v. Ghailani,—F. Supp. 2d—, 2011 WL 181757 (S.D.N.Y. 2011).

[78] The defense argued in essence that a conviction for conspiracy to commit a substantive offense is improper where a defendant is acquitted of committing the substantive offense itself and the proof necessary to support the substantive charge is identical to that required for a conspiracy conviction. The judge rejected that theory as a valid statement of the law. *See id.* at *13.

[79] *Id.* at *18.

[80] *Id.* at *15.

In: Terrorists, Enemy Combatant Detainees ...
Editors: Jian Sun and Miguel Masipag

ISBN: 978-1-61470-391-4

Chapter 2

ENEMY COMBATANT DETAINEES: *HABEAS CORPUS* CHALLENGES IN FEDERAL COURT*

Jennifer K. Elsea and Michael John Garcia

SUMMARY

After the Supreme Court held that federal courts have jurisdiction under the federal *habeas corpus* statute to hear legal challenges on behalf of persons detained at the U.S. Naval Station in Guantanamo Bay, Cuba, in connection with the conflict against Al Qaeda and associated groups (*Rasul v. Bush*), the Pentagon established administrative hearings, called "Combatant Status Review Tribunals" (CSRTs), to allow the detainees to contest their status as enemy combatants, and informed them of their right to pursue *habeas* relief in federal court. Lawyers subsequently filed dozens of petitions on behalf of the detainees in the District Court for the District of Columbia, where district court judges reached inconsistent conclusions as to whether the detainees have any enforceable rights to challenge their treatment and detention.

Congress subsequently passed the Detainee Treatment Act of 2005 (DTA) to divest the courts of jurisdiction to hear some detainees' challenges by eliminating the federal courts' statutory jurisdiction over *habeas* claims (as well as other causes of action) by aliens detained at Guantanamo. The DTA provided for limited appeals of CSRT determinations or final decisions of military commissions. After the Supreme Court rejected the view that the DTA left it without jurisdiction to review a *habeas* challenge to the validity of military commissions in the case of *Hamdan v. Rumsfeld*, Congress enacted the Military Commissions Act of 2006 (MCA) (P.L. 109-366) to authorize the President to convene military commissions and to amend the DTA to further reduce detainees' access to federal courts, including in cases already pending.

---

* This is an edited, reformatted and augmented version of a Congressional Research Service publication, CRS Report for Congress RL33180, from www.crs.gov, dated April 5, 2010.

In 2008, the Supreme Court ruled in *Boumediene v. Bush* that aliens detained at Guantanamo have the constitutional privilege of *habeas corpus*, and the judicial review mechanism provided by the MCA and DTA by which detainees could challenge the legality of their detention did not provide a constitutionally adequate *habeas* substitute. The immediate impact of the *Boumediene* decision is that detainees at Guantanamo may petition a federal district court for *habeas* review of the legality and possibly the circumstances of their detention, perhaps including challenges to the jurisdiction of military commissions. Several issues remain unresolved and are the subject of ongoing litigation, including the constitutional protections owed to detainees held at Guantanamo and other locations outside the United States; the substantive scope of military detention authority; the procedural standards used to assess the adequacy of evidence supporting a detainee's designation as an enemy belligerent; and the authority of federal *habeas* courts to compel the release of detainees determined to be unlawfully held into the United States if the Executive cannot effectuate their release to another country. The Supreme Court was expected to consider some of these issues in the case of *Kiyemba v. Obama*, but changed circumstances surrounding some of the petitioners resulted in the Court remanding the case back to the D.C. Circuit for further consideration.

In March 2009, the Obama Administration announced a new definitional standard for the government's authority to detain terrorist suspects, which is largely similar in scope to the "enemy combatant" standard used by the Bush Administration to detain terrorist suspects. The standard would permit the detention of members of the Taliban, Al Qaeda, and associated forces, along with persons who provide "substantial support" to such groups, regardless of whether such persons were captured away from the battlefield in Afghanistan. Courts that have considered the Executive's authority to detain under the AUMF and law of war have reached differing conclusions as to the scope of this detention authority. In January 2010, a D.C. Circuit panel held that support for or membership in an AUMF-targeted organization may constitute a sufficient ground to justify military detention.

INTRODUCTION

Following the terrorist attacks of 9/11, Congress passed the Authorization to Use Military Force (AUMF), which granted the President the authority "to use all necessary and appropriate force against those ... [who] planned, authorized, committed, or aided the terrorist attacks" against the United States.[1] Soon thereafter, President Bush issued a military order formulating guidelines for the detention and treatment of foreign belligerents captured in the "war on terror" and establishing military commissions to try some detainees for violations of the law of war.[2] Beginning in early 2002, the United States began transferring suspected foreign belligerents captured in the "war on terror" to the U.S. Naval Station in Guantanamo Bay, Cuba for preventive detention and potential prosecution for any war crimes they may have committed.

In 2004, the Supreme Court issued two key rulings concerning the Executive's authority to detain persons in the "war on terror." In *Hamdi v. Rumsfeld*,[3] a majority of the Court found that the 2001 AUMF permitted the preventive detention of enemy combatants captured during hostilities in Afghanistan, including those who were U.S. citizens. A divided Court found that persons deemed "enemy combatants" have the right to challenge their detention before a judge or other "neutral decision-maker." The *Hamdi* case concerned the rights of a U.S. citizen detained as an enemy combatant, and the Court did not decide the extent to which this right also applied to noncitizens held at Guantanamo and elsewhere. However, on the same day that *Hamdi* was decided, the Court issued an opinion in the case of *Rasul v. Bush*,[4] holding that the federal *habeas corpus* statute, 28 U.S.C. § 2241, provided federal courts with jurisdiction to consider *habeas corpus* petitions by or on behalf of persons detained at Guantanamo.

The Court's rulings in *Hamdi* and *Rasul* had two immediate consequences. First, the Department of Defense (DOD) established Combatant Status Review Tribunals (CSRTs), an administrative process to determine whether a detainee at Guantanamo was an "enemy combatant." Second, the U.S. District Court for the District of Columbia began to hear the dozens of *habeas* cases filed on behalf of the detainees, with different judges reaching conflicting conclusions as to whether the detainees had any enforceable rights available other than the bare right to petition for *habeas*.

After the Supreme Court granted certiorari to hear a challenge by one of the detainees to his trial by military tribunal, Congress passed the Detainee Treatment Act of 2005 (DTA)[5]. The DTA requires uniform standards for interrogation of persons in the custody of the DOD, and expressly bans cruel, inhuman, or degrading treatment of detainees in the custody of any U.S. agency. At the same time, however, it divested the courts of jurisdiction to hear challenges by those detained at Guantanamo Bay based on their treatment or living conditions. The DTA also eliminated the federal courts' statutory jurisdiction over *habeas* claims by aliens challenging their detention at Guantanamo Bay, but provided for limited appeals of status determinations made pursuant to the DOD procedures for CSRTs, along with final decisions by military commissions.

However, in the 2006 case of *Hamdan v. Rumsfeld*,[6] the Supreme Court interpreted the provision eliminating federal *habeas* jurisdiction as being inapplicable to cases that were pending at the time the DTA was enacted, permitting it to review the validity of military commissions established pursuant to President Bush's 2001 military order. The Court held that the military tribunals established by the President did not comply with the Uniform Code of Military Justice (UCMJ) or the law of war which the UCMJ incorporates, including the 1949 Geneva Conventions. In response to the *Hamdan* ruling, Congress enacted the Military Commissions Act of 2006 ("MCA" or "2006 MCA").[7] The act authorized the President to convene military commissions to try "unlawful alien combatants" for war crimes without complying with the parts of the UCMJ the earlier system was said to violate, and it also established procedural requirements for the commissions. Finally, the MCA expressly eliminated court jurisdiction over all pending and future causes of action by detainees, including *habeas* review, with the exception of the limited review process established under the DTA.

The complete elimination of *habeas corpus* review by Congress compelled the courts to address directly an issue they had avoided reaching in earlier cases: Does the constitutional writ of *habeas corpus* extend to noncitizens held at Guantanamo? The Constitution's Suspension Clause prohibits the suspension of *habeas corpus* except when public safety requires it in the case of invasion or surrender. The MCA did not purport to be a suspension of *habeas*, and the government did not make such a claim to the courts. Instead, the government argued that noncitizens detained at Guantanamo are entitled to no constitutional protections, including the privilege of *habeas corpus*. Therefore, it was argued, denying these persons access to *habeas* review would not run afoul of the Suspension Clause. In the 2008 case *Boumediene v. Bush*, the Court rejected this argument in a 5-4 opinion, and ruled that the constitutional privilege of *habeas* extends to Guantanamo detainees and cannot be extinguished by statute unless an adequate substitute is provided.[8]

As a result of the *Boumediene* decision, detainees currently held at Guantanamo may petition for *habeas* review of their designation and detention as enemy combatants. The judicial process established by the DTA was effectively nullified by a D.C. Circuit's ruling in January 2009 interpreting the *Boumediene* decision,[9] although Congress has not officially repealed it.[10] Several legal issues remain unsettled, including the scope of *habeas* review available to detainees, the remedy available for those persons found to be unlawfully held by the United States, and the extent to which other constitutional provisions extend to noncitizens held at Guantanamo and elsewhere.

Some of these issues were expected to be addressed by the Supreme Court this term in an appeal of a D.C. Circuit panel ruling in the case of *Kiyemba v. Obama*, in which the appellate court held that federal *habeas* courts lack the authority to order the release of Guantanamo detainees into the United States, even when those detainees are found to be unlawfully held and the government is unable to effectuate their release to a foreign country. After the Supreme Court granted certiorari to review the case, several countries agreed to resettle the *Kiyemba* petitioners. In March 2010, the Supreme Court vacated the appellate court's decision and remanded the case back to the circuit court for further consideration in light of these developments.[11]

On January 22, 2009, President Obama issued an Executive Order requiring that the Guantanamo detention facility be closed as soon as practicable, and no later than a year from the date of the Order.[12] The Order further requires specified officials to review all Guantanamo detentions to assess whether the detainee should continue to be held by the United States, be transferred or released to a third country, or be prosecuted by the United States for criminal offenses.[13] During the review process, the Secretary of Defense was required to take steps to ensure that all proceedings before military commissions and the United States Court of Military Commission Review were halted.[14] Although the imposed deadline for closing the Guantanamo detention facility was not met, the Obama Administration maintains that it intends to close the facility as expeditiously as possible. The closure of the Guantanamo detention facility and its resulting effects could have implications for legal challenges raised by detainees, particularly if detainees are brought to the United States, where they would arguably have a more clearly defined entitlement to additional constitutional protections.[15]

In March 2009, the Obama Administration announced a new definitional standard for the government's authority to detain terrorist suspects, which no longer employs the phrase "enemy combatant" to refer to persons who may be properly detained,[16] although the new standard is largely similar in scope to the "enemy combatant" standard used earlier. The Obama Administration standard would permit the detention of members of the Taliban, Al Qaeda, and associated forces, along with persons who provide "substantial support" (rather than merely "support") to such groups, regardless of whether these individuals were captured away from the battlefield in Afghanistan.[17] The Obama Administration indicated that this definitional standard does "not rely on the President's authority as Commander-in-Chief independent of Congress's specific authorization."[18]

The scope of the Executive's detention authority has been subject to ongoing litigation and conflicting rulings. In January 2010, a D.C. Circuit panel held in the case of *Al-Bihani v. Obama*[19] that support for or membership in an AUMF-targeted organization may be independently sufficient to justify military detention, without proof that the detainee committed any hostile act. In discussing the scope of the Executive's detention authority, the panel applied the standard that had been used by the Bush Administration rather than the slightly more limited standard applied by the Obama Administration, and disavowed the view that international law has relevance to the determination. The significance of this policy change and the circuit court's ruling remains to be seen. As of March 2010, reviewing courts have ruled that at least 11 detainees are lawfully held pursuant to the AUMF, while at least 33 have been held to be (or were conceded by the government to be) held without authorization.[20]

Also in January 2010, the Obama Administration reportedly completed its assessment of the nearly 200 detainees remaining at Guantanamo, determining that about 50 detainees will continue to be held without trial; that around 35 detainees will be prosecuted in military commission or federal court; and that suitable countries have been found to take the remaining detainees.[21] However, the transfer of 30 detainees of Yemeni nationality back to Yemen was stymied because an Al Qaeda affiliate in Yemen is suspected to have been behind the Christmas 2009 bombing attempt.[22] Additionally, Congress has balked at plans to bring detainees to the United States for continued, non-penal detention or for release.

This report provides an overview of the early judicial developments and the establishment of CSRT procedures; summarizes selected court cases related to the detentions and the use of military commissions; and discusses the Detainee Treatment Act, as amended by the Military Commissions Act of 2006 and the Military Commissions Act of 2009, analyzing its effects on detainee-related litigation in federal court. The report summarizes the Supreme Court's decision in *Boumediene* invalidating Congress's efforts to revoke the courts' habeas jurisdiction, and discusses some remaining issues and subsequent developments.

EARLY DEVELOPMENTS IN THE DETENTION AND TRIAL OF ENEMY COMBATANTS CAPTURED IN THE "WAR ON TERROR"

The Bush Administration determined in February 2002 that Taliban detainees are covered under the Geneva Conventions,[23] while Al Qaeda detainees are not,[24] but that none of the detainees qualifies for the status of prisoner of war (POW).[25] The Administration deemed all of them to be "unlawful enemy combatants," and claimed the right to detain them without trial or continue to hold them in preventive detention even if they are acquitted of criminal charges by a military tribunal. Fifteen of the detainees had been determined by the President to be subject to his military order ("MO") of November 13, 2001,[26] making them eligible for trial by military commission for war crimes offenses.[27] The Supreme Court, however, found that the procedural rules established by the Department of Defense to govern the military commissions were not established in accordance with the Uniform Code of Military Justice (UCMJ).[28] The following sections trace the judicial developments with respect to the detention of alleged enemy combatants.

Rasul v. Bush[29]

Petitioners were two Australians and twelve Kuwaitis (a petition on behalf of two U.K. citizens was mooted by their release) who were captured during hostilities in Afghanistan and were being held in military custody at the Guantanamo Bay Naval Base, Cuba. The Bush Administration argued, and the court below had agreed, that under the 1950 Supreme Court case *Johnson v. Eisentrager*,[30] "'the privilege of litigation' does not extend to aliens in military custody who have no presence in 'any territory over which the United States is sovereign.'" The Supreme Court distinguished *Rasul* by noting that *Eisentrager* concerned the *constitutional* right to *habeas corpus* rather than the right as implemented by statute. The *Rasul* Court did not reach the constitutional issue, but found authority for federal court jurisdiction in 28 U.S.C. § 2241, which grants courts the authority to hear applications for *habeas corpus* "within their respective jurisdictions," by any person who claims to be held "in custody in violation of the Constitution or laws or treaties of the United States."[31]

The Court also declined to read the statute to vary its geographical scope according to the citizenship of the detainee. Justice Kennedy, in a concurring opinion, would have found jurisdiction over the Guantanamo detainees based on the facts that Guantanamo is effectively a U.S. territory and is "far removed from any hostilities," and that the detainees are "being held indefinitely without the benefit of any legal proceeding to determine their status." Noting that the Writ of Habeas Corpus ("Writ") has evolved as the primary means to challenge executive detentions, especially those without trial, the Court held that jurisdiction over *habeas* petitions does not turn on sovereignty over the territory where detainees are held. Even if the *habeas* statute were presumed not to extend extraterritorially, as the government urged, the Court found that the "complete jurisdiction and control" the United States exercises under its lease with Cuba would suffice to bring the detainees within the territorial and historical scope of the Writ.

Without expressly overruling *Eisentrager*, the Court distinguished the cases at issue to find *Eisentrager* inapplicable. *Eisentrager* listed six factors that precluded those petitioners from seeking *habeas* relief: each petitioner "(a) is an enemy alien; (b) has never been or resided in the United States; (c) was captured outside of our territory and there held in military custody as a prisoner of war; (d) was tried and convicted by a Military Commission sitting outside the United States; (e) for offenses against laws of war committed outside the United States; (f) and is at all times imprisoned outside the United States."[32] The *Rasul* Court noted that the Guantanamo petitioners, in contrast, "are not nationals of countries at war with the United States, and they deny that they have engaged in or plotted acts of aggression against the United States; they have never been afforded access to any tribunal, much less charged with and convicted of wrongdoing; and for more than two years they have been imprisoned in territory over which the United States exercises exclusive jurisdiction and control."

As to the petitioners' claims based on statutes other than the *habeas* statute, which included the federal question statute[33] as well as the Alien Tort Statute,[34] the Court applied the same reasoning to conclude that nothing precluded the detainees from bringing such claims before a federal court.[35]

The Court's opinion left many questions unanswered. It did not clarify which of the *Eisentrager* (or *Rasul*) factors would control under a different set of facts.[36] The opinion did not address whether persons detained by the U.S. military abroad in locations where the

United States does not exercise full jurisdiction and control would have access to U.S. courts. The *Hamdan* opinion seems to indicate that a majority of the Court regarded *Eisentrager* as a ruling denying relief on the merits rather than a ruling precluding jurisdiction altogether.[37] Under this view, it may be argued, there was no statutory bar precluding detainees in U.S. custody overseas from petitioning for *habeas* relief in U.S. courts, although it may be substantially more difficult for such prisoners to identify a statutory or constitutional infraction that would enable them to prevail on the merits.

The Court did not decide the merits of the petitions, although in a footnote the majority opined that "Petitioners' allegations—that, although they have engaged neither in combat nor in acts of terrorism against the United States, they have been held in Executive detention for more than two years in territory subject to the long-term, exclusive jurisdiction and control of the United States, without access to counsel and without being charged with any wrongdoing—unquestionably describe 'custody in violation of the Constitution or laws or treaties of the United States.'" The opinion left to lower courts such issues as whether the detentions are authorized by Congress, who may be detained and what evidence might be adduced to determine whether a person is an enemy combatant, or whether the Geneva Conventions afford the detainees any protections. The Court did not address the extent to which Congress might alter federal court jurisdiction over detainees' *habeas* petitions, but *Boumediene* appears to foreclose the option of eliminating it completely, at least without an adequate substitute procedure. This issue is discussed more fully below.

Combatant Status Review Tribunals

In response to Supreme Court decisions in 2004 related to "enemy combatants," the Pentagon established procedures for Combatant Status Review Tribunals (CSRTs), based on the procedures the Army uses to determine POW status during traditional wars.[38] Detainees who are determined not to be enemy combatants are to be transferred to their country of citizenship or otherwise dealt with "consistent with domestic and international obligations and U.S. foreign policy."[39] CSRTs confirmed the status of at least 520 enemy combatants. Any new detainees that might be transported to Guantanamo Bay would go before a CSRT. The CSRTs are not empowered to determine whether the enemy combatants are unlawful or lawful, which led two military commission judges to hold that CSRT determinations are inadequate to form the basis for the jurisdiction of military commissions.[40] Military commissions must now determine whether a defendant is an unlawful enemy combatant in order to assume jurisdiction.[41]

CSRTs are administrative rather than adversarial, but each detainee has an opportunity to present "reasonably available" evidence and witnesses[42] to a panel of three commissioned officers to try to demonstrate that the detainee does not meet the criteria to be designated as an "enemy combatant," defined as "an individual who was part of or supporting Taliban or al Qaida forces, or associated forces that are engaged in hostilities against the United States or its coalition partners[,] ... [including] any person who has committed a belligerent act or has directly supported hostilities in aid of enemy armed forces."[43] Each detainee is represented by a military officer (not a member of the Judge Advocate General ("JAG") Corps)[44] and may elect to participate in the hearing or remain silent.[45] The government's evidence is presented by the recorder, who is a military officer, preferably a judge advocate.[46]

The CSRTs are not bound by the rules of evidence that would apply in court, and the government's evidence is presumed to be "genuine and accurate."[47] The government is required to present all of its relevant evidence, including evidence that tends to negate the detainee's designation, to the tribunal.[48] The CSRT is required to assess, "to the extent practicable, whether any statement derived from or relating to such detainee was obtained as a result of coercion and the probative value, if any, of any such statement."[49] Unclassified summaries of relevant evidence may be provided to the detainee.[50] The detainee's personal representative may view classified information and comment on it to the tribunal to aid in its determination[51] but does not act as an advocate for the detainee.[52] If the tribunal determines that the preponderance of the evidence is insufficient to support a continued designation as "enemy combatant" and its recommendation is approved through the chain of command, the detainee will be informed of that decision upon finalization of transportation arrangements (or earlier, if the task force commander deems it appropriate).[53]

In March 2002, the Pentagon announced plans to create a separate process for periodically reviewing the status of detainees.[54] The process, similar to the CSRT process, affords persons detained at Guantanamo Bay the opportunity to present to a review board, on at least an annual basis while hostilities are ongoing, information to show that the detainee is no longer a threat or that it is in the interest of the United States and its allies to release the prisoner. If new information with a bearing on the detainee's classification as an "enemy combatant" comes to light, a new CSRT may be ordered using the same procedures as described above.[55] The detainee's State of nationality may be allowed, national security concerns permitting, to submit information on behalf of its national.

PRE-*BOUMEDIENE V. BUSH* COURT CHALLENGES TO THE DETENTION POLICY

While the Supreme Court clarified in *Rasul* (and later *Boumediene*, discussed *infra*) that detainees currently held at Guantanamo have recourse to federal courts to challenge their detention, the extent to which they may enforce any rights they may have under the Geneva Conventions and other law continues to remain unclear. Prior to the enactment of the DTA provisions eliminating *habeas* review, the Justice Department argued primarily that *Rasul v. Bush* merely decided the issue of jurisdiction, but that the 1950 Supreme Court decision in *Johnson v. Eisentrager*[56] remained applicable to limit the relief to which the detainees may be entitled. While more than one district judge from the D.C. Circuit agreed,[57] others did not, holding for example that detainees have the right to the assistance of an attorney.[58] One judge found that a detainee has the right to be treated as a POW until a "competent tribunal" decides otherwise,[59] but the appellate court reversed. The following sections summarize the three most important decisions prior to the enactment of the 2006 MCA, including the cases that eventually reached the Supreme Court as *Boumediene v. Bush* and *Hamdan v. Rumsfeld.* The Court of Appeals for the D.C. Circuit had ordered these cases dismissed for lack of jurisdiction on the basis of the MCA,[60] but the Supreme Court reversed in both its *Hamdan* and *Boumediene* decisions, returning the cases to the district court for consideration on the merits. Also discussed is a Fourth Circuit case involving an alien, al-Marri, arrested in the United States and subsequently held in military custody as an enemy combatant. The

Supreme Court initially granted certiorari to review the appellate court's decision.[61] However, before the Court could consider the merits of the case, the government requested that the Court authorize al-Marri's release from military custody and transfer to civilian authorities to face criminal charges. The Court granted the government's request, vacated the appellate court's earlier judgment, and transferred the case back to the lower court with orders to dismiss it as moot.

Khalid v. Bush[62]

Seven detainees, all of whom had been captured outside of Afghanistan, sought relief from their detention at the Guantanamo Bay facility. U.S. District Judge Richard J. Leon agreed with the Bush Administration that Congress, pursuant to the 2001 AUMF, granted the President the authority to detain foreign enemy combatants outside the United States for the duration of the war against Al Qaeda and the Taliban, and that the courts have virtually no power to review the conditions under which such prisoners are held. Noting that the prisoners had been captured and detained pursuant to the President Bush's military order,[63] Judge Leon agreed with the government that "(1) non-resident aliens detained under [such] circumstances have no rights under the Constitution; (2) no existing federal law renders their custody unlawful; (3) no legally binding treaty is applicable; and (4) international law is not binding under these circumstances."[64]

Judge Leon rejected the petitioners' contention that their arrest outside of Afghanistan and away from any active battlefield meant that they could not be "enemy combatants" within the meaning of the law of war, finding instead that the AUMF contains no geographical boundaries,[65] and gives the President virtually unlimited authority to exercise his war power wherever enemy combatants are found.[66] The circumstances behind the off-battlefield captures did, however, apparently preclude the petitioners from claiming their detentions violate the Geneva Conventions.[67] Other treaties put forth by the petitioners were found to be unavailing because of their non-self-executing nature.[68]

The court declined to evaluate whether the conditions of detention were unlawful. Judge Leon concluded that "[w]hile a state of war does not give the President a 'blank check,' and the courts must have some role when individual liberty is at stake, any role must be limited when, as here, there is an ongoing armed conflict and the individuals challenging their detention are non-resident aliens."[69] He dismissed all seven petitions, ruling that "until Congress and the President act further, there is ... no viable legal theory under international law by which a federal court could issue a writ."

On appeal, the *Khalid* case was consolidated with *In re Guantanamo Detainee Cases* as *Boumediene v. Bush*.

In re Guantanamo Detainee Cases[70]

U.S. District Judge Joyce Hens Green interpreted *Rasul* more broadly, finding that the detainees do have rights under the U.S. Constitution and international treaties, and thus denied the government's motion to dismiss the 11 challenges before the court. Specifically, Judge Green held that the detainees are entitled to due process of law under the Fifth

Amendment, and that the CSRT procedures do not meet that standard. Interpreting the history of Supreme Court rulings on the availability of constitutional rights in territories under the control of the American government (though not part of its sovereign territory), Judge Green concluded that the inquiry turns on the fundamental nature of the constitutional rights being asserted rather than the citizenship of the person asserting them. Accepting that the right not to be deprived of liberty without due process of law is a fundamental constitutional right, the judge applied a balancing test to determine what process is due in light of the government's significant interest in safeguarding national security.[71] Judge Green rejected the government's stance that the CSRTs provided more than sufficient due process for the detainees. Instead, she identified two categories of defects. She objected to the CSRTs' failure to provide the detainees with access to material evidence upon which the tribunal affirmed their "enemy combatant" status and the failure to permit the assistance of counsel to compensate for the lack of access. These circumstances, she said, deprived detainees of a meaningful opportunity to challenge the evidence against them.

Second, in particular cases, the judge found that the CSRTs' handling of accusations of torture and the vague and potentially overbroad definition of "enemy combatant" could violate the due process rights of detainees. Citing detainees' statements and news reports of abuse, Judge Green noted that the possibility that evidence was obtained involuntarily from the accused or from other witnesses, whether by interrogators at Guantanamo or by foreign intelligence officials elsewhere, could make such evidence unreliable and thus constitutionally inadmissible as a basis on which to determine whether a detainee is an enemy combatant. Judge Green objected to the definition of "enemy combatant" because it appears to cover "individuals who never committed a belligerent act or who never directly supported hostilities against the U.S. or its allies." She noted that government counsel had, in response to a set of hypothetical questions, stated that the following could be treated as enemy combatants under the AUMF: "[a] little old lady in Switzerland who writes checks to what she thinks is a charity that helps orphans in Afghanistan but [what] really is a front to finance al-Qaeda activities, a person who teaches English to the son of an al Qaeda member, and a journalist who knows the location of Osama Bin Laden but refuses to disclose it to protect her source."[72] Judge Green stated that the indefinite detention of a person solely because of his contacts with individuals or organizations tied to terrorism, and not due to any direct involvement in terrorist activities, would violate due process even if such detention were found to be authorized by the AUMF.[73]

This case was consolidated with the *Khalid* decision and heard as *Boumediene v. Bush* by the D.C. Circuit Court of Appeals, and on appeal, the Supreme Court.

Hamdan v. Rumsfeld

Salim Ahmed Hamdan, who was captured in Afghanistan and is alleged to have worked for Osama Bin Laden as a bodyguard and driver, brought this challenge to the lawfulness of the Secretary of Defense's plan to try him for alleged war crimes before a military commission,[74] arguing that the military commission rules and procedures were inconsistent with the UCMJ[75] and that he had the right to be treated as a prisoner of war under the Geneva Conventions.[76] U.S. District Judge Robertson agreed, finding no inherent authority in the President as Commander-inChief of the Armed Forces to create such tribunals outside of the existing statutory authority, with which the military commission rules did not comply. He also concluded that the Geneva Conventions apply to the whole of the conflict in Afghanistan, including under their protections all persons detained in connection with the hostilities there,[77] and that Hamdan was thus entitled to be treated as a prisoner of war until his status was determined to be otherwise by a competent tribunal, in accordance with article 5 of the Third Geneva Convention (prisoners of war).

The D.C. Circuit Court of Appeals reversed, ruling that the Geneva Conventions are not judicially enforceable. Judge Williams wrote a concurring opinion, construing Common Article 3 to apply to any conflict with a non-state actor,[78] without regard to the geographical confinement of such a conflict within the borders of a signatory state. The Circuit Court interpreted the UCMJ language to mean that military commission rules have only to be consistent with those articles of the UCMJ that refer specifically to military commissions, and therefore need not be uniform with the rules that apply to courts-martial. After the appellate court decision was handed down, Congress passed the DTA, which revoked federal court jurisdiction to hear *habeas corpus* petitions and other causes of action brought by Guantanamo detainees. (The provisions of the DTA are discussed in greater detail *infra.*) The Supreme Court nevertheless granted review and reversed.

Jurisdiction

Before reaching the merits of the case, the Supreme Court declined to accept the government's argument that Congress, by passing the DTA, had stripped the Court of its jurisdiction to review *habeas corpus* challenges by or on behalf of Guantanamo detainees whose petitions had already been filed.[79] The Court also declined to dismiss the appeal as urged by the government on the basis that federal courts should abstain from intervening in cases before military tribunals that have not been finally decided,[80] noting the dissimilarities between military commission trials and ordinary courts-martial of service members pursuant to procedures established by Congress.[81] The government's argument that the petitioner had no rights conferred by the Geneva Conventions that could be adjudicated in federal court likewise did not persuade the Court to dismiss the case. Regardless of whether the Geneva Conventions provide rights enforceable in Article III courts, the Court found that Congress, by incorporating the "law of war" into UCMJ article 21,[82] brought the Geneva Conventions within the scope of law to be applied by courts. Justice Scalia, joined by Justices Thomas and Alito, dissented, arguing that the DTA should be interpreted to preclude the Court's review.

Presidential Authority

With respect to the authority to create the military commissions, the Court held that any power to create them must flow from the Constitution and must be among those "powers granted jointly to the President and Congress in time of war."[83] It disagreed with the government's position that Congress had authorized the commissions either when it passed the AUMF[84] or the DTA. Although the Court assumed that the AUMF activated the President's war powers, it did not view the AUMF as expanding the President's powers beyond the authorization set forth in the UCMJ. The Court also noted that the DTA, while recognizing the existence of military commissions, does not specifically authorize them. At most, these statutes "acknowledge a general Presidential authority to convene military commissions in circumstances where justified under the 'Constitution and laws,' including the law of war."[85]

The Geneva Conventions and the Law of War

The *habeas corpus* statute permits those detained under U.S. authority to challenge their detention on the basis that it violates any statute, the Constitution, or a treaty.[86] The D.C. Circuit nevertheless held that the Geneva Conventions are never enforceable in federal courts.[87] The Supreme Court disagreed, finding the Conventions were applicable as incorporated by UCMJ Article 21, because "compliance with the law of war is the condition upon which the authority set forth in Article 21 is granted."[88] In response to the alternative holding by the court below that Hamdan, as a putative member of Al Qaeda, was not entitled to any of the protections accorded by the Geneva Conventions, the Court concluded that Common Article 3 of the Geneva Conventions applies even to members of Al Qaeda, according to them a minimum baseline of protections, including protection from the "passing of sentences and the carrying out of executions without previous judgment pronounced by a regularly constituted court, affording all the judicial guarantees which are recognized as indispensable by civilized peoples."[89]

While recognizing that Common Article 3 "obviously tolerates a great degree of flexibility in trying individuals captured during armed conflict," and that "its requirements are general ones, crafted to accommodate a wide variety of legal systems," the Court found that the military commissions under M.C.O. No. 1 did not meet these criteria. In particular, the military commissions did not qualify as "regularly constituted" because they deviated too far, in the Court's view, from the rules that apply to courts-martial, without a satisfactory explanation of the need for such deviation.[90] Justice Alito, joined by Justices Scalia and Thomas, dissented, arguing that the Court is bound to defer to the President's plausible interpretation of the treaty language.

Analysis

While the *Hamdan* Court declared the military commissions as constituted under the President Bush's Military Order to be "illegal," it left open the possibility that changes to the military commission rules could cure any defects by bringing them within the law of war and conformity with the UCMJ, or by asking Congress to authorize or craft rules tailored to the armed conflict it authorized against those responsible for the 9/11 terrorist attacks. The Court did not resolve the extent to which the detainees, as aliens held outside of U.S. territory, have constitutional rights enforceable in federal court.

The decision may affect the treatment of detainees outside of their criminal trials; for example, in interrogations for intelligence purposes. Common Article 3 of the Geneva Conventions mandates that all persons taking no active part in hostilities, including those who have laid down their arms or been incapacitated by capture or injury, are to be treated humanely and protected from "violence to life and person," torture, and "outrages upon personal dignity, in particular, humiliating and degrading treatment." Insofar as these protections are incorporated in the UCMJ and other laws, it would seem the Court is ready to interpret and adjudicate them, to the extent it retains jurisdiction to do so.[91] It is not clear how the Court views the scope of the relevant armed conflict, however, because its decisions on the merits have been limited to cases arising out of hostilities in Afghanistan.[92]

The opinion reaffirms the holding in *Rasul v. Bush*[93] that the AUMF does not provide the President a "blank check," and, by finding in favor of a noncitizen held overseas, seems to have extended to non-citizens the *Hamdi* comment that

> [w]hatever power the United States Constitution envisions for the Executive in its exchanges with other nations or with enemy organizations in times of conflict, it most assuredly envisions a role for all three branches when individual liberties are at stake.[94]

The dissenting views also relied in good measure on actions taken by Congress, seemingly repudiating the view expressed earlier by the Executive that any efforts by Congress to legislate with respect to persons captured, detained, and possibly tried in connection with the armed conflict would be an unconstitutional intrusion into powers held exclusively by the President.[95] Expressly or implicitly, all eight participating Justices applied the framework set forth by Justice Jackson in his famous concurrence in the *Steel Seizures* case,[96] which accords greater deference to the President in cases involving national security where he acts with express congressional authority than when he acts alone. The differing views among the Justices seem to have been a function of their interpretation of the AUMF and other acts of Congress as condoning or limiting executive actions.[97] The Military Commissions Act likely resolves many issues regarding the scope of the President's authority to try detainees by military commission; however, the constitutionality of the various measures remains to be resolved.

Al-Marri

The case of Ali Saleh Kahlah al-Marri differs significantly from cases discussed above in that the petitioner, a lawful alien resident, was arrested and imprisoned within the United States. Whether a person in his position may lawfully be detained pursuant to the AUMF has not been fully resolved. The issue divided the Fourth Circuit, which initially found in favor in the petitioner but then reversed *en banc*, only to have the Supreme Court vacate the *en banc* opinion after the government charged the petitioner with a federal crime and moved him into the ordinary criminal justice system. The following section describes the facts of the case and the issues that divided the courts, which may return to relevance, especially if congressional efforts are successful in making military commissions the sole forum for trying persons who meet the definition of persons triable under the Military Commissions Act, as amended.[98]

Al-Marri, a Qatari student, was arrested in December 2001 in Peoria, IL, and transported to New York City, where he was held as a material witness for the grand jury investigating the 9/11 attacks. He was later charged with financial fraud and making false statements and transferred back to Peoria. Before his case went to trial, however, he was declared an "enemy combatant" and transferred to military custody in South Carolina. Al-Marri's counsel filed a petition for *habeas corpus* challenging al-Marri's designation and detention as an "enemy combatant." The petition was eventually dismissed for lack of jurisdiction by the U.S. Court of Appeals for the Seventh Circuit,[99] and a new petition was filed in the Fourth Circuit. In March 2005, Judge Floyd agreed with the government that the detention was authorized by the AUMF and transferred the case to a federal magistrate to examine the factual allegations supporting the government's detention of the petitioner as an enemy combatant.[100] The government provided a declaration asserting that al-Marri is closely associated with Al Qaeda and had been sent to the United States prior to September 11, 2001, to serve as a "sleeper agent" for Al Qaeda in order to "facilitate terrorist activities and explore disrupting this country's financial system through computer hacking."[101] The magistrate judge recommended the dismissal of the petition on the basis of information the government provided, which al-Marri did not attempt to rebut and which the magistrate judge concluded was sufficient for due process purposes in line with the *Hamdi* decision.[102] The district judge adopted the magistrate judge's report and recommendations in full, rejecting the petitioner's argument that his capture away from a foreign battlefield precluded his designation as an "enemy combatant."[103]

Al-Marri appealed, and the government moved to dismiss on the basis that section 7 of the 2006 MCA stripped the court of jurisdiction. The petitioner asserted that Congress did not intend to deprive him of his right to *habeas* or that, alternatively, the MCA is unconstitutional. The majority of the appellate panel avoided the constitutional question by finding that al-Marri does not meet the statutory definition as an alien who "has been determined by the United States to have been properly detained as an enemy combatant or is awaiting such determination."[104]

Turning to the merits, the majority found that al-Marri does not fall within the legal category of "enemy combatant" within the meaning of *Hamdi*, and that the government could continue to hold him only if it charges him with a crime, commences deportation proceedings, obtains a material witness warrant in connection with grand jury proceedings, or detains him for a limited time pursuant to the USA PATRIOT Act.[105] In so holding, the majority rejected the government's contention that the AUMF authorizes the President to order the military to seize and detain persons within the United States under the facts asserted by the government, or that, alternatively, the President has inherent constitutional authority to order the detention.

The government cited the *Hamdi* decision and the Fourth Circuit's decision in *Padilla v. Hanft*[106] to support its contention that al-Marri is an enemy combatant within the meaning of the AUMF and the law of war. The court, however, interpreted *Hamdi* as confirming only that "the AUMF is explicit congressional authorization for the detention of individuals in the *narrow category* ... [of] individuals who were 'part of or supporting forces hostile to the United States or coalition partners in Afghanistan and who engaged in an armed conflict against the United States there.'"[107] Likewise, Padilla, although captured in the United States, could be detained pursuant to the AUMF only because he had been, prior to returning to the United States, "'armed and present in a combat zone' in Afghanistan as part of Taliban forces during the conflict there with the United States."[108] The court explained that the two cases cited by the government, *Hamdi* and *Padilla*, involved situations similar to the World War II case *Ex parte Quirin*,[109] in which the Supreme Court agreed that eight German saboteurs could be tried by military commission because they were enemy belligerents within the meaning of the law of war.[110] In contrast, al-Marri's situation was to be likened to *Ex parte Milligan*,[111] the Civil War case in which the Supreme Court held that a citizen of Indiana accused of conspiring to commit hostile acts against the Union was nevertheless a civilian who was not amenable to military jurisdiction.[112] The court concluded that enemy combatant status rests, in accordance with the law of war, on affiliation with the military arm of an enemy government in an international armed conflict.

Judge Hudson dissented, arguing that the broad language of the AUMF, which authorized the President "to use all necessary and appropriate force against those nations, *organizations, or persons* he determines" were involved in the terrorist attacks of September 11, 2001, "would certainly seem to embrace surreptitious al Qaeda agents operating within the continental United States."[113] He would have found no meaningful distinction between the present case and *Padilla*.

The government petitioned for and was granted a rehearing *en banc*.[114] On rehearing, the narrowly divided Fourth Circuit full bench rejected the earlier panel's decision in favor of the government's position that al-Marri fit the legal definition of "enemy combatant," but also reversed the district court's decision that al-Marri was not entitled to present any more evidence to refute the government's case against him. Four of the judges on the panel would have retained the earlier decision, arguing that it was not within the court's power to expand the definition of "enemy combatant" beyond the law-of-war principles at the heart of the Supreme Court's *Hamdi* decision.[115] However, these four judges joined in Judge Traxler's opinion to remand for evidentiary proceedings in order "at least [to] place the burden on the Government to make an initial showing that normal due process protections are unduly burdensome and that the Rapp declaration is 'the most reliable available evidence,' supporting the Government's allegations before it may order al-Marri's military detention."[116]

Judge Traxler, whose opinion is controlling for the case although not joined in full by any other panel member, agreed with the four dissenting judges that the AUMF "grants the President the power to detain enemy combatants in the war against al Qaeda, including belligerents who enter our country for the purpose of committing hostile and war-like acts such as those carried out by the al Qaeda operatives on 9/11."[117] Accordingly, he would define "enemy combatant" in the present terrorism-related hostilities to include persons who "associate themselves with al Qaeda" and travel to the United States "for the avowed purpose of further prosecuting that war on American soil, ... even though the government cannot establish that the combatant also 'took up arms on behalf of that enemy and against our country in a foreign combat zone of that war.'"[118] Under this definition, American citizens arrested in the United States could also be treated as enemy combatants under similar allegations,[119] at least if they had traveled abroad and returned for the purpose of engaging in activity related to terrorism on behalf of Al Qaeda.

However, Judge Traxler did not agree that al-Marri had been afforded due process by the district court to challenge the factual basis for his designation as an enemy combatant. While recognizing that the *Hamdi* plurality had suggested that hearsay evidence might be adequate to satisfy due process requirements for proving enemy combatant status, Judge Traxler did not agree that such relaxed evidentiary standards are necessarily appropriate when dealing with a person arrested in the United States:

> Because al-Marri was seized and detained in this country,... he is entitled to habeas review by a civilian judicial court and to the due process protections granted by our Constitution, interpreted and applied in the context of the facts, interests, and burdens at hand. To determine what constitutional process al-Marri is due, the court must weigh the competing interests, and the burden-shifting scheme and relaxed evidentiary standards discussed in *Hamdi* serve as important guides in this endeavor. *Hamdi* does not, however, provide a cookie-cutter procedure appropriate for every alleged enemy-combatant, regardless of the circumstances of the alleged combatant's seizure or the actual burdens the government might face in defending the habeas petition in the normal way.[120]

In December 2008, the Supreme Court agreed to hear an appeal of the *Al-Marri* ruling,[121] potentially setting the stage for the Court to make a definitive pronouncement regarding the President's authority to militarily detain terrorist suspects apprehended away from the Afghan battlefield. However, on January 22, 2009, President Obama instructed the Attorney General, Secretary of Defense, and other designated officials to review the factual and legal basis for alMarri's continued detention as an enemy combatant, and "identify and thoroughly evaluate alternative dispositions."[122] This review culminated in criminal charges being brought against alMarri in the U.S. District Court for the Central District of Illinois, alleging that al-Marri provided material support to Al Qaeda and had conspired with others to provide material support to Al Qaeda.[123] The United States thereafter moved for the Supreme Court to dismiss al-Marri's appeal as moot and authorize his transfer from military to civilian custody pending his criminal trial. On March 6, 2009, the Court granted the government's application concerning the transfer of alMarri to civilian custody. It vacated the Fourth Circuit's judgment and remanded the case back to the appellate court with instructions to dismiss the case as moot.[124] Accordingly, the appellate court's earlier decision regarding the President's authority to detain terrorist suspects captured within the United States is no longer binding precedent in the Fourth Circuit. Al-Marri thereafter pled guilty in federal court to one count of conspiracy to provide material support to Al Qaeda,[125] and was sentenced to eight and a half years in prison.

The dismissal of al-Marri's case means that the President's legal authority to militarily detain terrorist suspects apprehended in the United States has not been definitively settled. Indeed, the transfer of al-Marri to civilian custody to face trial in federal court means that the United States no longer holds any terrorist suspect in military detention who was apprehended in the United States. Whether circumstances will arise either in the conflict with Al Qaeda or some other military conflict that will compel the Supreme Court to more definitively address the President's military detention authority remains to be seen.

DETAINEE TREATMENT ACT OF 2005 (DTA)

The DTA, passed after the Court's 2004 decision in *Rasul,* requires uniform standards for interrogation of persons in the custody of the Department of Defense,[126] and expressly bans cruel, inhuman, or degrading treatment of detainees in the custody of any U.S. agency.[127] The prohibited treatment is defined as that which would violate the Fifth, Eighth, and Fourteenth Amendments to the U.S. Constitution, as the Senate has interpreted "cruel, inhuman, or degrading" treatment banned by the U.N. Convention Against Torture.[128] The provision does not create a cause of action for detainees to ask a court for relief based on inconsistent treatment, and it divests the courts of jurisdiction to hear challenges by those detained at Guantanamo Bay based on their treatment or living conditions.[129] It also provides a legal defense to U.S. officers and agents who may be sued or prosecuted based on their treatment or interrogation of detainees.[130] This language appears to have been added as a compromise because the Bush Administration reportedly sought to have the Central Intelligence Agency excepted from the prohibition on cruel, inhuman and degrading treatment on the grounds that the President needs "maximum flexibility in dealing with the global war on terrorism."[131]

The DTA also includes a modified version of the "Graham-Levin Amendment,"[132] which requires the Defense Department to submit to the Armed Services and Judiciary Committees the procedural rules for determining detainees' status.[133] The amendment neither authorizes nor requires a formal status determination, but it does require that certain congressional committees be notified 30 days prior to the implementation of any changes to the rules. As initially adopted by the Senate, the amendment would have required these procedural rules to preclude evidence determined by the board or tribunal to have been obtained by undue coercion, however, the conferees modified the language so that the tribunal or board must assess, "to the extent practicable ... whether any statement derived from or relating to such detainee was obtained as a result of coercion" and "the probative value, if any, of any such statement."

The Graham-Levin Amendment also eliminated the federal courts' statutory jurisdiction over *habeas* claims by aliens detained at Guantanamo Bay, but provided for limited appeals of status determinations made pursuant to the DOD procedures for Combatant Status Review Tribunals (CSRTs). In June 2008, the Supreme Court invalidated the provision that eliminated *habeas corpus* jurisdiction, but stated that the DTA appellate process "remains intact,"[134] although it appears that the process is not an adequate substitute for *habeas* review.[135]. However, the D.C. Circuit held that the DTA appellate procedure is no longer good law, leaving *habeas* petitions as the only means of seeking review of detention.[136]

The DTA also provided for an appeal to the Court of Appeals for the District of Columbia Circuit of final sentences rendered by a military commission.[137] As initially enacted, the DTA required the court to review capital cases or cases in which the alien was sentenced to death or to a term of imprisonment for 10 years or more, and made review over convictions with lesser penalties discretionary.[138] The scope of review was limited to considering whether the decision applied the correct standards consistent with Military Commission Order No. 1 (implementing President Bush's Military Order) and whether those standards were consistent with the Constitution and laws of the United States, to the extent applicable.

THE MILITARY COMMISSIONS ACT OF 2006

After the Court's decision in *Hamdan*, the Bush Administration proposed legislation to Congress,[139] a version of which was enacted on October 17, 2006. The Military Commissions Act of 2006 (MCA or 2006 MCA) authorized the trial of certain detainees by military commission and prescribed detailed rules to govern their procedures.[140] The 2006 MCA also amended the DTA provisions regarding appellate review and *habeas corpus* jurisdiction. In 2009, Congress enacted the Military Commissions Act of 2009 (2009 MCA) as part of the National Defense Authorization Act for FY2010 (P.L. 111-84). The 2009 MCA modified many of the rules for military commissions to make them more closely resemble those used in courts-martial proceedings,[141] but made only minor modifications to existing laws concerning court jurisdiction to adjudicate claims raised by detainees.

Provisions Affecting Court Jurisdiction

The 2006 MCA expanded the DTA to make its review provisions the exclusive remedy for all aliens detained as enemy combatants anywhere in the world, rather than only those housed at Guantanamo Bay, Cuba.[142] It does not, however, require that all detainees undergo a CSRT or a military tribunal in order to continue to be confined. However, inasmuch as the U.S. Court of Appeals for the District of Columbia Circuit declared the DTA appellate procedures to be defunct in light of the Supreme Court's *Boumediene* decision, it appears that all challenges must now be brought by means of *habeas* review rather than under the DTA. The records of CSRT proceedings will likely be relevant to *habeas* determinations.

Appeals from the final decisions of military commissions continue to go to the United States Court of Appeals for the District of Columbia Circuit as they did under the DTA,[143] but are routed through an appellate body, the Court of Military Commission Review (CMCR). Review of decisions of a military commission may only concern matters of law, not fact.[144] Under the 2006 MCA, appeals could be based on inconsistencies with the procedures set forth by the act, or, to the extent applicable, the Constitution or laws of the United States. The 2009 MCA specifies that the circuit court may consider and take action regarding the sufficiency of the evidence used to support the commission's verdict.

Section 7 of the 2006 MCA revoked U.S. courts' jurisdiction to hear *habeas corpus* petitions by all aliens in U.S. custody as enemy combatants, including lawful enemy combatants, regardless of the place of custody. It replaced 28 U.S.C. § 2241(e), the *habeas* provision added by the DTA, with language providing that

> 1) No court, justice, or judge shall have jurisdiction to hear or consider an application for a writ of habeas corpus filed by or on behalf of an alien detained by the United States who has been determined by the United States to have been properly detained as an enemy combatant or is awaiting such determination.
> 2) Except as provided in paragraphs (2) [review of CSRT determinations] and (3) [review of final decisions of military commissions] of section 1005(e) of the Detainee Treatment Act of 2005 (10 U.S.C. 801 note), no court, justice, or judge shall have jurisdiction to hear or consider any other action against the United States or its agents relating to any aspect of the detention, transfer, treatment, trial, or conditions of confinement of an alien who is or was detained by the United States and has been determined by the United States to have been properly detained as an enemy combatant or is awaiting such determination.[145]

This amendment took effect on the date of its enactment, and applied to "all cases, without exception, pending on or after the date of [enactment] which relate to any aspect of the detention, transfer, treatment, trial, or conditions of detention of an alien detained by the United States since September 11, 2001." In *Boumediene v. Bush*, discussed *infra*, the Supreme Court held that MCA § 7 acted as an unconstitutional suspension of the writ of *habeas* corpus, and authorized Guantanamo detainees to petition federal district courts for *habeas* review of CSRT determinations of their enemy combatant status.

Under the DTA appeals provision, there was no apparent limit to the amount of time a detainee could spend awaiting a determination as to combatant status. Aliens who continue to be detained despite having been determined not to be enemy combatants were not permitted to challenge their continued detention or their treatment, nor were they able to protest their transfer to another country, for example, on the basis that they fear torture or persecution. However, these matters may be raised in *habeas* petition. The extent of relief the courts may be able to grant under *habeas* review is currently being litigated.

Provisions Regarding the Geneva Conventions

A continuing source of dispute in the detention and treatment of detainees is the application of the Geneva Convention. As noted previously, the *habeas corpus* statute has traditionally provided for, among other things, challenges to allegedly unlawful detentions based on rights found in treaties.[146] Thus, for instance, Common Article 3 of the 1949 Geneva Conventions, which prohibits the "passing of sentences and the carrying out of executions without previous judgment pronounced by a regularly constituted court, affording all the judicial guarantees which are recognized as indispensable by civilized peoples," has been used as a basis for challenging the confinement of detainees.[147]

Section 5 of the 2006 MCA (28 U.S.C. § 2241 note), however, specifically precludes the application of the Geneva Conventions to *habeas* or other civil proceedings.[148] Further, the MCA, as amended, provides that the Geneva Conventions may not be claimed as a basis for a private right of action by an alien who is subject to military commission proceedings.[149] However, Congress in the 2009 MCA removed language deeming that the military commission structure established by the act complies with the requirement under Common Article 3 of the Geneva Convention that trials be by a regularly constituted court.[150]

In addition, the act provides that the President shall have the authority to interpret the meaning of the Geneva Conventions.[151] The intended effect of this provision is unclear. While the President generally has a role in the negotiation, implementation, and domestic enforcement of treaty obligations,[152] this power does not generally extend to "interpreting" treaty obligations, a role more traditionally associated with courts.[153] In general, Congress is prohibited from exercising powers allocated to another branch of government.[154] In *United States v. Klein*,[155] the Supreme Court invalidated a law passed by Congress that was designed to frustrate an earlier finding of the Supreme Court as to the effect of a presidential pardon.[156] Similarly, a law that was specifically intended to grant the authority of the President to adjudicate or remedy treaty violations could violate the doctrine of separation of powers, as providing relief from acts in violation of treaties is a judicial branch function.[157] Instead, what appears to be the main thrust of this language is to establish the authority of the President within the Executive Branch to issue interpretative regulations by Executive Order.[158] However, the context in which this additional authority would be needed is unclear.

One possible intent of this provision is that the President is being given the authority to "interpret" the Geneva Convention for diplomatic purposes (e.g., to define treaty obligations and encourage other countries to conform to such definitions). This interpretation seems unlikely, as the President's power in this regard is already firmly established.[159] Another possible meaning is that the President is being given the authority to apply the Geneva Conventions to particular fact situations, such as specifying what type of interrogation techniques may be lawfully applied to a particular individual suspected of being an enemy combatant. This interpretation is possible, but it is not clear how the power to "interpret" would be significant in that situation, as the 2006 MCA precludes application of the Geneva Convention in those contexts in which such interrogations would be challenged—military commissions, *habeas corpus*, or any other civil proceeding.[160]

The more likely intent of this language would be to give the President the authority to promulgate regulations prescribing standards of behavior of employees and agents of federal agencies. For instance, this language might be seen as authorizing the President to issue regulations to implement how agency personnel should comply with the Geneva

Conventions, policies which might otherwise be addressed at the agency level. Thus, for instance, if the CIA had established internal procedures regarding how to perform interrogation consistent with the Geneva Convention, then this language would explicitly authorize the President to amend such procedures by Executive Order.[161] Whether the President already had such power absent this language is beyond the scope of this report.

POST-2006 MCA ISSUES AND DEVELOPMENTS

Shortly after the enactment of the 2006 MCA, the government filed motions to dismiss all of the *habeas* petitions in the D.C. Circuit involving detainees at Guantanamo Bay[162] and the petition of an alien then detained as an enemy combatant in a naval brig in South Carolina.[163]

Possible Application to U.S. Citizens

As originally enacted, the 2006 MCA provided that military commissions could exercise personal jurisdiction over alien "unlawful enemy combatants." Pursuant to modifications made by the 2009 MCA, military commissions may now exercise jurisdiction over alien "unprivileged enemy belligerents."[164] Despite the difference in nomenclature, the two terms are used to refer to similar categories of persons.

Some observers raised concern that the 2006 MCA permits the President to detain American citizens as enemy belligerents without trial.[165] The prohibition in the 2006 MCA with respect to *habeas corpus* petitions applied only to those filed by or on behalf of aliens detained by the United States as enemy combatants. However, both MCAs can be read by implication to permit the detention of U.S. citizens as enemy belligerents, although it does not permit their trial by military commission, which could affect their entitlement to relief using *habeas corpus* procedures.[166]

A plurality of the Supreme Court held in 2004 in *Hamdi v. Rumsfeld*,[167] that the President has the authority to detain U.S. citizens as enemy combatants pursuant to the AUMF,[168] but that the determination of combatant status is subject to constitutional due process considerations. The *Hamdi* plurality was limited to an understanding that the phrase "enemy combatant" means an "individual who ... was 'part of or supporting forces hostile to the United States or coalition partners' in Afghanistan and who 'engaged in an armed conflict against the United States' there,"[169] but left it to lower courts to flesh out a more precise definition. The U.S. Court of Appeals for the Fourth Circuit found that the definition continued to apply to a U.S. citizen who returned to the United States from Afghanistan and was arrested at the airport.[170] More recently, the Fourth Circuit appeared to have expanded the definition of "enemy combatant" to individuals arrested in the United States on suspicion of planning to participate in terrorist acts without necessarily having engaged in hostilities in Afghanistan, but this ruling was part of a judgment that was thereafter vacated by the Supreme Court. (See discussion of *Al-Marri*, *supra*.)

In theory, the executive branch could detain a citizen as an enemy belligerent and argue that the definition of "unprivileged enemy belligerent" provided in the 2009 MCA, which does not explicitly limit its definitional scope to aliens, bolsters the detention authority already possessed by virtue of the AUMF. Constitutional due process would apply, and the citizen could petition for *habeas corpus* to challenge his detention. However, under the 2006 MCA the citizen-combatant would not be able to assert rights based on the Geneva Convention in support of his contention that he is not an enemy belligerent. In that sense, U.S. citizens could be affected by the 2006 and 2009 MCAs even though they do not directly apply to U.S. citizens.

On the other hand, since the 2009 MCA's definition for unprivileged enemy belligerent applies on its face only for the purposes of chapter 47a of Title 10, U.S. Code (providing for the trial by military commission of alien unprivileged enemy belligerents), it may be argued that outside of that context, the terms "enemy belligerent" and "enemy combatant" should be understood in the ordinary sense, that is, to include only persons who participate directly in hostilities against the United States. This interpretation seems unlikely, given that it would also mean that this narrower definition of "enemy belligerent" was also meant to apply in the context of the 2006 MCA's *habeas corpus* provisions, such that some aliens who fall under the jurisdiction of a military commission under the 2006 MCA would nevertheless have been able to argue that their right to petition for *habeas corpus* or pursue any other cause of action in U.S. court is unaffected, a reading that does not seem consistent with Congress's probable intent. Further, it does not appear that Congress meant to apply a different definition of "enemy belligerent" to persons depending on their citizenship. Congress could specify that U.S. citizens captured in the context of the armed conflict against terrorist organizations be subject to trial in U.S. court for treason or a violation of any other statute, or prescribe procedures for determining whether U.S. citizens are subject to detention as enemy belligerents, if constitutional, but it has not done so.

DTA Challenges to Detention

At the same time as it was considering the *Boumediene* case, the D.C. Circuit was reviewing several challenges brought pursuant to the DTA in which detainees contested CSRT determinations that they are properly detained as "enemy combatants." The first of these cases to advance involved Haji Bismullah, who was captured in Afghanistan in 2003, and Husaifa Parhat and six other detainees, all ethnic Chinese Uighers captured in Pakistan in December 2001. In January 2009, the D.C. Circuit ruled that the judicial review system established under by the DTA had been effectively nullified by the Supreme Court's ruling in *Boumediene*, meaning that detainees could only challenge the legality of their confinement via *habeas corpus* review.

Bismullah v. Gates

At issue was a series of motions filed by both parties seeking to establish procedures governing access to classified information, attorneys' access to clients, and other matters. The petitioners sought to have the court adopt rules similar to what the district court had ordered when the cases were before it on petitions of *habeas corpus*. The government sought to establish rules restricting scope of discovery and attorney-client communication to what it viewed as the proper scope of the court's review, that is, the CSRT proceedings.

The D.C. Circuit in July 2007 issued an order rejecting the government's motion to limit the scope of the court's review to the official record of the CSRT hearings (*Bismullah I*).[171] Rather, the court decided, in order to determine whether a preponderance of evidence supported the CSRT determinations, it must have access to *all* the information a CSRT "is authorized to obtain and consider, pursuant to the procedures specified by the Secretary of Defense." The court denied the petitioners' motion for discovery, at least for the time being, stating there was no need for additional evidence to challenge a CSRT's ruling that specific evidence or a witness was not reasonably available. And, because the DTA does not authorize the court to hold a status determination invalid as "arbitrary and capricious," there was no need for it to evaluate the conduct of other detainees' CSRTs. The court also denied as unnecessary the petitioners' motion to appoint a special master.

The court also promised to enter a protective order to implement guidelines for handling classified and sensitive information and for government monitoring of attorney client written communications ("legal mail"). Again stressing its mandate under the DTA to determine whether a preponderance of the evidence supports a CSRT's status determination, the court found that counsel for the detainees, to aid in their capacity to assist the court, should be presumed to have a "need to know" all government information concerning their clients except for highly sensitive information, in which case the government could present the evidence to the court *ex parte*. The court rejected the government's proposal that would have allowed the government, rather than the court, to determine what unclassified information would be required to be kept under seal. With respect to legal mail, the court agreed to the government's proposal to have mail from attorneys to detainees reviewed by a "privilege team," composed of Department of Defense personnel not involved in the litigation, to redact information not pertinent to matters within the court's limited scope of review.

The government asked the panel to reconsider the ruling based on its belief that the order would require the government to undertake an overly burdensome search of all relevant federal agencies in order to create a new record for each detainee that would be entirely different from the record reviewed by the CSRT for that case. The court denied the request for rehearing, explaining its view that its previous order would not require a search for information that is not "reasonably available" (*Bismullah II*).[172] The court also suggested that the government might instead convene new CSRTs to reconfirm the detainees' status, this time ensuring that the relevant documents are retained for the purpose of review under the DTA. The government also objected to the requirement that it turn over classified information to the petitioners' counsel on the basis of the risk to intelligence sources and methods as well as the burden of conducting the necessary reviews to determine which information must be turned over. The court rejected the argument, pointing out that DOD regulations declare classified information to be not reasonably available where the originating agency declines to authorize its use in the CSRT process. In light of this fact, the court suggested, the burden of reviewing the information should not be as great as the government had argued.

The government then asked for an *en banc* hearing, but the D.C. Circuit, evenly divided, declined.[173] The government then sought expedited review at the Supreme Court, urging the Court to decide the cases concurrently with the *Boumediene* case, but the Court took no action on the request.[174] Instead, it granted certiorari and vacated the decision, remanding for reconsideration in light of its decision in *Boumediene*.[175] On August 22, 2008, the D.C. Circuit reinstated without explanation its decisions in *Bismullah I* and *Bismullah II*, presumably because it did not find the *Boumediene* ruling to conflict with its decisions in these cases.[176]

The government subsequently petitioned for a rehearing of the case, arguing that the Supreme Court's ruling in *Boumediene* effectively nullified the system of circuit court review established by the DTA, as Congress had not intended for detainees to have two judicial forums in which to challenge their detention.[177] The D.C. Circuit granted the government's motion for rehearing, and on January 9, 2009, a three-judge panel held that, in light of the Supreme Court's ruling in *Boumediene* restoring detainees' ability to seek *habeas* review of the legality of their detention, the appellate court no longer had jurisdiction over petitions for review filed pursuant to the DTA. Writing for the panel, Judge Douglas H. Ginsburg described both the text of the DTA and the subsequent jurisdiction-stripping measures of the 2006 MCA, stating they left no doubt that Congress understood review under DTA to be a substitute for and not a supplement to *habeas corpus* and hence the exclusive means by which a detainee could contest the legality of his detention in a court."[178] In the aftermath of *Boumediene*, Judge Ginsburg wrote, the DTA "can no longer function in a manner consistent with the intent of Congress."[179] Accordingly, the court held that the DTA may no longer serve as an avenue of judicial review of detainees' claims, as Congress had intended this review process to be available to detainees only in the absence of the availability of *habeas* review. In January 2009, a review panel considering new information determined that Bismullah was not an enemy combatant, and he was repatriated to Afghanistan.[180]

Parhat v. Gates

In October 2007, while the government's petition to the Supreme Court for certiorari in the *Bismullah* case was pending, the government produced to the counsel of Husaifa Parhat, one of the parties to the *Bismullah* case, a record (including both classified and unclassified material) of what was actually presented to Parhat's CSRT. Parhat subsequently filed a separate motion to the D.C. Circuit requesting review of the CSRT's determination that he was an enemy combatant. In June 2008, a three-judge panel for the D.C. Circuit ruled in the case of *Parhat v. Gates* that petitioner had been improperly deemed an "enemy combatant" by a CSRT, the first ruling of its kind by a federal court. Because the court's opinion contained classified information, only a redacted version has been released.[181]

Parhat, an ethnic Chinese Uighur captured in Pakistan in December 2001, was found to be an "enemy combatant" by the CSRT on account of his affiliation with a Uighur independence group known as the East Turkistan Islamic Movement (ETIM), which was purportedly "associated" with Al Qaeda and the Taliban and engaged in hostilities against the United States and its coalition partners. The basis for Parhat's alleged "affiliation" with the ETIM was that an ETIM leader ran a camp in Afghanistan where Parhat had lived and received military training. For his part, Parhat denied membership in the ETIM or engagement in hostilities against the United States, and claimed he traveled to Afghanistan solely to join the resistance against China, which was not alleged to have been a coalition partner of the United States.

The Circuit Court agreed with Parhat that the record before the CSRT did not support the finding that he was an "enemy combatant," as that term had been defined by the DOD, and accordingly the CSRT's determination was not supported by a "preponderance of the evidence" and "consistent with the standards and procedures specified by the Secretary of

Defense for Combatant Status Review Tribunals," as required by the DTA.[182] The DOD defined an "enemy combatant" as

> an individual who was part of or supporting Taliban or al Qaida forces, or associated forces that are engaged in hostilities against the United States or its coalition partners. This includes any person who has committed a belligerent act or has directly supported hostilities in aid of enemy armed forces.[183]

Both parties agreed that for a detainee who is not a member of the Taliban or Al Qaeda to be deemed an enemy combatant under this definition, the government must demonstrate by a preponderance of the evidence that (1) the detainee was part of or supporting "forces"; (2) those forces are associated with Al Qaeda or the Taliban; and (3) the forces are engaged in hostilities against the United States or its coalition partners.[184]

The circuit court found that the evidence presented by the government to support the second and third elements was insufficient to support the CSRT's determination that Parhat was an enemy combatant. Most significantly, the court found that the principal evidence presented by the government regarding these elements—four government intelligence documents describing ETIM activities and the group's relationship with Al Qaeda and the Taliban—did not "provide any of the underlying reporting upon which the documents' bottom-line assertions are founded, nor any assessment of the reliability of that reporting."[185] As a result, the circuit court found that neither the CSRT nor the reviewing court itself were capable of assessing the reliability of the assertions made by the documents. Accordingly "those bare assertions cannot sustain the determination that Parhat is an enemy combatant,"[186] and the CSRT's designation was therefore improper. The circuit court stressed that it was not suggesting that hearsay evidence could never reliably be used to determine whether a person was an enemy combatant, or that the government must always submit the basis for its factual assertions to enable an assessment of its claims. However, evidence "must be presented in a form, or with sufficient additional information, that permits the [CSRT] and court to assess its reliability."[187]

Having found that the evidence considered by the CSRT was insufficient to support the designation of Parhat as an enemy combatant, the circuit court next turned to the question of remedy. Although Parhat urged the court to order his release or transfer to a country other than China, the court declined to grant such relief, postulating that the government might wish to hold another CSRT in which it could present additional evidence to support Parhat's designation as an enemy combatant. While acknowledging that the DTA did not expressly grant the court release authority over detainees, the court stated that there was nonetheless "a strong argument ... [that release authority] is implicit in our authority to determine whether the government has sustained its burden of proving that a detainee is an enemy combatant,"[188] and indicated that it would not "countenance 'endless do-overs'" in the CSRT process.

The circuit court also noted that following the Supreme Court's ruling in *Boumediene,* Parhat could pursue immediate *habeas* relief in federal district court, where he would "be able to make use of the determinations we have made today regarding the decision of his CSRT, and ... raise issues that we did not reach" before a court which unquestionably would have the power to order his release.[189]

The continuing viability of the circuit court's ruling in *Parhat* is unclear given the Court's subsequent ruling in *Bismullah* that the DTA review process has been nullified.

However, the circuit court panel in *Bismullah* implied that, despite its determination that the DTA review process was no longer available to detainees, its ruling in *Parhat* remains in force.[190]

The government declined to reconvene CSRTs for Parhat and 16 other Uighurs detained at Guantanamo, and no longer considers them enemy combatants. However, the DOD continues to maintain custody over them pending their transfer to a third country. The government was initially unable to effectuate their transfer to a country where they would not face a substantial risk of torture or persecution. Although some of the Uighurs have successfully been transferred to other countries,[191] several remain at Guantanamo. The Uighurs filed *habeas* petitions with the U.S. District Court for D.C., and requested that they be released into the United States pending the court's final judgment on their *habeas* petitions. In October 2008, District Court Judge Ricardo M. Urbina found that the government had no authority to detain the petitioners and ordered their release into the United States, [192] at least until they may be transferred to a third country.

The government quickly filed an emergency motion with the D.C. Circuit to temporarily stay Judge Urbina's ruling pending the circuit court's disposition of a government motion for a stay pending appeal. The emergency motion was granted by a three-judge panel of the circuit court.[193] Later, the panel granted the government's motion for expedited review of the district court's order and, in a 2-1 decision, a stay of the Uighurs' transfer pending review of the district court's ruling.[194] In February 2009, the circuit panel reversed the district court, finding that the constitutional writ of *habeas* did not entitle petitioners to the "extraordinary remedy" of being released into the United States in light of long-standing jurisprudence recognizing the "exclusive power of the political branches to decide which aliens may, and which aliens may not, enter the United States."[195] The Supreme Court subsequently agreed to hear an appeal of the circuit court's ruling.[196] However, the United States was thereafter able to find countries willing to resettle the *Kiyemba* petitioners, and several have in fact been transferred.[197] Five of the *Kiymemba* petitioners remain detained at Guantanamo, apparently having rejected current offers for resettlement. Because the Supreme Court had granted certiorari on the understanding that no remedy was available for the petitioners other than release into the United States, it vacated the appellate court's ruling and remanded the case to circuit court to consider the ramifications of the new circumstances surrounding the petitioners' detention.[198] It remains to be seen whether the appellate court will reaffirm its previous ruling regarding the federal *habeas* courts' authority to release detainees into the United States.

BOUMEDIENE V. BUSH[199]

The petitioners in *Boumediene* were aliens detained at Guantanamo who sought *habeas* review of their continued detention. Rather than pursuing an appeal of their designation as enemy combatants by CSRTs using the DTA appeals process, the petitioners sought to have the district court decisions denying *habeas* review reversed on the basis that the 2006 MCA's "courtstripping"[200] provision was unconstitutional.[201] On appeal, the D.C. Circuit affirmed, holding that the 2006 MCA stripped it and all other federal courts of jurisdiction to consider petitioners' *habeas* applications. Relying upon its earlier opinion in *Al Odah v. United*

States[202] and the 1950 Supreme Court case *Johnson v. Eisentrager*,[203] in which the Supreme Court found that the constitutional writ of *habeas* was not available to enemy aliens imprisoned for war crimes in post-WWII Germany, the D.C. Circuit held that the 2006 MCA's elimination of *habeas* jurisdiction did not operate as an unconstitutional suspension of the writ, because aliens held by the United States in foreign territory do not have a constitutional right to *habeas*.[204] Consequently, the court did not examine whether the DTA provides an adequate substitution for *habeas* review.

The Supreme Court initially denied the petitioners' request for review,[205] with three Justices dissenting to the denial and two Justices explaining the basis for their support.[206] In June 2007, however, the Court reversed its denial and granted certiorari to consider the consolidated cases of *Boumediene* and *Al Odah*. In a 5-4 opinion authored by Justice Kennedy, the Court reversed the D.C. Circuit and held that petitioners had a constitutional right to *habeas* that was withdrawn by the 2006 MCA in violation of the Constitution's Suspension Clause.[207]

Constitutional Right to *Habeas*

The petitioners in *Boumediene* argued that they possess a constitutional right to *habeas*, and that the 2006 MCA deprived them of this right in contravention of the Suspension Clause, which prohibits the suspension of the writ of *habeas* except "when in Cases of Rebellion or Invasion the public Safety may require it." The 2006 MCA did not expressly purport to be a formal suspension of the writ of *habeas*, and the government did not make such a claim to the Court. Instead, the government argued that aliens designated as enemy combatants and detained outside the *de jure* territory of the United States have no constitutional rights, including the constitutional privilege to *habeas*, and that therefore stripping the courts of jurisdiction to hear petitioners' *habeas* claims did not violate the Suspension Clause.

The Court began its analysis by surveying the history and origins of the writ of *habeas corpus*, emphasizing the importance placed on the writ for the Framers, while also characterizing its prior jurisprudence as having been "careful not to foreclose the possibility that the protections of the Suspension Clause have expanded along with post-1789 developments that define the present scope of the writ."[208] The Court characterized the Suspension Clause as not only a "vital instrument" for protecting individual liberty, but also a means to ensure that the judiciary branch would have, except in cases of formal suspension, "a time-tested device, the writ, to maintain the delicate balance of governance" between the branches and prevent "cyclical abuses" of the writ by the executive and legislative branches.[209] The Court stated that the separation-of-powers doctrine and the history shaping the design of the Suspension Clause informed its interpretation of the reach and purpose of the Clause and the constitutional writ of *habeas*.

The Court found the historical record to be inconclusive for resolving whether the Framers would have understood the constitutional writ of *habeas* as extending to suspected enemy aliens held in foreign territory over which the United States exercised plenary, but not *de jure* control. Nonetheless, the Court interpreted the Suspension Clause as having full effect at Guantanamo. While the Court did not question the government's position that Cuba maintains legal sovereignty over Guantanamo under the terms of the 1903 lease giving the

U.S. plenary control over the territory, it disagreed with the government's position that "at least when applied to non-citizens, the Constitution necessarily stops where *de jure* sovereignty ends."[210]

Instead, the Court characterized its prior jurisprudence as recognizing that the Constitution's extraterritorial application turns on "objective factors and practical concerns."[211] Here, the Court emphasized the functional approach taken in the *Insular Cases*, where it had assessed the availability of constitutional rights in incorporated and unincorporated territories under the control of United States.[212] Although the government argued that the Court's subsequent decision in *Eisentrager* stood for the proposition that the constitutional writ of *habeas* does not extend to enemy aliens captured and detained abroad, the Court found this reading to be overly constrained. According to the Court, interpreting the *Eisentrager* ruling in this formalistic manner would be inconsistent with the functional approach taken by the Court in other cases concerning the Constitution's extraterritorial application,[213] and would disregard the practical considerations that informed the *Eisentrager* Court's decision that the petitioners were precluded from seeking *habeas*.

Based on the language found in the *Eisentrager* decision and other cases concerning the extraterritorial application of the Constitution, the Court deemed at least three factors to be relevant in assessing the extraterritorial scope of the Suspension Clause: (1) the citizenship and status of the detainee and the adequacy of the status determination process; (2) the nature of the site where the person is seized and detained; and (3) practical obstacles inherent in resolving the prisoner's entitlement to the writ.

Applying this framework, the Court characterized petitioners' circumstances in the instant case as being significantly different from those of the detainees at issue in *Eisentrager*. Among other things, the Court noted that unlike the detainees in *Eisentrager*, the petitioners denied that they were enemy combatants, and the government's control of the post-WWII, occupied German territory in which the *Eisentrager* detainees were held was not nearly as significant nor secure as its control over the territory where the petitioners are located. The Court also found that the procedural protections afforded to Guantanamo detainees in CSRT hearings are "far more limited [than those afforded to the *Eisentrager* detainees tried by military commission], and, we conclude, fall well short of the procedures and adversarial mechanisms that would eliminate the need for habeas corpus review."[214]

While acknowledging that it had never before held that noncitizens detained in another country's territory have any rights under the U.S. Constitution, the Court concluded that the case before it "lack[ed] any precise historical parallel."[215] In particular, the Court noted that the Guantanamo detainees have been held for the duration of a conflict that is already one of the longest in U.S. history, in territory that, while not technically part of the United States, is subject to complete U.S. control. Based on these factors, the Court concluded that the Suspension Clause has full effect at Guantanamo.

Adequacy of *Habeas Corpus* Substitute

Having decided that petitioners possessed a constitutional privilege to *habeas corpus*, the Court next assessed whether the court-stripping measure of MCA § 7 was impermissible under the Suspension Clause. Because the MCA did not purport to be a formal suspension of the writ, the question before the Court was whether Congress had provided an adequate substitute for *habeas corpus*. The government argued that the 2006 MCA complied with the Suspension Clause because it applied the DTA's review process to petitioners, which the government claimed was a constitutionally adequate *habeas* substitute.

Though the Court declined to "offer a comprehensive summary of the requisites for an adequate substitute for *habeas corpus*," it nonetheless deemed the *habeas* privilege, at minimum, as entitling a prisoner "to a meaningful opportunity to demonstrate that he is being held pursuant to 'the erroneous application or interpretation' of relevant law," and empowering a court "to order the conditional release of an individual unlawfully detained," though release need not be the exclusive remedy or appropriate in every instance where the writ is granted.[216] Additionally, the necessary scope of *habeas* review may be broader, depending upon "the rigor of any earlier proceedings."[217]

The Court noted that petitioners identified a myriad of alleged deficiencies in the CSRT process which limited a detainee's ability to present evidence rebutting the government's claim that he is an enemy combatant. Among other things, cited deficiencies include constraints upon the detainee's ability to find and present evidence at the CSRT stage to challenge the government's case; the failure to provide a detainee with assistance of counsel; limiting the detainee's access to government records other than those that are unclassified, potentially resulting in a detainee being unaware of critical allegations relied upon by the government to order his detention; and the fact that the detainee's ability to confront witnesses may be "more theoretical than real,"[218] given the minimal limitations placed upon the admission of hearsay evidence.

While the Court did not determine whether the CSRTs, as presently constituted, satisfy due process standards, it agreed with petitioners that there was "considerable risk of error in the tribunal's findings of fact."[219] "[G]iven that the consequence of error may be detention for the duration of hostilities that may last a generation or more, this is a risk too serious to ignore."[220] The Court held that for either the writ of *habeas* or an adequate substitute to function as an effective remedy for petitioners, a court conducting a collateral proceeding must have the ability to (1) correct errors in the CSRT process; (2) assess the sufficiency of the evidence against the detainee; and (3) admit and consider relevant exculpatory evidence that was not introduced in the prior proceeding.

The Court held that the DTA review process is a facially inadequate substitute for *habeas* review. It listed a number of potential constitutional infirmities in the review process, including the absence of provisions (1) empowering the D.C. Circuit to order release from detention; (2) permitting petitioners to challenge the President's authority to detain them indefinitely; (3) enabling the appellate court to review or correct the CSRT's findings of fact; and (4) permitting the detainee to present exculpatory evidence discovered after the conclusion of CSRT proceedings. As a result, the Court deemed 2006 MCA § 7's application of the DTA review process to petitioners as failing to provide an adequate substitute for *habeas*, therefore effecting an unconstitutional suspension of the writ.

In light of this conclusion, the Court held that petitioners could immediately pursue *habeas* review in federal district court, without first obtaining review of their CSRT designations from the D.C. Circuit as would otherwise be required under the DTA review process. While prior jurisprudence recognized that prisoners are generally required to exhaust alternative remedies before seeking federal *habeas* relief, the Court found that petitioners in the instant case were entitled to a prompt *habeas* hearing, given the length of their detention. The Court stressed, however, that except in cases of undue delay, federal courts should generally refrain from considering *habeas* petitions of detainees being held as enemy combatants until after the CSRT had an opportunity to review their status. Acknowledging that the government possesses a "legitimate interest in protecting sources and methods of intelligence gathering," the Court announced that it expected courts reviewing Guantanamo detainees *habeas* claims to use "discretion to accommodate this interest to the greatest extent possible," so as to avoid "widespread dissemination of classified information."[221]

Implications of *Boumediene*

As a result of the *Boumediene* decision, detainees currently held at Guantanamo may petition a federal district court for *habeas* review of status determinations made by a CSRT. However, the full consequences of the *Boumediene* decision are likely to be significantly broader. While the petitioners in *Boumediene* sought *habeas* review of their designation as enemy combatants, the Court's ruling that the constitutional writ of *habeas* extends to Guantanamo suggests that detainees may also seek judicial review of claims concerning unlawful conditions of treatment or confinement or to protest a planned transfer to the custody of another country.[222]

The conduct of trials before military commissions at Guantanamo may also be affected by *Boumediene*, as enemy combatants may now potentially raise constitutional arguments against their trial and conviction. Aliens convicted of war crimes before military commissions may also potentially seek *habeas* review of their designation as an enemy combatant by the CSRT, a designation that served as a legal requisite for their subsequent prosecution before a military commission.

Although the *Boumediene* Court held that DTA review procedures were an inadequate substitute for *habeas*, it made "no judgment as to whether the CSRTs, as currently constituted, satisfy due process standards," and emphasized that "both the DTA and the CSRT process remain intact."[223] Whether these procedures violate due process standards, facially or as applied in a given case, and whether a particular detainee is being unlawfully held, are issues that will be addressed by the District Court when reviewing the *habeas* claims of Guantanamo detainees.

Over 200 *habeas* petitions have been filed on behalf of Guantanamo detainees in the U.S. District Court for the District of Columbia. In the aftermath of the *Boumediene* ruling, the District Court adopted a resolution for the coordination and management of Guantanamo cases. The resolution calls for all current and future Guantanamo cases to be transferred by the judge to whom they have been assigned to Senior Judge Thomas F. Hogan, who has been designated to coordinate and manage all Guantanamo cases so that they may be "addressed as expeditiously as possible as required by the Supreme Court in *Boumediene v. Bush*.... "[224] Judge Hogan is responsible for identifying and ruling on procedural issues common to the cases. The transferring judge will retain the case for all other purposes, though Judge Hogan is to confer with those judges whose cases raise common substantive issues, and he may address those issues with the consent of the transferring judge. District Court Judges Richard J. Leon and Emmet G. Sullivan have declined to transfer their cases for coordination, and it is possible that the three judges may reach differing opinions regarding issues common to their respective cases.[225] Litigation concerning detainees' *habeas* claims remains ongoing. Final rulings have been reached in several cases. In some instances, detainees have been ordered released (including Lakhdar Boumediene), while in others, detention has been deemed lawful.[226]

Executive Order to Close Guantanamo and Halt Military Commission Proceedings

On January 22, 2009, President Barack Obama issued Executive Order 13492, requiring that the Guantanamo detention facility be closed as soon as practicable, and no later than a year from the date of the Order.[227] Any persons who continue to be held at Guantanamo at the time of closure are to be either transferred to a third country for continued detention or release, or transferred to another U.S. detention facility. The Order further requires specified officials to review all Guantanamo detentions to assess whether the detainee should continue to be held by the United States, transferred or released to a third country, or be prosecuted by the United States for criminal offenses.[228] Reviewing authorities are required to identify and consider the legal, logistical, and security issues that would arise in the event that some detainees are transferred to the United States. The Order also requires reviewing authorities to assess the feasibility of prosecuting detainees in an Article III court. During the review period, the Secretary of Defense was required to take steps to ensure that all proceedings before military commissions and the United States Court of Military Commission Review were halted.

Although the deadline for the closure of the Guantanamo detention facility has not been met, the Administration has stated that it remains committed to closing the facility as expeditiously as possible. The Administration's efforts to close the detention facility have been limited, in part, by congressional measures limiting the transfer of detainees into the United States. In the first session of the 111th Congress, several appropriations and authorizations measures were enacted which effectively barred funds from being used to transfer any detainee into the United States for release or purposes other than prosecution, and restrict funds from being used to transfer detainees into the country to face prosecution prior to the submission of certain reports to Congress.[229]

The full implications of these actions upon ongoing litigation involving persons currently detained at Guantanamo remain to be seen. However, the closure of the Guantanamo detention facility would raise a number of legal issues with respect to the individuals presently interned there, particularly if those detainees are transferred to the United States. The nature and scope of constitutional protections owed to detainees within the United States may be different than those available to persons held at Guantanamo or elsewhere. This may have implications for the continued detention or prosecution of persons transferred to the United States. Although the scope of constitutional protections owed to Guantanamo detainees remains a matter of legal dispute, it is clear that the procedural and substantive due process protections of the Constitution apply to all persons within the United States, regardless of their citizenship.[230] Accordingly, detainees transferred to the United States might be able to more successfully pursue legal challenges against aspects of their detention that allegedly infringe upon constitutional protections owed to them.[231]

REDEFINING U.S. DETENTION AUTHORITY

In March 2009, the Obama Administration announced a new definitional standard for the government's authority to detain terrorist suspects, which does not use the phrase "enemy combatant" to refer to persons who may be properly detained.[232] Under this new definition, the Administration claims that:

> The President has the authority to detain persons that the President determines planned, authorized, committed, or aided the terrorist attacks that occurred on September 11, 2001, and persons who harbored those responsible for those attacks. The President also has the authority to detain persons who were part of, or substantially supported, Taliban or al-Qaida forces or associated forces that are engaged in hostilities against the United States or its coalition partners, including any person who has committed a belligerent act, or has directly supported hostilities, in aid of such enemy armed forces.[233]

This definitional standard is largely similar to that used by the Bush Administration to detain terrorist suspects as "enemy combatants." Like the previous administration, the Obama Administration claims the power to militarily detain members of the Taliban or Al Qaeda, regardless of whether such persons were captured away from the battlefield in Afghanistan.[234] However, there are a few differences in the standard used by the Bush and Obama Administrations. Most notably, whereas the Bush Administration claimed the authority to detain persons who supported Al Qaeda, the Taliban, or associated forces, the standard announced by the Obama Administration expressly requires such support to be "substantial." While the Obama Administration claims that activities constituting "substantial support" will be developed in application to individual cases, it has stated that it would not cover "unwitting or insignificant" support.[235]

The Obama Administration has stated that this definitional standard is based upon the authority provided by the AUMF, as informed by the laws of war. The Administration has also claimed that this standard does "not rely on the President's authority as Commander-in-Chief independent of Congress's specific authorization."[236] The Bush Administration had previously argued that, separate from the authority provided by the AUMF, the President has the independent authority as Commander-in-Chief to order the detention of terrorist suspects. While the Obama Administration has not expressly rejected this claim, it appears that the Administration will not rely upon the notion of inherent constitutional authority to serve as a legal basis for the detention of terrorist suspects.

The full implications of this change in language and intent remain to be seen.[237] One issue that is subject to debate is the Executive's authority under the AUMF and traditional law-of-war principles to detain members of Al Qaeda or the Taliban who did not directly participate in battlefield hostilities. The nature of activities constituting "substantial support" for the groups may also merit significant judicial attention.

The scope of the Executive's detention authority under the AUMF and the law of war has been subject to conflicting rulings in the D.C. Circuit. In 2009, several *habeas* courts reached different conclusions regarding the scope of the President's military detention authority. A few district court judges held that the Executive has authority to detain persons who were "part of" or "substantially supported" Al Qaeda, the Taliban, or associated forces, so long as those terms are understood to include only those persons who were members of the enemy organizations' *armed forces* at the time of capture.[238] Other district court judges held that that the Executive has authority under the AUMF and the law of war to detain persons who were "part of" the Taliban, Al Qaeda, or associated forces, but lacks authority to detain non-members who provide "support" to such organizations (though such support may be considered when determining whether a detainee was "part of" one of these groups).[239]

In January 2010, a three-judge panel of the D.C. Circuit Court of Appeals considered the scope of Executive's detention authority in the case of *Al-Bihani v. Obama*.[240] In an opinion supported in full by two members of the panel,[241] the appellate court endorsed the definitional standard for the Executive's detention authority that had initially been asserted by the Bush Administration (a standard which was later somewhat circumscribed by the Obama Administration[242]); namely, that the President may detain those persons who were "part of or supporting Taliban or al Qaeda forces, or associated forces that are engaged in hostilities against the United States or its coalition partners."[243] While the panel concluded that either support for or membership in an AUMFtargeted organization may be independently sufficient to justify detention, it declined "to explore the outer bounds of what constitutes sufficient support or indicia of membership to meet the detention standard."[244] It did, however, note that this standard would, for example, permit the detention of a "civilian contractor" who "purposefully and materially supported" an AUMFtargeted organization through "traditional food operations essential to a fighting force and the carrying of arms."[245] Notwithstanding the government's reliance on the law of war to interpret the scope of the AUMF and seemingly in conflict with Supreme Court discussion of the issue, the panel rejected the idea that the international law of war has any relevance to the courts' interpretation of the scope of the detention power conferred by the AUMF.[246] The standard endorsed by the panel will be controlling for the D.C. Circuit unless the decision is overturned either by the Circuit Court of Appeals sitting *en banc* or the Supreme Court, or unless Congress takes up Judge Brown's separate invitation to craft appropriate *habeas* standards for detainee cases.[247]

CONSTITUTIONAL CONSIDERATIONS AND OPTIONS FOR CONGRESS

The Supreme Court decision in *Boumediene* holding that the DTA violates the Constitution's Suspension Clause (article I, § 9, cl. 2) leaves open a number of constitutional questions regarding the scope of the Writ of Habeas Corpus and options open to Congress to make rules for the detention of suspected terrorists. The following sections provide a brief background of *habeas corpus* in the United States, outline some proposals for responding to the *Boumediene* holding, and discuss relevant constitutional considerations.

The Writ of Habeas Corpus (*ad subjiciendum*), also known as the Great Writ, has its origin in Fourteenth Century England.[248] It provides the means for those detained by the government to ask a court to order their warden to explain the legal authority for their detention. In the early days of the Republic, its primary use was to challenge executive detention without trial or bail, or pursuant to a ruling by a court without jurisdiction, but the writ has expanded over the years to include a variety of collateral challenges to convictions or sentences based on alleged violations of fundamental constitutional rights.[249] The *habeas* statute provides jurisdiction to hear petitions by persons claiming that they are held "in custody in violation of the Constitution or laws or treaties of the United States."[250] A court reviewing a petition for *habeas corpus* does not determine the guilt or innocence of the petitioner; rather, it tests the legality of the detention and the custodian's authority to detain. If the detention is not supported by law, the detainee is to be released.[251] Minor irregularities in trial procedures that do not amount to violations of fundamental constitutional rights are generally to be addressed on direct appeal.[252]

Article I, § 9, cl. 2, of the Constitution provides: "The Privilege of the Writ of Habeas Corpus shall not be suspended, unless when in Cases of Rebellion or Invasion the public Safety may require it." Given the emphasis the *Rasul* Court had placed on the distinction between the statutory and constitutional entitlement to *habeas corpus*, it might have seemed reasonable to suppose that Congress retained the power to revoke by statute what it had earlier granted without offending either the Court or the Constitution, without regard to establishing a public safety justification. However, as the *Boumediene* case demonstrates, the special status accorded the Writ by the Suspension Clause complicates matters.

The relevance of the distinction between a "statutory" and a "constitutional" privilege of *habeas corpus* is not entirely clear. The federal courts' power to review petitions under *habeas corpus* has historically relied on statute,[253] but it has been explained that the Constitution obligates Congress to provide "efficient means by which [the Writ] should receive life and activity."[254] While the Court has stated that "at the absolute minimum, the Suspension Clause protects the writ 'as it existed in 1789,'"[255] it has also presumed that "the Suspension Clause of the Constitution refers to the writ as it exists today, rather than as it existed in 1789."[256] The *Boumediene* Court declined to adopt a date of reference by which the constitutional scope of the writ is to be judged.[257] Accordingly, it remains unclear whether statutory enhancements of *habeas* review can ever be rolled back without implicating the Suspension Clause.[258] The constitutionally mandated scope of the writ may turn on the same kinds of "objective factors and practical considerations" that the Court stated would determine the territorial scope of the writ.

Options for Congress

Under *Boumediene*, it appears that Congress's ability to revoke altogether the courts' jurisdiction over *habeas* petitions for certain classes of persons is constrained by the Constitution, but Congress has the power to impose some procedural regulations that may limit how courts consider such cases.[259] Congress retains the option of withdrawing *habeas* jurisdiction if it provides an effective and adequate alternative means of pursuing relief.[260] The Court's opinion in *Boumediene* did not fully delineate the lower bounds of what the Court might consider as necessary either to preserve the constitutional scope of the writ or to provide an adequate substitute, but indicated that the prisoners are entitled to "a meaningful opportunity to demonstrate that [they are] being held pursuant to the erroneous application or interpretation of relevant law."[261] A more direct option to affect the outcome of *habeas* cases brought by detainees may involve enacting a clear statutory definition of who may be detained and the purpose of the detention, along with an appropriate procedure designed to distinguish those who meet the definition from those who do not. Such an approach could potentially increase certainty with respect to courts' decisions regarding whether the detention of particular alleged enemy combatants comports with statutes and treaties, although constitutionally based claims may remain less predictable.

Congress could formally suspend the writ with respect to the detainees, although it is unclear whether Congress's views regarding the requirements of public safety are justiciable.[262] If they are, then a reviewing court's assessment of the constitutionality of *habeas*-suspending legislation would likely turn on whether Al Qaeda's terrorist attacks upon the United States qualify as a "rebellion or invasion," and whether the court finds that "the public safety" requires the suspension of the writ.

Congress might be able to impose some limitations upon judicial review of CSRT determinations if it strengthened the procedural protections afforded to detainees in CSRT status hearings. Legislation addressing some or all of the potential procedural inadequacies in the CSRT process identified in *Boumediene* might permit judicial review of CSRT determinations to be further streamlined.

In 2008, Attorney General Michael Mukasey recommended that Congress enact new legislation to eliminate the DTA appeals process and make *habeas corpus* the sole avenue for detainees to challenge their detention in civilian court, and also to eliminate challenges to conditions of confinement or transfers out of U.S. custody. In a speech before the American Enterprise Institute on July 21, 2008,[263] Attorney General Mukasey discussed this suggestion along with five other points he felt Congress should address:

- Courts should be prohibited from ordering that an alien captured and detained abroad be brought to the United States for court proceedings, or be admitted and released into the United States.
- Procedures should be put in place to ensure that intelligence information, including sources and methods, are protected from disclosure to terrorist suspects.
- Detainees awaiting trial by military commission should be prevented from bringing *habeas* petitions until the completion of their trials.
- Congress should reaffirm the authority to detain as enemy combatants persons who have "engaged in hostilities or purposefully supported al Qaeda, the Taliban, and associated organizations."
- Congress should establish sensible procedures for *habeas* challenges by assigning one district court exclusive jurisdiction over the cases, with one judge deciding common legal issues; by adopting "rules that strike a reasonable balance between the detainees' rights to a fair hearing ... and our national security needs ..." that would "not provide greater protection than we would provide to American citizens held as enemy combatants in this conflict"; and ensuring that court proceedings "are not permitted to interfere with the mission of our armed forces."

Other proposals that have been floated include the creation of a new national security court to authorize preventive detention of terror suspects[264] or the use of civilian or military courts to prosecute all detainees who cannot be released to their home country or another country willing to take them. Among the issues associated with prosecuting all of the detainees in civilian court is that the detainees may not have committed any crimes cognizable in federal court. Persons accused of engaging in terrorist acts (including attempts, conspiracies and the like) against the United States could likely be prosecuted,[265] but jurisdiction over offenses involving the provision of material support to a terrorist organization abroad is somewhat more limited, and for acts occurring prior to 2004, included only persons subject to the jurisdiction of the United States.[266]

Congress could also take no action and allow the courts to address the issues in the course of deciding the *habeas* petitions already docketed.

Scope of Challenges

Whether Congress enacts legislation to guide the courts or permits courts to resolve the *habeas* cases as they now stand, courts will be faced with determining the scope of the writ as it applies to detainees in Guantanamo and perhaps elsewhere outside the United States. Although the *Boumediene* Court held that DTA review procedures were an inadequate substitute for *habeas,* it expressly declined to assess "the content of the law that governs" the detention of aliens at Guantanamo.[267] Nonetheless, the Supreme Court identified a number of potential deficiencies in the status review process that necessitated *habeas* review of CSRT determinations, including the detainee's lack of counsel during the hearings; the presumption of validity accorded to the government's evidence; procedural and practical limitations upon the detainee's ability to present evidence rebutting the government's charges against him and to confront witnesses; potential limitations on the detainee's ability to introduce exculpatory evidence; and limitations on the detainee's ability to learn about the nature of the government's case against him to the extent that it is based upon classified evidence.[268] Whether these procedures violate due process standards, facially or as applied in a given case, and whether a particular detainee is being unlawfully held, are issues that will be addressed by the district court when reviewing the *habeas* claims of Guantanamo detainees.

Boumediene considered challenges to the legality of detention, the issue at the heart of most of the *habeas* challenges brought by Guantanamo detainees to date. However, there are also some cases challenging the conditions under which a detainee is being held. These two categories of challenges may involve different procedural routes and the application of different constitutional rights. The extent to which Congress may limit the scope of challenges Guantanamo detainees may bring may turn on the unresolved question of which constitutional rights apply to aliens detained in territory abroad. If detainees are transferred into the United States, the degree to which Congress may limit their access to the courts may be subject to further constitutional constraints.

The Supreme Court has not directly addressed whether there must exist a judicial forum to vindicate all constitutional rights. Justice Scalia has pointed out that there are particular cases, such as political questions cases, where all constitutional review is in effect precluded.[269] Other commentators point to sovereign immunity and the ability of the government to limit the remedies available to plaintiffs.[270] However, the Court has, in cases involving particular rights, generally found a requirement that effective judicial remedies must be available.[271] Although the extent of constitutional rights enjoyed by aliens outside the territory of the United States is subject to continuing debate, the right to liberty enjoyed by aliens within the United States, except when deprived of it in accordance with due process of law, seems well established.

The Fact and Length of Detention

Unlike the appeals process under the DTA, which is no longer available to detainees as a result of the D.C. Circuit's decision in *Bismullah*,[272] *habeas* challenges may also permit challenges to detention not based solely on the adequacy of CSRT procedures. It is unclear how much of a role CSRT proceedings will play in *habeas* cases or whether courts will abstain from hearing cases that have not yet received a CSRT ruling (should such a case occur). There is no statutory requirement that all detainees receive a CSRT determination in order to be detained, nor that detainees receive any kind of a hearing within any certain period of time after their capture. This might have left some detainees without effective means to pursue a DTA challenge. Moreover, it appears that some detainees who were determined by CSRTs to be properly classified as enemy combatants have been released from Guantanamo without a new determination, which may call into question the importance of the CSRT procedure as the primary means for obtaining release and therefore, the sole focus of a collateral challenge. Detainees may also be transferred or released based on the results of periodic reviews conducted by Administrative Review Boards (ARBs)[273] to determine whether the detainee is no longer a threat or that it is in the interest of the United States and its allies to release the prisoner. The DTA provided no opportunity to appeal the result of an ARB finding and no means of challenging a decision not to convene a new CSRT to consider new evidence.[274]

The scope and standard for *habeas* review involving detainees has been the subject of several orders by judges for the U.S. District Court for the District of Columbia. In such proceedings, the government has the burden of demonstrating, by a preponderance of the evidence, the lawfulness of the petitioner's detention.[275] The government is also required to explain its legal justification for detaining the petitioner, including, where appropriate, the standard it uses to define the scope of its detention authority.[276]

The government is also required to provide the petitioner with all reasonably available exculpatory evidence.[277] In December 2008, Senior Judge Thomas F. Hogan, who is coordinating and managing most Guantanamo cases for the D.C. District Court, issued a case management order that, among other things, requires the government to disclose any evidence it has relied upon to justify the petitioner's detention.[278] With respect to classified information, Judge Hogan's order requires the government, unless granted an exception by the district court judge considering the case's merits, to "provide the petitioner's counsel with the classified information, provided the petitioner's counsel is cleared to access such information. If the government objects to providing the petitioner's counsel with the classified information, the government shall move for an exception to disclosure." There is no requirement that classified information be provided to a petitioner himself. Moreover, the order rescinds the requirement of an earlier case management order that petitioners receive an "adequate substitute" for any classified information disclosed to the court or petitioners' counsel.[279]

In January 2010, a D.C. Circuit panel held in the case of *Al-Bihani v. Obama* that the procedural protections afforded in *habeas* cases involving wartime detainees do not need to mirror those provided to persons in the traditional criminal law context. Judge Janice Rogers Brown, writing for herself and another member of the panel, argued that a lower procedural standard may exist in *habeas* cases involving challenges to wartime detention, as "national security interests are at their zenith and the rights of the alien petitioner [are] at their nadir."[280] The government needs only to support its detention using a "preponderance of evidence" standard.[281] The panel also held that *habeas* courts assessing the validity of a petitioner's detention could properly consider hearsay evidence proffered by the government in support of his detention. According to the majority opinion,[282] "the question a *habeas* court must ask when presented with hearsay is not whether it is admissible—it is always admissible—but what probative weight to ascribe to whatever indicia of reliability it exhibits."[283]

Conditions of Detention

Although it appears less common for challenges to prison conditions to be entertained under *habeas* review, such cases have been heard by federal courts on *habeas* petitions.[284] Persons incarcerated in federal prisons may also ask a district court to address such complaints using their general jurisdiction to consider claims that arise under the Constitution,[285] by means of a writ of mandamus.[286] These writs, which are directed against government officials, have been used to require those officials to act in compliance with constitutional requirements. Although these challenges are often denied on the merits or on procedural grounds, cases have been brought based on the First Amendment,[287] Sixth Amendment,[288] Eighth Amendment[289] and various other grounds.[290]

The *Boumediene* Court declined to discuss whether challenges to conditions of detention are within the constitutional scope of the writ as it applies to Guantanamo detainees.[291] A variety of challenges has been raised by detainees in Guantanamo regarding conditions of their detention, including such issues as whether prisoners can be held in solitary confinement,[292] when they can be transferred,[293] or whether they can have contact with relatives.[294] Although some of these were brought as *habeas corpus* cases,[295] Guantanamo detainees have also sought relief from the courts using the All Writs Act,[296] principally to prevent their transfer to other countries without notice,[297] but for other reasons too.[298] Use of the All Writs Act by a court is an extraordinary remedy, generally not invoked if there is an alternative remedy available.[299]

In April 2009, a D.C. Circuit panel interpreted *Boumediene* as invalidating the MCA's court-stripping provisions with respect "to all *habeas* claims brought by Guantanamo detainees, not simply with respect to so-called 'core' *habeas* claims."[300] In that case, the panel found that *habeas* courts could consider not only Guantanamo detainees challenges to the legality of their detention, but also their proposed transfer to another country (though *habeas* review of such transfers may be quite limited).[301] Accordingly, whether Guantanamo detainees may challenge their conditions of confinement may depend on whether a reviewing court considers these conditions to be "a proper subject of ... *habeas* relief."[302] *Habeas* courts have thus far rejected challenges by Guantanamo detainees relating to their conditions of detention.[303]

The rejection of challenges to conditions of confinement may be based, at least in part, upon the opinion that any such claim by Guantanamo detainees does not derive from a constitutional protection to which they are entitled. In February 2009, a D.C. Circuit panel held in the case of *Kiyemba v. Obama* that the Constitution's due process protections did not extend to non-citizen detainees held at Guantanamo.[304] In October 2009, the Supreme Court granted certiorari to review the *Kiyemba* ruling. On March 1, 2010, the Supreme Court vacated the appellate court's opinion and remanded the case back to the appellate court for further consideration in light of new developments surrounding the *Kiyemba* petitioners' detention. It remains to be seen whether the appellate court will reaffirm its earlier ruling regarding the Constitution's application to detainees held at Guantanamo, or whether the issue will even be reached by the court. Presuming that the circuit court's earlier constitutional analysis is reaffirmed, the ability of non-citizen detainees held outside the United States to challenge the conditions of their detention may be quite limited. If detainees currently held at Guantanamo are transferred into the United States, however, they might be able to more successfully pursue legal challenges against aspects of their detention that allegedly infringe upon constitutional protections owed to them.

Available Remedy

Under Title 28, U.S. Code, a court conducting *habeas* review must "award the writ or issue an order directing the respondent to show cause why the writ should not be granted, unless it appears from the application that the detainee is not entitled to it."[305] The court can order either party to expand the record by submitting additional information bearing on the petition.[306] The court may order hearings to assist it in determining the facts, and is authorized to "dispose of the matter as law and justice require,"[307] or in criminal cases, to vacate a sentence, grant a new trial, or order that a prisoner be released.[308]

By contrast, the DTA review procedures did not address the remedies available to detainees who prevail in a challenge. Detainees who succeed in persuading a CSRT that they are not enemy combatants do not have an express right to release or even a right initially to be informed of the CSRT's decision. If the CSRT Director approves a finding that a detainee is no longer an enemy combatant, the detainee may be held for as long as it takes the government to arrange for his transfer to his home country or another country willing to provide asylum, during which time he need not be told of the CSRT's conclusion.[309] According to one report of unclassified CSRT records, in the event the CSRT Director disapproves of the finding, new CSRTs may be convened, apparently without notifying or permitting the participation of the detainee, although the government might present new evidence to the new panel.[310]

The Supreme Court viewed the lack of an express power permitting the courts to order the release of a detainee as a factor relevant to the DTA's inadequacy as a substitute proceeding.[311] In the context of CSRT determinations, the government suggested to the Court that remand for new CSRT proceedings would be the appropriate remedy for a determination that an error of law was made or that new evidence must be considered.[312] Whether such a remedy would be acceptable probably depends on whether measures are taken to decrease the risk of error under the CSRT procedures.

The available remedy for Guantanamo detainees found to be unlawfully held by the United States is an issue of ongoing litigation. The typical remedy for *habeas* claims is the release of the individual being unlawfully detained.[313] But given that detainees are being held in a military facility in Cuba, it is unclear whether the order of their release is a practical remedy, particularly in cases where the government is unable to effectuate a detainee's transfer to a third country. Whether or not a court would have the power to craft a *habeas* remedy for Guantanamo detainees that permits their entry into the United States remains unresolved. The Supreme Court has recognized that *habeas* relief "is at its core, an equitable remedy,"[314] and judges have broad discretion to fashion an appropriate remedy for a particular case. On the other hand, in the immigration context, courts have long recognized that the political branches have plenary authority over whether arriving aliens may enter the United States.[315]

As previously discussed, in October 2008, a federal district court ordered the release into the United States of 17 Guantanamo detainees who were no longer considered enemy combatants, finding that the political branches' plenary authority in the immigration context did not contravene the petitioners' entitlement to an effective remedy to their unauthorized detention.[316] However, the D.C. Circuit panel stayed the district court's order pending appellate review,[317] and subsequently reversed the district court's decision in the case of *Kiyemba v. Obama*, decided in February 2009. Writing for the majority of the panel, Judge Randolph stated that federal courts lacked the authority to order a non-citizen detainee's entry and release into the United States. In reaching this conclusion, the majority opinion cited long-standing Supreme Court jurisprudence in the immigration context which recognized and sustained, "without exception ... the exclusive power of the political branches to decide which aliens may, and which aliens may not, enter the United States, and on what terms."[318] According to the majority, this jurisprudence made clear that it was "not within the province of any court, unless expressly authorized by law, to review the determination of the political branch of the Government to exclude a given alien."[319]

The *Kiyemba* majority held that the district court lacked the legal authority to override the Executive's determination not to admit the petitioners into the United States. The majority held that the district court's order was not supported by federal statute or treaty. The majority also found that aliens held at Guantanamo were not protected by the Due Process Clause of the Constitution, and the district court's order therefore could not be based upon a liberty interest owed to the petitioners under the Constitution. The *Kiyemba* majority also found that the district court's order was improper to the extent that it was based on the notion that where there is a legal right, there must also be a remedy. The majority stated that it did "not believe the maxim reflects federal statutory or constitutional law."[320] While acknowledging that the Supreme Court's decision in *Boumediene* made clear that the constitutional writ of *habeas* extended to Guantanamo detainees, the *Kiyemba* majority held that the constitutional writ of *habeas* did not entitle petitioners to the "extraordinary remedy" of being ordered transferred and released into the United States.[321]

Writing separately from the *Kiyemba* majority, Judge Rogers argued that the majority's opinion was "not faithful to *Boumediene* and would compromise both the Great Writ as a check on arbitrary detention and the balance of powers over exclusion and admission and release of aliens into the United States."[322] She would have found that the Executive has no independent authority to detain aliens to prevent their entry into the United States, and would have held that a *habeas* court has the power to order the conditional release of a Guantanamo detainee into the United States when the Executive lacks authority to detain him. Nonetheless, she concurred with the majority's judgment that the district court's order was improper, because the lower court had not considered whether the Executive was authorized to detain the petitioners pursuant to U.S. immigration laws even after it had determined that they were not "enemy combatants."

In October 2009, the Supreme Court agreed to review the appellate court's ruling.[323] Following the Supreme Court's grant of certiorari, however, several *Kiyemba* petitioners were resettled in foreign countries, and the United States was able to find countries willing to settle the remaining petitioners (although five petitioners have rejected these countries' offers for resettlement). On March 1, 2010, the Supreme Court vacated the appellate court's opinion and remanded the case in light of these developments. Because the Supreme Court had granted certiorari on the understanding that no remedy was available for the petitioners other than release into the United States, it returned the case to the D.C. Circuit to review the ramifications of the new circumstances.[324] Litigation in *Kiyemba* remains ongoing.

Extraterritorial Scope of Constitutional Writ of Habeas

In *Boumediene*, the Supreme Court held that the constitutional writ of *habeas* extended to persons detained at Guantanamo, even though they are held outside the *de jure* sovereign territory of the United States. Left unresolved in the Court's discussion of the extraterritorial application of the Constitution is the degree to which the writ of *habeas* and other constitutional protections applies to aliens detained in foreign locations other than Guantanamo (e.g., at military facilities in Afghanistan and elsewhere, or at any undisclosed U.S. detention sites overseas). In April 2009, a federal district court held that the constitutional writ of *habeas* extended to at least some detainees held by the United States at the Bagram Theater Internment Facility in Afghanistan.[325]

The *Boumediene* Court indicated that it would take a functional approach in resolving such issues, taking into account "objective factors and practical concerns" in deciding whether the writ extended to aliens detained outside U.S. territory. Practical concerns mentioned in the majority's opinion as relevant to an assessment of the writ's extraterritorial application include the degree and likely duration of U.S. control over the location where the alien is held; the costs of holding the Suspension Clause applicable in a given situation, including the expenditure of funds to permit *habeas* proceedings and the likelihood that the proceedings would compromise or divert attention from a military mission; and the possibility that adjudicating a *habeas* petition would cause friction with the host government.[326] The *Boumediene* Court declined to overrule the Court's prior decision in *Eisentrager*, in which it found that convicted enemy aliens held in post-WWII Germany were precluded from seeking *habeas* relief. Whether enemy aliens are held in a territory that more closely resembles post-WWII Germany than present-day Guantanamo may influence a reviewing court's assessment of whether the writ of *habeas* reaches them, as well as its assessment of the merits of the underlying claims.

In April 2009, District Court Judge John D. Bates found in the case of *Al Maqaleh v. Gates* that the constitutional writ of *habeas* may extend to non-Afghan detainees currently held by the United States at the Bagram Theater Internment Facility in Afghanistan, when those detainees had been captured outside of Afghanistan but were transferred to Bagram for long-term detention as enemy combatants. Judge Bates held that the circumstances surrounding the detention of the petitioners in *Al Maqaleh* were "virtually identical to the detainees in *Boumediene* – they are [non-U.S.] citizens who were ... apprehended in foreign lands far from the United States and brought to yet another country for detention"[327] Applying the factors discussed in *Boumediene* as being relevant to a determination of the extraterritorial scope of the writ of *habeas corpus*, Judge Bates concluded that the writ extended to three of the four petitioners at issue in *Al Maqaleh*, who were not Afghan citizens. The constitutional writ was not found to extend to a fourth petitioner who was an Afghan citizen, however, because review of his *habeas* petition could potentially cause friction with the Afghan government.[328] This ruling has been appealed. Presuming that the ruling is upheld, it could have significant ramifications for U.S. detention policy, as at least some foreign detainees held outside the United States or Guantanamo could seek review of their detention by a U.S. court. On September 14, 2009, the DOD announced modifications to the administrative process used to review the status of aliens held at Bagram, which would afford detainees greater procedural rights. The modified process does not contemplate judicial review of administrative determinations regarding the detention of persons at Bagram.[329]

Use of Habeas Petitions to Challenge the Jurisdiction of Military Commissions

Whether detainees who are facing prosecution by a military commission may challenge the jurisdiction of such tribunals prior to the completion of their trial remains unsettled, although the district court has so far declined to enjoin military commissions.[330] Supreme Court precedent suggests that *habeas corpus* proceedings may be invoked to challenge the jurisdiction of a military court even where *habeas corpus* has been suspended.[331] *Habeas* may remain available to defendants who can make a colorable claim not to be enemy belligerents within the meaning of the MCA, and therefore to have the right not to be subject to military trial at all, perhaps without necessarily having to await a verdict or exhaust the appeals process.[332] Interlocutory challenges contesting whether the charges make out a valid violation of the law of war, for example, seem less likely to be entertained on a *habeas* petition.[333]

CONCLUSION

The Executive's policy of detaining wartime captives and suspected terrorists at the Guantanamo Bay Naval Station has raised a host of novel legal questions regarding, among other matters, the relative powers of the President and Congress to fight terrorism, as well as the power of the courts to review the actions of the political branches. The DTA was Congress's first effort to impose limits on the President's conduct of what the Bush Administration termed the "Global War on Terror" and to prescribe a limited role for the courts. The Supreme Court's decision striking the DTA provision that attempted to eliminate the courts' *habeas* jurisdiction may be seen as an indication that the Court will continue to play a role in determining the ultimate fate of the detainees at Guantanamo. However, the Court did not foreclose all options available to Congress to streamline *habeas* proceedings involving detainees at Guantanamo or elsewhere in connection with terrorism. Instead, it indicated that the permissibility of such measures will be weighed in the context of relevant circumstances and exigencies.

As a general matter, the courts did not accept the Bush Administration's view that the President has inherent constitutional authority to detain those he suspects may be involved in international terrorism. Rather, the courts have looked to the language of the AUMF and other legislation to determine the contours of presidential power. The Supreme Court has interpreted the AUMF with the assumption that Congress intended for the President to pursue the conflict in accordance with traditional law-of-war principles, and has upheld the detention of a "narrow category" of persons who fit the traditional definition of "enemy belligerent" under the law of war. Other courts have been willing to accept a broader definition of enemy belligerency to permit the detention of individuals who were not captured in circumstances suggesting their direct participation in hostilities against the United States, but a plurality of the Supreme Court warned that a novel interpretation of the scope of the law of war might cause their understanding of permissible executive action to unravel. Consequently, Congress may be called upon to consider legislation to support the full range of authority asserted by the executive branch in connection with the "war on terror." In the event the Court finds that the detentions in question are fully supported by statutory authorization, whether on the basis of existing law or new enactments, the key issue is likely to be whether the detentions comport with due process of law under the Constitution. In the event that detainees currently held at Guantanamo are transferred into the United States, such persons may receive more significant constitutional protections. These protections may inform executive policy, legislative proposals, and judicial rulings concerning matters relating to detainees' treatment, continued detention, and access to federal courts.

End Notes

[1] P.L. 107-40.

[2] Order on Detention, Treatment, and Trial of Certain Non-Citizens in the War Against Terrorism, November 13, 2001, 66 Federal Register 57833 (2001)(hereinafter "MO" or "military order").

[3] 542 U.S. 507 (2004).

[4] 542 U.S. 466 (2004).

[5] P.L. 109-148, Title X; P.L. 109-163, Title XIV.

[6] Hamdan v. Rumsfeld, 548 U.S. 557 (2006).

[7] P.L. 109-366.

[8] Boumediene v. Bush, 553 U.S. 723 (2008).

[9] Bismullah v. Gates, 551 F.3d 1068 (D.C. Cir. 2009).

[10] P.L. 111-84, § 1803(b), 123 Stat. 2612, struck section 1005(e)(3) of the "Detainee Treatment Act of 2005" (title X of P.L. 109-359; 10 U.S.C. 801 note) pertaining to appellate review of military commission decisions, but left intact paragraph 2, pertaining to appellate review of CSRT proceedings, as well as language similar to paragraph 3 passed as section 1405(e)(3) of title XIV of P.L. 109-163, which continues to refer to pre-MCA military commissions. (The reference to P.L. 109-359 should probably be P.L. 109-148.)

[11] Kiyemba v. Obama, 130 S.Ct. 1235 (2010).

[12] Executive Order 13492, "Review and Disposition of Individuals Detained at the Guantanamo Bay Naval Base and Closure of Detention Facilities," 74 *Federal Register* 4897, January 22, 2009.

[13] *Id.* at § 4.

[14] *Id.* at § 7.

[15] For further discussion, see CRS Report R40139, *Closing the Guantanamo Detention Center: Legal Issues*, by Michael John Garcia et al.

[16] Department of Justice, "Department of Justice Withdraws 'Enemy Combatant' Definition for Guantanamo Detainees," press release, March 13, 2009, http://www.usdoj.gov/opa/pr/2009/March/09-ag-232.html (hereinafter "DOJ Press Release"); In re Guantanamo Bay Detainee Litigation, Respondents' Memorandum Regarding the Government's Detention Authority Relative to Detainees Held At Guantanamo Bay, No. 08-0442, filed March 13, 2009 (D.D.C.) (hereinafter "Detention Authority Memorandum").

[17] Detention Authority Memorandum, *supra* footnote 16, at *7-8.

[18] DOJ Press Release, *supra* footnote 16.

[19] Al-Bihani v. Obama, 590 F.3d 866 (D.C. Cir. 2010).

[20] Charts listing *habeas* challenges by Guantanamo detainees in which final rulings had been reached as of January 2010 are available at Chisun Lee, "An Examination of 41 Gitmo Detainee Lawsuits," *Pro Publica*, updated January 22, 2010, http://www.propublica.org/special/an-examination-of-31-gitmo-detainee-lawsuits-722; and Benjamin Wittes, Robert Chesney & Rabea Benhalim, *The Emerging Law of Detention: The Guantánamo Habeas Cases as Lawmaking*, Brookings Institute, January 22, 2010, available at http://www.brookings.edu/papers/2010/ 0122_guantanamo_wittes_chesney.aspx (hereinafter "Brookings *Habeas* Report") (also discussing broader implications of these *habeas* rulings). Since that time, publicly available final rulings have also been issued in Al-Adahi v. Obama, 2010 WL 811280, 2010 WL 811282, No. 05-280 (D.D.C. Mar. 10, 2010) (denying *habeas* petition by two detainees in separate orders). Some judicial orders issued in *habeas* cases are classified, and in a few cases, redacted versions of those orders are not yet available. *See* Jess Bravin, "Gitmo Detainee Ordered Released," WALL STREET JOURNAL, March 23, 2010, at A46 (reporting that a federal *habeas* judge granted a detainee's *habeas* petition in a classified order, and that a redacted version is expected to be released in the coming weeks).

[21] *See* Charlie Savage, *Detainees Will Still Be Held, but Not Tried, Official Says*, NY TIMES, Jan. 22, 2010.

[22] *Id.*

[23] The two most relevant conventions are the Geneva Convention Relative to the Treatment of Prisoners of War, August 12, 1949, 6 U.S.T. 3317 (hereinafter "GPW"); and the Geneva Convention Relative to the Protection of Civilian Persons in Time of War, August 12, 1949, 6 U.S.T. 3516 (hereinafter "GC").

[24] White House Memorandum, "Humane Treatment of al Qaeda and Taliban Detainees" (February 7, 2002), available at http://www.washingtonpost.com/wp-srv/nation/documents/020702bush.pdf.

[25] For more history and analysis, see CRS Report RL31367, *Treatment of "Battlefield Detainees" in the War on Terrorism*, by Jennifer K. Elsea.

[26] Order on Detention, Treatment, and Trial of Certain Non-Citizens in the War against Terrorism, November 13, 2001, 66 *Federal Register* 57833 (2001)(hereinafter "MO" or "military order").

[27] For an analysis of the military commission rules, see CRS Report RL33688, *The Military Commissions Act of 2006: Analysis of Procedural Rules and Comparison with Previous DOD Rules and the Uniform Code of Military Justice*, by Jennifer K. Elsea.

[28] Chapter 47 of title 10, U.S. Code, 10 U.S.C. § 801 *et seq.*

[29] 542 U.S. 466 (2004).

[30] 339 U.S. 763 (1950).

[31] *Rasul*, 542 U.S. at 478-79. When *Eisentrager* was decided in 1950, the *Rasul* majority found, the "respective jurisdictions" of federal district courts were understood to extend no farther than the geographical boundaries of the districts (citing Ahrens v. Clark, 335 U.S. 188 (1948)). According to the Court, that understanding was altered by a line of cases, recognized in Braden v. 30th Judicial Circuit Court of Ky., 410 U.S. 484 (1973), as overruling the statutory interpretation that had established the "inflexible jurisdictional rule" upon which *Eisentrager* was implicitly based. Justice Scalia, with Chief Justice Rehnquist and Justice Thomas, dissented, arguing that the *habeas* statute on its face requires a federal district court with territorial jurisdiction over the detainee. The dissenters would have read *Braden* as distinguishing *Ahrens* rather than overruling it. For more analysis of the *Rasul* opinion, see CRS Report RS21884, *The Supreme Court 2003 Term: Summary and Analysis of Opinions Related to Detainees in the War on Terrorism*, by Jennifer K. Elsea.

[32] *Rasul*, 542 U.S. at 475 (citing *Eisentrager*, 339 U.S. at 777).

[33] 28 U.S.C. § 1331("The district courts shall have original jurisdiction of all civil actions arising under the Constitution, laws, or treaties of the United States.").

[34] 28 U.S.C. § 1350 ("The district courts shall have original jurisdiction of any civil action by an alien for a tort only, committed in violation of the law of nations or a treaty of the United States.").

[35] *Rasul*, 542 U.S. at 484 ("nothing in *Eisentrager* or in any of our other cases categorically excludes aliens detained in military custody outside the United States from the 'privilege of litigation' in U.S. courts"). Congress has amended Title 28, U.S. Code, to prohibit such actions, which the courts have so far upheld. 28 U.S.C. § 2241(e)(1).

[36] The Court noted that "*Eisentrager* made quite clear that all six of the facts critical to its disposition were relevant only to the question of the prisoners' *constitutional* entitlement to habeas corpus." *Rasul*, 542 U.S. at 476 (emphasis original).

[37] *Hamdan*, 548 U.S. at 626 (characterizing the *Eisentrager* decision, 339 U.S. 763, 790(1950), as having rejected the treaty claim "on the merits"). Justice Kennedy's *Boumediene* opinion rejected the view that *Eisentrager* imposed a strict jurisdictional test based solely on the sovereignty of the territory involved, finding instead that all of the "practical considerations" considered in the opinion were integral to the ultimate holding. *Boumediene*, 128 S.Ct. at 2257.

[38] *See* Department of Defense (DOD) Fact Sheet, "Combatant Status Review Tribunals," available at http://www.defenselink.mil/news/Jul2004/d20040707factsheet.pdf. CSRT proceedings are modeled on the procedures of Army Regulation (AR) 190-8, Enemy Prisoners of War, Retained Personnel, Civilian Internees and Other Detainees (1997), which establishes administrative procedures to determine the status of detainees under the Geneva Conventions and prescribes their treatment in accordance with international law. It does not include a category for "unlawful" or "enemy" combatants, who would presumably be covered by the other categories.

[39] *See* DOD Press Release, "Combatant Status Review Tribunal Order Issued" (June 7, 2004), available at http://www.defenselink.mil/releases/2004/nr20040707-0992.html; Memorandum from the Deputy Secretary of Defense to the Secretary of the Navy, Order Establishing Combatant Status Review Tribunal, July 7, 2004 (hereinafter "CSRT Order"), available at http://www.defenselink.mil/news/Jul2004/d20040707review.pdf; Memorandum from Deputy Secretary of Defense, Implementation of Combatant Status Review Tribunals

Procedures for Enemy Combatants Detained at U.S. Naval Base Guantanamo Bay, Cuba, July 14, 2006 (hereinafter "CSRT Implementing Directive"), available at http://www.defenselink.mil/news/Aug2006/ d20060809CSRTProcedures.pdf.

[40] *See* Josh White and Shailagh Murray, *Guantanamo Ruling Renews The Debate Over Detainees*, WASH. POST, June 6, 2007, at A3.

[41] United States v. Khadr, No. 07-001, (U.S.C.M.C.R. September 7, 2007) (finding CSRT designation alone insufficient to confer jurisdiction on military commission, but holding that the military commission judge has the inherent authority to determine the status of the accused). The Military Commissions Act of 2009 amended the MCA accordingly. *See* 10 U.S.C. § 948d ("A military commission is a competent tribunal to make a finding sufficient for jurisdiction.").

[42] Witnesses from within the U.S. Armed Forces are not "reasonably available" if their participation, as determined by their commanders, would adversely affect combat or support operations. CSRT Implementing Directive, *supra* footnote 39, at encl. 1, para. G(9)(a). All other witnesses, apparently including those from other agencies, are not "reasonably available" if they decline to attend or cannot be reached, or if security considerations prevents their presence. *Id.* at encl. 1, para. G(9)(b). It is unclear who makes the security determination. Non-government witnesses appear at their own expense. Testimony is under oath and may be provided in writing or by telephone or video.

[43] CSRT Order, *supra* footnote 39, at 1.

[44] CSRT Implementing Directive, *supra* footnote 39, at encl. 1, para. B.

[45] *Id.* at encl. 1, para. F.

[46] *Id* at encl. 1, para. C(2). In an affidavit submitted in DTA litigation, the government acknowledged that it has not utilized the procedures set forth in the CSRT Implementing Directive. *See* Bismullah v. Gates, 501 F.3d 178, 194-95 (D.C. Cir. 2007) (order on motions) (Rogers, J. Concurring) (citing differences between written procedures and those described by Rear Admiral James M. McGarrah in the *Boumediene* case). Rather than having a JAG officer in the rank of O-3 or above compile government information, the Department of Defense has utilized research, collection, and coordination teams to gather information to be assessed by a "case writer" who has "received approximately two weeks of training." *Id.* at 94. Thus, the reporter assigned to represent the government's case may not have had access to all government information.

[47] CSRT Implementing Directive, *supra* footnote 39 , at encl. 1, para. G(7) & (11).

[48] *Id.* at encl. 1, para. G(8).

[49] *Id.* at encl. 10.

[50] *Id.* at encl. 1, para. E(3)(a).

[51] *Id.* at encl. 1, para. H(7).

[52] *Id.* at encl. 2, para. D (the personal representative is required to explain to the represented detainee that he or she is neither the attorney or advocate for the detainee, and that any information provided by the detainee is not confidential).

[53] *Id.* at encl. 1, para. I(9)-(10).

[54] *See* DOD Press Release, "DoD Announces Draft Detainee Review Policy" (March 3, 2004), available at http://www.defenselink.mil/releases/2004/nr20040303-0403.html; Memorandum from Deputy Secretary of Defense, Revised Implementation of Administrative Review Procedures for Enemy Combatants Detained at U.S. Navy Base, Guantanamo Bay, Cuba (July 14, 2006), available at http://www.defenselink.mil/news/ Aug2006/ d20060809ARBProceduresMemo.pdf.

[55] CSRT Implementing Directive, *supra* footnote 39, at encl. 10 (implementing Detainee Treatment Act provisions).

[56] 339 U.S. 763 (1950) (holding that the federal courts did not have jurisdiction to hear a petition on behalf of German citizens who had been convicted by U.S. military commissions in China because the writ of *habeas corpus* was not available to "enemy alien[s], who at no relevant time and in no stage of [their] captivity [have] been within [the court's] jurisdiction").

[57] Khalid v. Bush, 355 F. Supp. 2d 311 (D.D.C. 2005); Hamdan v. Rumsfed, 464 F. Supp.2d 9 (D.D.C. 2006).

[58] Al Odah v. United States, 346 F. Supp. 2d 1 (D.D.C. 2004).

[59] Hamdan v. Rumsfeld, 344 F. Supp. 2d 152 (D.D.C. 2004), *rev'd* 415 F.3d 33 (D.C. Cir.), *rev'd* 548 U.S. 557 (2006).

[60] Boumediene v. Bush, 476 F.3d 981 (D.C. Cir. 2007).

[61] 129 S.Ct. 680 (U.S. 2008). Al-Marri also petitioned separately for relief from certain conditions of detention. Al-Marri v. Gates, Case No. 05-2259 (D.S.C. filed March 13, 2008). In March 2009, shortly after his transfer to civilian custody, Al-Marri filed with the court a notice of voluntary dismissal of the case.

[62] 355 F. Supp. 2d 311 (D.D.C. 2005), *vacated and dismissed sub nom.* Boumediene v. Bush, 476 F.3d 981 (D.C. Cir. 2007), *rev'd* 553 U.S. 723, 128 S.Ct. 2229 (2008).

[63] Although the MO authorized detention as well as trial by military commissions, only fifteen of the detainees were formally designated as subject to the MO.

[64] 355 F. Supp. 2d at 314.

[65] *Id.* at 320.

[66] *Id.* at 318. Judge Leon wrote: The President's ability to make the decisions necessary to effectively prosecute a Congressionally authorized armed conflict must be interpreted expansively. Indeed, the Constitution does not delegate to Congress the power to "conduct" or to "make" war; rather, Congress has been given the power to "declare" war. This critical distinction lends considerable support to the President's authority to make the operational and tactical decisions necessary during an ongoing conflict. Moreover, there can be no doubt that the President's power to act at a time of armed conflict is at its strongest when Congress has specifically authorized the President to act.

[67] *Id.* at 326.

[68] *Id.* at 327. It may be argued that the *habeas* statute itself (28 U.S.C. § 2241), which authorizes challenges of detention based on treaty violations, provided a means for private enforcement, at least prior to its amendment by the 2006 MCA. *See Eisentrager*, 339 U.S. at 789 (while noting that the 1929 Geneva Convention did not provide for private enforcement, considering but rejecting the *habeas* claim that the treaty vitiated jurisdiction of military commission).

[69] *Id.* at 330 (citations omitted).

[70] 355 F. Supp. 2d 443 (D.D.C. 2005), *vacated and dismissed sub nom.* Boumediene v. Bush, 476 F.3d 981 (D.C. Cir. 2007), *rev'd* Boumediene v. Bush, 553 U.S. 723, 128 S.Ct. 2229 (2008).

[71] *Id.* at 465 (citing *Hamdi v. Rumsfeld*).

[72] *Id.* at 475 (internal citations omitted).

[73] *Id.* at 476.

[74] 344 F. Supp. 2d 152 (D.D.C. 2004), 415 F.3d 33 (D.C. Cir. 2005), *rev'd* 548 U.S. 557 (2006).

[75] 10 U.S.C. §§ 801, *et seq.*

[76] There are four Conventions, the most relevant of which is The Geneva Convention Relative to the Treatment of Prisoners of War, August 12, 1949, 6 U.S.T. 3317 (hereinafter "GPW").

[77] 344 F. Supp. 2d at 161.

[78] GPW art. 3. For a discussion of Common Article 3, see CRS Report RL31367, *Treatment of "Battlefield Detainees" in the War on Terrorism*, by Jennifer K. Elsea.

[79] *Hamdan*, 548 U.S. at 583-584. To resolve the question, the majority employed canons of statutory interpretation supplemented by legislative history, avoiding the question of whether the withdrawal of the Court's jurisdiction would constitute a suspension of the Writ of Habeas Corpus, or whether it would amount to impermissible "court-stripping." Justice Scalia, joined by Justices Alito and Thomas in his dissent, interpreted the DTA as a revocation of jurisdiction.

[80] *Id.* at 577-578. The court below had also rejected this argument, 413 F.3d 33, 36 (D.C. Cir. 2005).

[81] *See id.* (stating that the bodies established by the Department of Defense to review the decisions of military commissions "clearly lack the structural insulation from military influence that characterizes the Court of Appeals for the Armed Forces.... ").

[82] 10 U.S.C. § 821 ("The provisions of [the UCMJ] conferring jurisdiction upon courts-martial do not deprive military commissions, provost courts, or other military tribunals of concurrent jurisdiction with respect to offenders or offenses that by statute or by the law of war may be tried by military commissions, provost courts, or other military tribunals.")

[83] *Hamdan*, 548 U.S. at 591 (citing Congress's powers to "declare War ... and make Rules concerning Captures on Land and Water," Art. I, §8, cl. 11, to "raise and support Armies," *Id.*, cl. 12, to "define and punish ... Offences against the Law of Nations," *Id.*, cl. 10, and "To make Rules for the Government and Regulation of the land and naval Forces," *Id.*, cl. 14.).

[84] P.L. 107-40, 115 Stat. 224 (2001).

[85] *Hamdan*, 548 U.S. at 594-595.

[86] 28 U.S.C. § 2241(c)(3)(permitting petitions by prisoners "in custody in violation of the Constitution or laws or treaties of the United States").

[87] *See* 415 F.3d at 39 (citing Johnson v. Eisentrager, 339 U.S. 763, 789, n. 14(1950)).

[88] *Hamdan*, 548 U.S. at 628.

[89] GPW art. 3 § 1(d). The identical provision is included in each of the four Geneva Conventions and applies to any "conflict not of an international character." The majority declined to accept the President's interpretation of Common Article 3 as inapplicable to the conflict with Al Qaeda and interpreted the phrase "in contradistinction to a conflict between nations," which the Geneva Conventions designate a "conflict of international character." *Hamdan*, 548 U.S. at 630.

[90] *Id.* at 633-634 (plurality opinion); *id.* (Kennedy, J., concurring) at 651. Justice Stevens, joined by Justices Ginsburg, Breyer, and Souter, further based their conclusion on the basis that M.C.O. No. 1 did not meet all criteria of art. 75 of Protocol I to the Geneva Conventions of 1949, adopted in 1977 (Protocol I). While the United States is not party to Protocol I, the plurality noted that many authorities regard it as customary international law.

[91] The MCA explicitly prohibits detainees from raising the Geneva Conventions as a source of rights in any U.S. court. MCA § 5, *codified at* 28 U.S. C. § 2441 note.

[92] Like the Bush Administration, the Obama Administration interprets the language regarding Common Article 3 as affirming that the current operations against Al Qaeda, regardless of where they take place or in what form, constitute an armed conflict; however, the opinion may be read more narrowly to apply only to hostilities in Afghanistan and other areas of active armed conflict.

[93] 542 U.S. 466 (2004).

[94] 542 U.S. 507, 535 (2004).

[95] *See, e.g., Oversight of the Department of Justice: Hearing Before the Senate Judiciary Committee*, 107th Cong. (2002) (testimony of Attorney General John Ashcroft) (arguing that a statute that could be read to interfere with the executive power to detain enemy combatants must be interpreted otherwise to withstand constitutional scrutiny).

[96] Youngstown Sheet & Tube Co. v. Sawyer, 343 U.S. 579 (1952).

[97] For information about relevant legislation, see CRS Report RL31600, *The Department of Defense Rules for Military Commissions: Analysis of Procedural Rules and Comparison with Proposed Legislation and the Uniform Code of Military Justice*, by Jennifer K. Elsea.

[98] *See, e.g.*, H.R. 4111, H.R. 4463, H.R. 4415, and H.R. 4127 (111th Cong.).

[99] Al-Marri v. Rumsfeld, 360 F.3d 707 (7th Cir. 2004), *cert. denied* 543 U.S. 809 (2004).

[100] Al-Marri v. Hanft, 378 F. Supp.2d 673 (D. S.C. 2005) (order denying summary judgment).

[101] Al-Marri v. Pucciarelli, 534 F.3d 213, 220 (4th Cir. 2008)(Motz, J., concurring)(citing declaration Jeffrey N. Rapp, Director of the Joint Intelligence Task Force for Combating Terrorism).

[102] Al-Marri v. Wright, 443 F. Supp. 2d 774 (D. S.C. 2006) (citing Hamdi v. Rumsfeld, 542 U.S. 507 (2004)). With respect to the "due process hearing" required to establish that an enemy combatant is properly held, the *Hamdi* plurality stated that: enemy combatant proceedings may be tailored to alleviate their uncommon potential to burden the Executive at a time of ongoing military conflict. Hearsay, for example, may need to be accepted as the most reliable available evidence from the Government in such a proceeding. Likewise, the Constitution would not be offended by a presumption in favor of the Government's evidence, so long as that presumption remained a rebuttable one and fair opportunity for rebuttal were provided. Thus, once the Government puts forth credible evidence that the habeas petitioner meets the enemy-combatant criteria, the onus could shift to the petitioner to rebut that evidence with more persuasive evidence that he falls outside the criteria.

[103] *Id.* at 778-80.

[104] The court held that the 2006 MCA requires a two-step process for determining whether persons are properly detained as enemy combatants, but that the President's determination of the petitioner's "enemy combatant" status fulfilled only the first step. The court next found that al-Marri could not be said to be awaiting such a determination within the meaning of the MCA, inasmuch as the government was arguing on the merits that the presidential determination had provided all of the process that was due, and the government had offered the possibility of bringing al-Marri before a CSRT only as an alternative course of action in the event the petition were dismissed. Further, the majority looked to the legislative history of the MCA, from which it divined that Congress did not intend to replace *habeas* review with the truncated review available under the amended DTA in the case of aliens within the United States, who it understood to have a constitutional as opposed to merely statutory entitlement to seek *habeas* review. AlMarri v. Wright , 487 F.3d 160, 172 (4th Cir. 2007), *vacated sub nom.* Al-Marri v. Pucciarelli, 534 F.3d 213 (2008)(*per curiam*).

[105] *Id.* at 196.

[106] 423 F.3d 386 (4th Cir. 2005). The government is no longer holding Jose Padilla as an enemy combatant, having turned him over to civil authorities for trial on charges associated with terrorism.

[107] *Al-Marri*, 487 F.3d at 180 (citing *Hamdi*, 542 U.S. at 516-17)(emphasis in original).

[108] *Id.* (citing *Padilla*, 423 F.3d at 390-91).

[109] 317 U.S. 1 (1942).

[110] *Al-Marri*, 487 F.3d at 179 (citing *Quirin*, 317 U.S. at 37-38; *Hamdi*, 542 U.S. at 519; *Padilla*, 423 F.3d at 391).

[111] 71 U.S. (4 Wall.) 2 (1866).

[112] *Al-Marri*, 487 F.3d at 189.

[113] *Id.* at 196 (Hudson, J., dissenting).

[114] Al-Marri v. Pucciarelli, 534 F.3d 213 (4th Cir. 2008)(*per curiam*). The intervening Supreme Court decision in *Boumediene* led the court to reject the government's contention that the 2006 MCA had divested the court of jurisdiction.

[115] *Id.* at 227-232 (Motz, J. concurring)(citing *Hamdi*, 542 U.S. at 518). Judge Motz, joined by three other judges, characterized leading precedents as sharing two characteristics: they look to law-of-war principles to determine who fits within the "legal category" of enemy combatant; and following the law of war, they rest enemy combatant status on affiliation with the military arm of an enemy nation. Under their interpretation of the law of war, there is no combatant status in non-international armed conflict, where detention is controlled by domestic law. For a discussion of U.S. practice with respect to the wartime detention of suspected enemies, whether civilians or combatants, see CRS Report RL31724, *Detention of American Citizens as Enemy Combatants*, by Jennifer K. Elsea.

[116] *Al-Marri*, 534 F.3d at 553 (Motz, J. concurring).

[117] *Id.* at 253-254 (Traxler, J., concurring).

[118] *Id.* at 258-259 (Traxler, J., concurring). Judge Traxler further suggested that the types of activities that would distinguish a combatant from a civilian enemy would include violent activities. *See id.* at 261 (describing the allegations that al-Marri "directly allied himself with al Qaeda abroad, volunteered for assignments (including a martyr mission), received training and funding from al Qaeda abroad, was dispatched by al Qaeda to the United States as an al Qaeda operative with orders to serve as a sleeper agent, and was tasked with facilitating and ultimately committing terrorist attacks against the United States within this country"). The dissenting judges suggested similar definitions for determining who may be treated as an "enemy combatant." *See id.* at 285 (Williams, J., concurring in part and dissenting in part)(defining enemy combatant covered by the AUMF as "an individual who meets two criteria: (1) he attempts or engages in belligerent acts against the United States, either domestically or in a foreign combat zone; (2) on behalf of an enemy force"); *id.* at 323-324 (Wilkinson, J., concurring in part and dissenting in part)(proposing two-part test in which "an 'enemy' is any individual who is (1) a member of (2) an organization or nation against whom Congress has declared war or authorized the use of military force" and a combatant is " a person who knowingly plans or engages in conduct that harms or aims to harm persons or property for the purpose of furthering the military goals of an enemy nation or organization").

[119] *See id.* at 279-280 (Gregory, J., concurring).

[120] *Id.* at 272. Judge Traxler formulated a general rule under which such enemy combatants "would be entitled to the normal due process protections available to all within this country, including an opportunity to confront and question witnesses against him[, unless] the government can demonstrate to the satisfaction of the district court that this is impractical, outweighed by national security interests, or otherwise unduly burdensome because of the nature of the capture and the potential burdens imposed on the government to produce non-hearsay evidence and accede to discovery requests, [in which case] alternatives should be considered and employed." *Id.* at 273.

[121] 129 S.Ct. 680 (2008).

[122] Memorandum from President Barack Obama to the Attorney General and Other Officials, "Review of the Detention of Ali Saleh Kahlah al-Marri," January 22, 2009, available at http://www.whitehouse.gov/the_press_office/ ReviewoftheDetentionofAliSalehKahlah/ (hereinafter "al-Marri Memo").

[123] Department of Justice, "Ali Al-Marri Indicted for Providing Material Support to Al-Qaeda," press release, February 27, 2009, http://www.usdoj.gov/opa/pr/2009/February/09-ag-177.html.

[124] Al-Marri v. Spagone, 129 S.Ct. 1545 (U.S. 2009).

[125] Department of Justice, "Ali Al-Marri Pleads Guilty to Conspiracy to Provide Material Support to Al-Qaeda," press release, April 30, 2009, http://www.usdoj.gov/opa/pr/2009/April/09-nsd-415.html.

[126] Section 1002 of P.L. 109-148 requires the DOD to follow the Army Field Manual for intelligence interrogation. *See* Department of the Army Field Manual 2-22.3 (FM 34-52), Human Intelligence Collector Operations (2006).

[127] Section 1003 of P.L. 109-148. *See* CRS Report RL33655, *Interrogation of Detainees: Requirements of the Detainee Treatment Act*, by Michael John Garcia.

[128] Section 1003(d) of P.L. 109-148. For more information, see CRS Report RL32438, *U.N. Convention Against Torture (CAT): Overview and Application to Interrogation Techniques*, by Michael John Garcia.

[129] Section 1005 of P.L. 109-148 (denying aliens in military custody privilege to file writ of *habeas corpus* or "any other action against the United States or its agents relating to any aspect of the[ir] detention ... ").

[130] Section 1004 of P.L. 109-148 provides a defense in litigation related to "specific operational practices," involving detention and interrogation where the defendant: did not know that the practices were unlawful and a person of ordinary sense and understanding would not know the practices were unlawful. Good faith reliance on advice of counsel should be an important factor, among others, to consider in assessing whether a person of ordinary sense and understanding would have known the practices to be unlawful.

[131] *See* Eric Schmitt, *Exception Sought in Detainee Abuse Ban*, N.Y. TIMES, October 25, 2005, at 16.

[132] 151 CONG. REC. S12667 (daily ed. November 10, 2005)(introduced by Sen. Graham, passed by roll call vote, 49 - 42), as amended by S.Amdt. 2524, 151 CONG. REC. S12771 (daily ed. November 14, 2005).

[133] The amendment refers to both the Combatant Status Review Tribunals ("CSRTs"), the initial administrative procedure to confirm the detainees' status as enemy combatants, and the Administrative Review Boards, which were established to provide annual review that the detainees' continued detention is warranted.

[134] *Boumediene*, 128 S.Ct. at 2275 (2008).

[135] Under the appellate process prescribed by the DTA, the D.C. Circuit Court of Appeals had exclusive jurisdiction to hear appeals of any status determination made by a "Designated Civilian Official," but the review was limited to a consideration of whether the determination was made consistently with applicable DOD procedures, including whether it was supported by the preponderance of the evidence, but allowing a rebuttable presumption in favor of the government. Detainees were permitted to appeal status determinations on the basis that, "to the extent the Constitution and laws of the United States are applicable, whether the use of such standards and procedures to make the determination is consistent with the Constitution and laws of the United States." Jurisdiction was to cease if the detainee were transferred from DOD custody. Congress in 2006 amended one version of the DTA to provide that jurisdiction would cease in the event the detainee was transferred from U.S. custody. Compare P.L. 109-163, title XIV, § 1405(e)(2) and P.L. 109-148, div. A, title X, § 1005(e)(2), as amended by P.L. 109-366 § 10, 10 U.S.C. § 801 note.

[136] Bismullah v. Gates, 551 F.3d 1068 (D.C. Cir. 2009).

[137] P.L. 109-163, title XIV, § 1405(e)(3) and P.L. 109-148, div. A, title X, § 1005(e)(3), both codified at 10 U.S.C. § 801 note.

[138] The first version of the DTA, P.L. 109-148, was amended by the 2006 MCA, P.L. 109-366 § 9 to change the reference from military commissions pursuant to President Bush's military order to refer to the military commissions established pursuant to the MCA and to make review "as of right" for all verdicts, irrespective of the sentence, but the version of the DTA passed in P.L. 109-163 was not amended. The amended version of the DTA was amended again by the 2009 MCA to strike paragraph 3 altogether, P.L. 111-84, title XVIII § 1803(b), 123 stat. 2574, 2612. Appeals of military commission at the D.C. Circuit are now covered by 10 U.S.C. § 950g, although the first version of the DTA, (P.L. 109-148) was neither amended nor repealed.

[139] Senator Frist introduced the Bush Administration's proposal as the "Bringing Terrorists to Justice Act of 2006," S. 3861. The Senate Armed Services Committee reported favorably a bill called the "Military Commissions Act of 2006" (S. 3901), which was in many respects similar to the Administration's proposal, but varied with respect to jurisdiction and some rules of evidence. The House Armed Services Committee approved H.R. 6054, also called the "Military Commissions Act of 2006," which closely tracked the Bush Administration's proposal. After reaching an agreement with the White House with respect to several provisions in S. 3901, Senator McCain introduced S. 3930, again entitled the "Military Commissions Act of 2006." Representative Hunter subsequently introduced a modified version of H.R. 6054 as H.R. 6166, which the House of Representatives passed on September 28, 2006. A manager's amendment to S. 3930, substantially identical to the bill passed by the House, was passed by the Senate the following day.

[140] P.L. 109-366. For a further description of the procedures associated with these military commissions, see CRS Report RL33688, *The Military Commissions Act of 2006: Analysis of Procedural Rules and Comparison with Previous DOD Rules and the Uniform Code of Military Justice*, by Jennifer K. Elsea; and CRS Report R40752, *The Military Commissions Act of 2006 (MCA): Background and Proposed Amendments*, by Jennifer K. Elsea.

[141] For discussion, see CRS Report R40932, *Comparison of Rights in Military Commission Trials and Trials in Federal Criminal Court*, by Jennifer K. Elsea.

[142] P.L. 109-148 § 1005, as amended by P.L. 109-366 § 10. Section 1405 of P.L. 109-163 was not amended.

[143] 2006 MCA § 5.

[144] 10 U.S.C. § 950g(d) (as amended).

[145] 2006 MCA § 7. See also, CRS Report R40752, *The Military Commissions Act of 2006 (MCA): Background and Proposed Amendments*, by Jennifer K. Elsea.

[146] 28 U.S.C. § 2241.

[147] GPW art. 3 § 1(d). *See Hamdan*, 548 U.S. at 630-632 (noting the application of this provision of the Geneva Conventions to detainees through the UCMJ Article 21).

[148] 2006 MCA § 5(a) (28 U.S.C. § 2241 note) provides that "No person may invoke the Geneva Conventions or any protocols thereto in any habeas corpus or other civil action or proceeding to which the United States, or a current or former officer, employee, member of the Armed Forces, or other agent of the United States is a party as a source of rights in any court of the United States or its States or territories."

[149] 10 U.S.C. § 948b(e) provides that "No alien unprivileged enemy belligerent subject to trial by military commission under this chapter may invoke the Geneva Conventions as a basis for a private right of action." Previously, under the 2006 MCA, the Geneva Conventions were not available "as a source of rights" in military commissions. Prior 10 U.S.C. § 948b(g).

[150] Prior 10 U.S.C. § 948b(f), provided that a military commission is a "regularly constituted court, affording all the necessary 'judicial guarantees which are recognized as indispensable by civilized peoples' for purposes of common Article 3 of the Geneva Conventions."

[151] 2006 MCA § 6(a)(3)(A) (18 U.S.C. § 2441 note) provides that "the President has the authority for the United States to interpret the meaning and application of the Geneva Conventions and to promulgate higher standards and administrative regulations for violations of treaty obligations which are not grave breaches of the Geneva Conventions."

[152] *See, e.g., id.* (President is given power to promulgate higher standards and administrative regulations for violations of treaty obligations).

[153] *See, e.g.*, 2006 MCA § 6(a)(3)(B)(18 U.S.C. § 2441 note)("No foreign or international source of law shall supply a basis for a rule of decision in the courts of the United States in interpreting the prohibitions enumerated in subsection (d) of such section 2441.").

[154] *See* Dickerson v. United States, 530 U.S. 428, 438 (2000)(striking down congressional statute purporting to overturn the Court's Fourth Amendment ruling in *Miranda v. Arizona*); City of Boerne v. Flores, 521 U.S. 507, 519 (1997)(Congress' enforcement power under the Fourteenth Amendment does not extend to the power to alter the Constitution); Plaut v. Spendthrift Farm, 514 U.S. 211, 225 (Congress may not disturb final court rulings).

[155] 80 U.S. (13 Wall.) 128 (1871).

[156] The Court struck down the law, essentially holding that the Congress had an illegitimate purpose in passage of the law. "[T]he language of the proviso shows plainly that it does not intend to withhold appellate jurisdiction except as a means to an end. Its great and controlling purpose is to deny to pardons granted by the President the effect which this court had adjudged them to have.... It seems to us that this is not an exercise of the acknowledged power of Congress to make exceptions and prescribe regulations to the appellate power." 80 U.S. at 146. The Court also found that the statute impaired the effect of presidential pardon, and thus "infringe[ed] the constitutional power of the Executive." *Id.* at 147.

[157] *See generally* Miller v. French, 530 U.S. 327, 350-51 (2000)(Souter, J., concurring).

[158] 2006 MCA § 6(a)(3)(B), *codified at* 18 U.S.C. § 2441 note..

[159] "If the country with which the treaty is made is dissatisfied with the action of the legislative department, it may present its complaint to the executive head of the government, and take such other measures as it may deem essential for the protection of its interests. The courts can afford no redress. Whether the complaining nation has just cause of complaint, or our country was justified in its legislation, are not matters for judicial cognizance." Whitney v. Robertson 124 U.S. 190, 194 (1888).

[160] 2006 MCA § 5(a), *codified at* 28 U.S.C. § 2241 note. *See also* Al-Bihani v. Obama, 590 F.3d 866, 875 (D.C. Cir. 2010) (2006 MCA precluded petitioner from raising claim that government's failure to accord him prisoner of war status violated Geneva Convention requirements). Because *habeas* petitions and other claims by persons properly deemed to be enemy combatants were precluded by the DTA and the MCA, it appears that section 5 of the 2006 MCA was intended to prohibit other detainees, including U.S. citizens and prisoners of war, from asserting rights under the Geneva Conventions in a petition for *habeas corpus* or other civil proceeding, but only against the United States. Section 1405(e) of P.L. 109-63; 2006 MCA, §7(a). *See also* Noriega v. Pastrana, 564 F.3d 1290 (11th Cir. 2009) (MCA precluded petitioner, a designated prisoner of war under the Geneva Conventions, from invoking Conventions in challenge to his proposed extradition to France), *cert. denied*, 130 S.Ct. 1002 (2010).

[161] Executive Order 13340, *Interpretation of the Geneva Conventions Common Article 3 as Applied to a Program of Detention and Interrogation Operated by the Central Intelligence Agency*, 72 Fed. Reg. 40707 (July 20, 2007), *revoked by* Executive Order 13341, *Ensuring Lawful Interrogations*, 74 Fed. Reg. 4893 (January 22, 2009) .

[162] *See* Karen DeYoung, *Court Told It Lacks Power in Detainee Cases*, WASH. POST, October 20, 2006, at A18 (reporting notice submitted by Justice Department to courts of intention to move for dismissal of pending enemy combatant cases).

[163] Al-Marri v. Wright, 487 F.3d 160 (4th Cir. 2007), *vacated sub nom.* Al-Marri v. Pucciarelli, 534 F.3d 213 (4th Cir. 2008) (*per curiam*).

[164] 10 U.S.C. § 948c.

[165] *See, e.g.*, Scott Shane and Adam Liptak, *Detainee Bill Shifts Power to President*, N.Y. TIMES, September 30, 2006, at A1.

[166] The MCAs' provisions concerning persons subject to trial before military commissions were recognized in a recent D.C. Circuit opinion as providing guidance as to the category of persons subject to military detention in the conflict with Al Qaeda and the Taliban. In *Al-Bihani v. Obama*, 590 F.3d 866 (D.C. Cir. 2010), the majority found that "the government's detention authority logically covers a category of persons no narrower than is covered by its military commission authority [under the MCA]...[At a minimum,] any person subject to a military commission trial is also subject to detention.... *Id.* at 872.

[167] 542 U.S. 507 (2004).

[168] P.L. 107-40, 115 Stat. 224 (2001).

[169] 542 U.S. at 516.

[170] Padilla v. Hanft, 423 F.3d 386 (4th Cir. 2005).

[171] Bismullah v. Gates, 501 F.3d 178 (*Bismullah I*), *reh'g denied* 503 F.3d 137(D.C. Cir. 2007) (*Bismullah II*).

[172] *Bismullah II*, 503 F. 3d 137 (D.C. Cir. 2007).

[173] Bismullah v. Gates, 514 F.3d 1291 (D.C. Cir. 2008).

[174] Gates v. Bismullah (U.S., filed February 14, 2008) (07-1054).

[175] Gates v. Bismullah, 128 S.Ct. 2960 (2008). The D.C. Circuit's determination of how to carry out its mandate under the DTA was a matter of interest to the Supreme Court as it was considering *Boumediene*, and may have had some bearing on the ultimate determination that the DTA procedures are not an adequate substitute for the writ of *habeas corpus*. Accordingly, it may be worthwhile to review some of the shortcomings described by the dissent, the only opinion of the panel that addressed the adequacy of the DTA procedures as a substitute for *habeas corpus*. Judge Janice Rogers Brown, concurring separately in *Bismullah I*, set forth a number of issues she felt call into question the fairness of the CSRT proceedings. For example, she noted that the detainee bears the burden of proving that he is not an "enemy combatant"—a term she described as elastic in nature, even though the detainee may not be aware of the information he is expected to rebut, all without the assistance of counsel. *See Bismullah I*, 501 F.3d at 193 (Rogers, J. Concurring). Further, the record presented to the CSRT is limited by the Executive, and the detainee's only recourse for seeking further evidence is through the DTA review process. If the detainee is successful in obtaining new evidence, his remedy appears to be a new CSRT. *Id.* Finally, she noted evidence that the CSRTs do not necessarily follow their own regulations regarding the collection and presentation of evidence. *Id.* (citing differences between written procedures and those described by Rear Admiral James M. McGarrah in the *Boumediene* case).

[176] Bismullah v. Gates, Case No. 06-1197, Order (D.C. Cir. August 22, 2008) (*per curium*), available at http://www.scotusblog.com/wp/wp-content/uploads/2008/08/bismullah-order-8-22-08.pdf.

[177] Bismullah v. Gates, 551 F.3d 1068 (D.C. Cir. 2009). In a previous case, the government had argued for abeyance of a detainee's petition for review of his detention under DTA procedures pending conclusion of *habeas* proceedings. The D.C. Circuit granted the government's motion for abeyance, and raised the possibility in *dicta* that the *Boumediene* had foreclosed direct Circuit Court review under the DTA. Basardh v. Gates, 545 F.3d 1068 (D.C. Cir. 2008).

[178] *Bismullah*, 551 F.3d at 1075.

[179] *Id.*

[180] William Glaberson, *Rulings of Improper Detentions as the Bush Era Closes*, NY TIMES, Jan. 18, 2009.

[181] Parhat v. Gates, 532 F.3d 834 (D.C. Cir. 2008).

[182] Although Parhat argued that the DOD's regulatory definition of "enemy combatant" exceeded the scope authorized by the 2001 AUMF, the Circuit Court declined to reach this issue, finding that the government provided insufficient evidence to demonstrate that Parhat met the DOD's own regulatory definition.

[183] *Parhat*, 532 F.3d at 838, quoting Dept. of Def. Order Establishing Combatant Status Review Tribunal (July 7, 2004), at 1.

[184] *Id.*
[185] *Id.* at 846-847.
[186] *Id.* at 847.
[187] *Id.* at 849.
[188] *Parhat*, 532 F.3d at 850 .
[189] *Id.* at 851.
[190] *Bismullah*, 551 F.3d at 1075, n, 2.
[191] *See* William Glaberson, *6 Detainees Are Freed as Questions Linger*, NY TIMES, June 11, 2009 (discussing transfer of four Uighur detainees to Bermuda).
[192] In re Guantanamo Bay Detainee Litigation, 581 F.Supp.2d 33 (D.D.C. 2008).
[193] Kiyemba v. Bush, No. 08-5424, Order (D.C. Cir., October 8, 2008) (*per curiam*).
[194] Kiyemba v. Bush, No. 08-5424, 2008 WL 4898963, Order (D.C. Cir., October 20, 2008) (*per curiam*).
[195] Kiyemba v. Obama, 555 F.3d 1022, 1025, 1028 (D.C. Cir. 2009).
[196] Kiyemba v. Obama, 130 S.Ct. 458 (2009).
[197] *See* Andrei Scheinkman et al., "The Guantanamo Docket," NY TIMES, at http://projects.nytimes.com/guantanamo [hereinafter "Guantanamo Docket"] (providing information regarding current and former Guantanamo population, including countries to which former detainees have been transferred).
[198] Kiyemba v. Obama, 130 S.Ct. 1235 (2010).
[199] For further discussion, see CRS Report RL34536, *Boumediene v. Bush: Guantanamo Detainees' Right to Habeas Corpus*, by Michael John Garcia.
[200] The practice of divesting courts of jurisdiction over particular issues is sometimes referred to as "court-stripping."
[201] *In re* Guantanamo Cases, 355 F. Supp. 2d 443 (D.D.C. 2005) and Khalid v. Bush, 355 F. Supp. 2d 311 (D.D.C. 2005), *consolidated, vacated and dismissed sub nom.* Boumediene v. Bush, 476 F.3d 981 (D.C. Cir. 2007).
[202] Al Odah v. United States, 321 F.3d 1134 (D.C. Cir 2003), *rev'd sub nom* Rasul v. Bush, 542 U.S. 466 (2004).
[203] 339 U.S. 763 (1950).
[204] 476 F.3d 981 (D.C. Cir. 2007). Judge Randolph, joined by Judge Sentelle, found that the measure does not constitute a suspension of the Writ within the meaning of the Constitution because the majority was "aware of no case prior to 1789 going the detainees' way," and were thus convinced that "the writ in 1789 would not have been available to aliens held at an overseas military base leased from a foreign government." Judge Rogers, in dissent, would have given greater deference to the Supreme Court's *Rasul* opinion, in which it drew a distinction between the situation faced by the Guantanamo detainees and the post-WWII convicts, 542 U.S. 466, 475 (2004), and in which it found the naval base to be within the historical scope of the Writ. *Boumediene*, 476 F.3d at 1002 (Rogers, J., dissenting))(citing Sierra Club v. EPA, 322 F.3d 718, 724 (D.C. Cir. 2003)).
[205] Boumediene v. Bush, 127 S.Ct. 1478 (2007).
[206] Justice Stevens, joined by Justice Kennedy, wrote a statement explaining their view that, "despite the obvious importance of the issues raised," the petitioners should first exhaust remedies available under the DTA unless the petitoners can show that the government is causing delay or some other ongoing injury that would make those remedies inadequate. *Id.* at 1478. Justice Breyer, joined by Justices Souter and Ginsburg, would have granted certiorari to provide immediate attention to the issues. The dissenters viewed it as unlikely that further treatment by the lower courts might elucidate the issues, given that the 2006 MCA limits jurisdiction to the Court of Appeals for the D.C. Circuit, which had already indicated that Guantanamo detainees have no constitutional rights. Justices Breyer and Souter would have granted expedited consideration.
[207] U.S. CONST. Art. 1, § 9, cl. 2.
[208] *Boumediene*, 128 S.Ct. 2229 at 2248 (citing INS v. St. Cyr, 533 U. S. 289, 300-301(2001)).
[209] *Id.* at 2247.
[210] *Id.* at 2253.
[211] *Id.* at 2258.
[212] *See* De Lima v. Bidwell, 182 U. S. 1 (1901); Dooley v. United States, 182 U. S. 222 (1901); Armstrong v. United States, 182 U. S. 243 (1901); Downes v. Bidwell, 182 U. S. 244; Hawaii v. Mankichi, 190 U. S. 197 (1903); Dorr v. United States, 195 U. S. 138 (1904).
[213] *Boumediene*, 128 S.Ct. 2229 at 2255-56, 2258 (discussing plurality opinion in Reid v. Covert, 354 U. S. 1 (1957)). In his concurring opinion in *Reid*, Justice Harlan argued that whether a constitutional provision has extraterritorial effect depends upon the "particular circumstances, the practical necessities, and the possible

alternatives which Congress had before it" and, in particular, whether judicial enforcement of the provision would be "impracticable and anomalous." *Reid*, 354 U.S. at 74-75 (Harlan, J., concurring in result).

[214] *Id.* at 2260.

[215] *Id.* at 2262.

[216] *Boumediene*, 128 S. Ct. 2229 at 2266-67.

[217] *Id.* at 2268.

[218] *Id.* at 2269.

[219] *Id.* at 2270.

[220] *Id.*

[221] *Id.* at 2275.

[222] *See Boumediene*, 128 S. Ct. at 2274 ("In view of our holding we need not discuss the reach of the writ with respect to claims of unlawful conditions of treatment or confinement.").

[223] *Id.* at 2275. Whether the 2006 MCA continues to preclude judicial consideration of such claims is a subject that has not been definitely resolved. In the aftermath of *Boumediene*, district court judges have continued to give effect to MCA § 7(a)(2), which bars judicial review of claims relating to conditions of detainees' confinement. *See* Khadr v. Bush, 587 F.Supp.2d 225, 235 (D.D.C.,2008) ("the Supreme Court appears to have left ... [the MCA's bar on judicial review of conditions of detention] undisturbed"); *In re* Guantanamo Bay Detainee Litigation, 577 F.Supp.2d 312, 314 (D.D.C.2008) (Hogan, J.) ("Cognizant of the long-standing rule of severability, this Court, therefore, holds that MCA § 7(a)(2) remains valid and strips it of jurisdiction to hear a detainee's claims that 'relat[e] to any aspect of the detention, transfer, treatment, trial, or conditions of confinement ... '"). *See also In re* Guantanamo Bay Detainee Litigation, 570 F.Supp.2d 13 (D.D.C.2008) (Urbina, J.) (holding that MCA § 7(a)(2) was not invalidated by *Boumediene*, but declining to decide whether constitutional writ of *habeas* permits challenges to conditions of confinement).

[224] U.S. Dist. Court for the District of Columbia, Resolution of the Executive Session, July 1, 2008, available at http://www.dcd.uscourts.gov/public-docs/system/files/Guantanamo

[225] For further discussion of recent *habeas* cases, see BENJAMIN WITTES *ET AL.*, BROOKINGS INSTITUTION, THE EMERGING LAW OF DETENTION: THE GUANTÁNAMO HABEAS CASES AS LAWMAKING 2010), available at http://www.brookings.edu/~/media/Files/rc/papers/2010/0122_guantanamo_wittes_chesney/0122_guantanamo_wittes_chesney.pdf.

[226] *See, e.g.,* Sliti v. Bush, 592 F.Supp.2d 46 (D.D.C. 2008); *Boumediene*, 579 F. Supp. 2d, at 198 (denying one *habeas* petition and granting five others).

[227] Executive Order 13492, "Review and Disposition of Individuals Detained at the Guantanamo Bay Naval Base and Closure of Detention Facilities," 74 *Federal Register* 4897, January 22, 2009.

[228] *Id.* at § 4. The Order specifies that the review would be conducted by the Attorney General (who was also to coordinate the review process), the Secretary of Defense, the Secretary of State, the Secretary of Homeland Security, the Director of National Intelligence, the Chairman of the Joint Chiefs of Staff, as well as other officers or full- or part-time employees of the U.S. government (as determined by the Attorney General, with the concurrence of the relevant department head) with intelligence, counterterrorism, military, or legal expertise.

[229] Supplemental Appropriations Act, 2009 (P.L. 111-32), Department of Homeland Security Appropriations Act, 2010 (P.L. 111-83), National Defense Authorization Act for Fiscal Year 2010 (P.L. 111-84), the Department of the Interior, Environment, and Related Agencies Appropriations Act, 2010 (P.L. 111-88), the Consolidated Appropriations Act, 2010 (P.L. 111-117), and the Department of Defense Appropriations Act, 2010 (P.L. 111-118).

[230] Zadvydas v. Davis, 533 U.S. 678, 693 (2001) ("the Due Process Clause applies to all 'persons' within the United States, including aliens, whether their presence here is lawful, unlawful, temporary or permanent").

[231] For further discussion and analysis, see CRS Report R40139, *Closing the Guantanamo Detention Center: Legal Issues*, by Michael John Garcia et al.

[232] DOJ Press Release, *supra* footnote 16; Detention Authority Memorandum, *supra* footnote 16

[233] Detention Authority Memorandum, *supra* footnote 16, at *2.

[234] Detention Authority Memorandum, *supra* footnote 16 at *7-8.

[235] *Id.* at *2.

[236] DOJ Press Release, *supra* footnote 16.

[237] It should also be noted that the new definitional standard announced in the Detention Authority Memorandum, *supra* footnote 16, refers only to detainees held by the United States at Guantanamo, and not those persons detained at other facilities (e.g., the Bagram Air Base in Afghanistan). However, the Obama Administration

subsequently made clear in court filings and congressional reports that the same definitional standard would also be used to justify the detention of suspected belligerents held at Bagram. *See* Department of Justice, Brief for Respondent-Appellants, filed September 14, 2009, Al Maqaleh v. Gates, No. 09-5265 (D.C. Cir.) (employing same definitional framework for detention authority as used with respect to detainees held at Guantanamo) (hereinafter "DOJ Brief"); Letter from Phillip Cater, Dep. Asst. Sec. Defense for Detainee Policy, to Sen. Carl Levin, Chairman of Sen. Armed Serv. Comm., July 14, 2009 (included as attachment to DOJ Brief, *supra*) (hereinafter "Bagram Policy Guidance"). Both the DOJ Brief and Bagram Policy Guidance are available at http://www.scotusblog.com/wp/wp-content/uploads/2009/09/USBagram-brief-9-14-09.pdf.

238 Gherebi v. Obama, 609 F.Supp.2d 43 (D.D.C., 2009) (Walton, J.); Al-Adahi v. Obama, 2009 WL 2584685 (D.D.C., August 21, 2009) (Kessler, J.).

239 Hamlily v. Obama, 616 F.Supp.2d 63 (D.D.C. 2009) (Bates, J.); Mattan v. Obama, 618 F. Supp. 2d 24 (D.D.C. 2009) (Lamberth, C.J.). In assessing whether an individual was "part of" the Taliban, Al Qaeda, or associated forces, several *habeas* judges have considered whether "the individual functions or participates within or under the command structure of the organization—i.e. whether he receives and executes orders or directions." *Hamlily*, 616 F.Supp.2d at 75; Al Odah v. United States, 648 F. Supp. 2d 1, 6 (D.D.C., August 24, 2009) (Kollar-Kotelly, J.) (citing *Hamlily*); Awad v. Obama, 646 F. Supp. 2d 20, 23 (D.D.C., August 12, 2009) (Robertson, J.) (same).

240 Al-Bihani v. Obama, 590 F.3d 866 (D.C. Cir. 2010).

241 A third member of the panel issued a separate opinion concurring with the majority's judgment. However, the opinion did not clearly endorse the majority's view as to scope of the Executive's detention authority. *See id.*, at 883- 884 (Williams, J., concurring) (arguing that petitioner was detainable on account of being "part of" an AUMF-targeted organization, but not deciding whether a person could be detained on account of "support" for a targeted organization that he was not also a "part of").

242 *See supra* footnote 16. In contrast, the Obama Administration espouses a standard that specifies that such support must be "substantial."

243 *Al-Bihani*,.590 F.3d at 872.

244 *Id.* at 873.

245 *Id.* The panel found that even if petitioner was not a member of an AUMF-targeted organization, his service as a cook for a military brigade affiliated with Taliban and Al Qaeda forces, in addition to his accompaniment of the brigade during military operations, constituted sufficient grounds for his detention. *Id.*

246 *Id.* at 871. *See also id.* at 885 (Williams, J., concurring in part and concurring in the judgment) (contrasting majority position with the Supreme Court plurality opinion in *Hamdi*, 542 U.S. at 521 statement that the Court's understanding of the AUMF "is based on longstanding law-of-war principles").

247 *Id.* at 882 (Brown, J. concurring).

248 For a general background and description of related writs, see 39 AM. JUR. 2d. *Habeas Corpus* § 1 (1999).

249 *See generally* S. DOC. NO. 108-17 at 848 *et seq.*

250 Rasul v. Bush, 542 U.S. 466 (2004).

251 *Ex parte* Watkins, 28 U.S. (3 Pet.) 193, 201 (1830) (Marshall, C.J.) ("The writ of habeas corpus is a high prerogative writ, known to the common law, the great object of which is the liberation of those who may be imprisoned without sufficient cause.").

252 39 AM. JUR. 2d. *Habeas Corpus* § 27 (1999).

253 *Ex parte* Bollman, 8 U.S. (4 Cr.) 75 (1807).

254 *Id.* at 94.

255 INS v. St. Cyr, 533 U.S. 289, 301 (U.S. 2001).

256 Felker v. Tupin, 518 U.S. 663 (1996)(citing *Swain*, 430 U.S. 372).

257 *See Boumediene*, 128 S.Ct. at 2248 (" The Court has been careful not to foreclose the possibility that the protections of the Suspension Clause have expanded along with post-1789 developments that define the present scope of the writ.").

258 *Cj St. Cyr*, 533 U.S. at 340 n.5 (2001) (Scalia, J., dissenting)("If ... the writ could not be suspended within the meaning of the Suspension Clause until Congress affirmatively provided for habeas by statute, then surely Congress may subsequently alter what it had initially provided for, lest the Clause become a one-way ratchet.").

259 *Cj Felker*, 518 U.S. 663 (Holding that restrictions on successive petitions for *habeas corpus* by prisoners convicted in state courts did not suspend the writ, but merely applied a modified *res judicata* rule to control abuse of the writ); *Boumediene*, 128 S.Ct. 2229 at 2276-77 (explaining that some reasonable regulations on *habeas* cases to relieve governmental burden or preserve security will be permissible).

[260] *See* United States v. Hayman, 342 U.S. 205 (1952); Hill v. United States, 368 U.S. 424 (1962); *Swain* , 430 U.S. 372 (1977); *Felker*, 518 U.S. 651 (1996); *St. Cyr*, 533 U.S. 289.

[261] *Boumediene*, 128 S.Ct. 2229 at 2266.

[262] The *Boumediene* Court did not address the matter because the 2006 MCA did not purport to act as a formal suspension of the writ. *Boumediene*, 128 S.Ct. at 2262.

[263] The Attorney General's prepared statement is available at http://www.scotusblog.com/wp/mukasey-curb-courts-powers-on-detainees

[264] *See* Improving Detainee Policy: Handling Terrorism Detainees within the American Justice System, Hearing before the Senate Judiciary Committee, June 4, 2008. For a review and criticism of some proposals, see the Constitution Project, *A Critique of "National Security Courts,"* available at http://www.constitutionproject.org/pdf/Critique_of_the_National_Security_Courts.pdf.

[265] *See, e.g.*, 18 U.S.C. § 2332 (prescribing penalties for homicides of U.S. nationals abroad and other violence directed at the United States, so long as the act is "intended to coerce, intimidate, or retaliate against a government or a civilian population"); 18 U.S.C. § 2232b (acts of terrorism transcending national boundaries).

[266] *See* 18 U.S.C. § 2339B (provision of material support to designated terrorist organization prior to amendment by P.L. 108-458, § 6603(d), December 17, 2004); *see also* 18 U.S.C. § 2339 (proscribing harboring or concealing terrorists, but only after October 26, 2001 enactment of P.L. 107-56, title VIII, § 803(a)). The *Ex Post Facto* Clause prevents prosecution for charges that would not have been applicable when the offense occurred, U.S. CONST. art. 1, § 9, cl. 3.

[267] *Boumediene*, 128 S. Ct. 2229 at 67.

[268] *See id.* at 37-38, 54-56.

[269] Webster v. Doe, 486 U.S. 592, 612-13 (Scalia, J., dissenting).

[270] Bartlett v. Bowen, 816 F.2d 695, 719-720 (1987)(Bork, J., dissenting).

[271] *See e.g.*, First English Evangelical Lutheran Church of Glendale v. Los Angeles County, 482 U.S. 304 (1987)(holding that the Constitution mandates effective remedies for takings).

[272] *Bismullah*, 551 F.3d at 1075.

[273] *See* DOD Press Release, "DoD Announces Draft Detainee Review Policy" (March 3, 2004), available at http://www.defenselink.mil/releases/2004/nr20040303-0403.html; Memorandum from Deputy Secretary of Defense, Revised Implementation of Administrative Review Procedures for Enemy Combatants Detained at U.S. Navy Base, Guantanamo Bay, Cuba (July 14, 2006), available at http://www.defenselink.mil/news/Aug2006/ d20060809ARBProceduresMemo.pdf.

[274] CSRT Implementing Directive, *supra* footnote 39, at encl. 10 (implementing Detainee Treatment Act provisions).

[275] *See In re* Guantanamo Bay Detainee Litigation, No. 08-0442, 2008 WL 4858241, Order, at *3 (D.D.C. November 6, 2008) (Hogan, J.) (hereinafter "November Order").

[276] *See id.* at * 1; el Gharani v. Bush, 593 F.Supp.2d 144 (D.D.C. 2009) (Leon, J.) (finding that when the government justifies the detention of a *habeas* petitioner on the ground that he is an "enemy combatant," it must provide a definition of the term).

[277] *See* November Order, *supra* footnote 275, at *1. *See also* Boumediene v. Bush, No. 04-1166, Order (D.D.C. August 27, 2008) (Leon, J.), available at http://www.scotusblog.com/wp/wp-content/uploads/2008/08/leon-case-manage-order8-27-08.pdf (requiring government to provide "any evidence contained in the material reviewed in developing the return for the petitioner, and in preparation for the hearing for the petitioner, that tends materially to undermine the Government's theory as to the lawfulness of petitioner's detention"). *Habeas* judges have found that information compiled by the Task Force established under Executive Order 134992 (concerning the proposed closure of the Guantanamo detention facility) is "reasonably available evidence" that may be considered in the context of a Guantanamo detainee's *habeas* petition. *See, e.g.*, Bin Attash v. Obama, 628 F.Supp.2d 24, 38 (D.D.C. 2009) (citing rulings in several *habeas* cases).

[278] *In re* Guantanamo Bay Detainee Litigation, No. 08-0442, 2008 WL 5245890, Order, at *1 (D.D.C., December 16, 2008) (Hogan, J.).

[279] November Order, *supra* footnote 275, at *2.

[280] Al-Bihani v. Obama, 590 F.3d 866, 878 (D.C. Cir. 2010). The majority also noted that it did not "endeavor to identify what standard would represent the minimum required by the Constitution," and the court did not need to address whether a "some evidence, reasonable suspicion, or probable cause standard of proof could constitutionally suffice for preventative detention of non-citizens seized abroad who are suspected of being terrorist threats to the United States." *Id.* at 878, n. 4.

[281] *Id.*at 878.

[282] *Id.* at 879. Senior Judge Stephen F. Williams, the third member of the *Al-Bihani* panel, declined to join the majority's analysis regarding the procedures used by the *habeas* court to review the petitioner's claim, finding this discussion unnecessary "since the facts that Al Bihani says are correct readily yield a ruling that his detention is legally permissible." *Id.* at 886 (Williams, J., concurring in part and concurring in judgment).

[283] *Id.* at 879.

[284] "A motion pursuant to § 2241 generally challenges the execution of a federal prisoner's sentence, including such matters as the administration of parole, computation of a prisoner's sentence by prison officials, prison disciplinary actions, prison transfers, type of detention and prison conditions." Jiminian v. Nash, 245 F.3d 144 (2d Cir. 2001). *See, e.g.,* Rickenbacker v. United States, 365 F. Supp. 2d 347 (E.D.N.Y. 2005) (challenging failure to provide drug and psychiatric treatment in accordance with sentencing court's recommendation).

[285] 28 U.S.C. § 1331. *See* Caldwell v. Miller, 790 F.2d 589 (7th Cir. 1986).

[286] Russell Donaldson, *Mandamus, under 28 U.S.C.A. §1361, To Obtain Change in Prison Condition or Release of Federal Prisoner,* 114 A.L.R. Fed. 225 (2005). Relief in mandamus is generally available where: (1) the plaintiff can show a clear legal right to the performance of the requested action; (2) the duty of the official in question is clearly defined and nondiscretionary; (3) there is no other adequate remedy available to the plaintiff; (4) there are other separate jurisdictional grounds for the action. *Id.* at 1(a). A writ of mandamus may issue only where "the duty to be performed is ministerial and the obligation to act peremptory, and clearly defined. The law must not only authorize the demanded action, but require it; the duty must be clear and undisputable." Ali v. Ashcroft, 350 F. Supp. 2d 28, 65 (D.D.C. 2004), *quoting* Shoshone-Bannock Tribes v. Reno, 56 F.3d 1476, 1479 (D.C. Cir. 1995).

[287] *See* Long v. Parker, 390 F.2d. 816 (3rd Cir. 1968) (prisoner suit to obtain access to religious weekly newspaper stated a valid cause of action worthy of a factual hearing).

[288] Stover v. Carlson, 413 F. Supp. 718 (D. Conn. 1976) (ending federal prison practice of opening privileged communications outside of prisoner's presence).

[289] Fullwood v. Clemmer, 206 F. Supp. 370 (D.D.C. 1962) (keeping prisoner in solitary confinement for more than two years for minor disciplinary infractions violates the Eighth Amendment). It should be noted that where a prisoner has not yet been convicted of a crime, a challenge to conditions of detentions may sound in Due Process rather than as an Eighth Amendment challenge. Bell v. Wolfish, 441 U.S. 520 (1979).

[290] *See generally* Donaldson, *supra* footnote 286.

[291] *See Boumediene*, 128 S. Ct. 2229 at 2274 ("In view of our holding we need not discuss the reach of the writ with respect to claims of unlawful conditions of treatment or confinement.").

[292] Paul Shukovsky, *Terrorism Suspect's Suit Tells of U.S. Abuse: Documents in Guantanamo Case Describe Extreme Isolation,* SEATTLE POST-INTELLIGENCER, August 6, 2004, at A1.

[293] Al-Anazi v. Bush, 370 F. Supp. 2d 188 (D.D.C. 2005).

[294] Josh White, *Lawyers Seek Improved Conditions for Suicidal Detainee*, WASH. POST, November 5, 2005, at A8.

[295] *See, e.g., In re* Guantanamo Detainee Cases, 355 F. Supp. 2d 443, 480-81 (D.D.C. 2005)(rejecting claims on other grounds).

[296] All Writs Act, 28 U.S.C. § 1651.

[297] Belbach v. Bush, 520 F.3d 452, 456 (D.C. Cir. 2008) (holding the 2006 MCA leaves intact the presumptive jurisdiction of federal courts to inquire into the constitutionality of a jurisdiction-stripping statute). *See also* Al Ansi v. Bush, No. 08-1923, 2008 WL 5412360, Order (D.D.C., December 29, 2008) (requiring government to give court and petitioner's counsel 30 days' notice prior to releasing or transferring petitioner from Guantanamo).

[298] *See* El-Banna v. Bush, No. 04-1144, 2005 WL 1903561 (D.D.C. July 18, 2005) (seeking preservation of records relating to treatment of detainees).

[299] Al-Anazi v. Bush, 370 F. Supp. 2d 188, 196 (D.D.C. 2005).

[300] Kiyemba v. Obama, 561 F.3d 509, 512-513 (D.C. Cir. 2009), *cert. denied*, 2010 WL 1005960, 78 USLW 3302 (U.S. Mar. 22, 2010).

[301] *Id.* at 513-514 (when executive branch has determined that a detainee will not be tortured if transferred to a particular country, a *habeas* court may not second-guess this assessment).

[302] *Id.* at 513.

[303] *See supra* footnote 223.

[304] Kiyemba v. Obama, 555 F.3d 1022, 1026-1027 (D.C. Cir. 2009), *cert. granted*, 130 S.Ct. 458 (2009), *vacated*, 130 S.Ct. 1235 (2010).

[305] 28 U.S.C. § 2243.

[306] Rules Governing § 2255 Cases, Rule 7, 28 U.S.C.A. foll. § 2255 (applicable to prisoners subject to sentence of a federal court).

[307] 28 U.S.C. § 2243.

[308] 28 U.S.C. § 2255.

[309] CSRT Implementing Directive, *supra* footnote 39 at encl. 1, para. I(9)-(10).

[310] *See* Mark Denbeaux *et al.*, *No-Hearing Hearings, CSRT: The Modern Habeas Corpus?*, at 37-40 (2006), available at http://law.shu.edu/news/final_no_hearing_hearings_report.pdf. The named author is a professor at Seton Hall University School of Law and serves as counsel to two Guantanamo detainees.

[311] *Boumediene*, 128 S.Ct. at 2271.

[312] *See* Gov't Br. in Opp. to Pet. for Reh'g, Boumediene v. Bush, No. 16-1195 (U.S.).

[321] *Id.* at 1028.

[322] *Id.* at 1032 (Rogers, J., concurring).

[323] 130 S.Ct. 458 (2009).

[324] 130 S.Ct. 1235 (2010).

[325] Al Maqaleh v. Gates, 604 F.Supp.2d 205 (D.D.C. 2009).

[326] *Boumediene,* 128 S.Ct. at 2261-62.

[327] *Al Maqaleh*, 604 F. Supp. 2d at 208.

[328] *Id.* at 229-230.

[329] Under this new system, detainees would undergo a case review within 60 days of incarceration, with periodic review occurring roughly every six months thereafter. Further, U.S. military members shall act as personal representatives to assist detainees during the review process. DOJ Brief, *supra* footnote 237; Bagram Policy Guidance, *supra* footnote 237; Gerry J. Gilmore, "Bagram Detention Facility to Implement Case Review Panels," *American Forces Press Service*, September 14, 2009, http://www.defenselink.mil/news/newsarticle.aspx?id=55831.

[330] *See* Khadr v. United States, No. 07-1405 (D.C. Cir. June 20, 2008); Hamdan v. Gates, No. 04-1519 (JR) (D.D.C. July 18, 2008)(order denying injunction of military commission proceedings).

[331] *See Ex parte* Milligan, 71 U.S. (4 Wall.) 2, 115-16 (1866); *cf. Ex parte* Quirin, 317 U.S. 1, 24-25 (1942)(dismissing contention that presidential proclamation stripped Court of authority to review case, stating that "nothing in the Proclamation precludes access to the courts for determining its applicability to the particular case").

[332] Schlesinger v. Councilman, 420 U.S. 738, 759 (1975)(finding judicial abstention is not appropriate in cases in which individuals raise "'substantial arguments denying the right of the military to try them at all,'" and in which the legal challenge "turn[s] on the status of the persons as to whom the military asserted its power"); United States *ex rel.* Toth v. Quarles, 350 U.S. 11, 76 (1955). *But see* Al Odah v. Bush, 593 F. Supp. 2d 53 (D.D.C. 2009) (court would stay consideration of *habeas* claims during course of military commission proceedings, but stay would not occur until charges were referred to commission); Khadr v. Bush, 587 F. Supp. 2d 225 (D.D.C. 2008) (ordering stay in *habeas* case to the extent that it raised issues that have been, will be, or can be raised in military commission proceedings against petitioner and the subsequent appeals process).

[333] *Cf.* New v. Cohen, 129 F.3d 639, 643 (D.C. Cir. 1997).

In: Terrorists, Enemy Combatant Detainees …
Editors: Jian Sun and Miguel Masipag
ISBN: 978-1-61470-391-4

Chapter 3

TERRORIST MATERIAL SUPPORT: AN OVERVIEW OF 18 U.S.C. 2339A AND 2339B*

Charles Doyle

SUMMARY

The material support statutes, 18 U.S.C. 2339A and 2339B, have been among the most frequently prosecuted federal anti-terrorism statutes. Section 2339A outlaws:

(1)(a) attempting to,
(b) conspiring to, or
(c) actually
(2)(a) providing material support or resources, or
(b) concealing or disguising
(i) the nature,
(ii) location,
(iii) source, or
(iv) ownership of material support or resources
(3) knowing or intending that they be used
(a) in preparation for,
(b) in carrying out,
(c) in preparation for concealment of an escape from, or
(d) in carrying out the concealment of an escape from
(4) an offense identified as a federal crime of terrorism.
Section 2339B outlaws:
(1)(a) attempting to provide,
(b) conspiring to provide, or
(c) actually providing

* This is an edited, reformatted and augmented version of a Congressional Research Service publication, CRS Report for Congress R41333, from www.crs.gov, dated July 19, 2010.

(2) material support or resources
(3) to a foreign terrorist organization
(4) knowing that the organization
 (a) has been designated a foreign terrorist organization, or
 (b) engages, or has engaged, in "terrorism" or "terrorist activity."

The sections use a common definition for the term "material support or resources:" any service or tangible or intangible property. The Supreme Court recently held that the forms of material support in the challenge before it were not unconstitutionally vague nor was their proscription inconsistent with the First Amendment's freedom of speech and freedom of association requirements. Violations of either section are punishable by imprisonment for not more than 15 years. Although neither section creates a civil cause of action for victims, treble damages and attorneys fees may be available for some victims under 18 U.S.C. 2333. Section 2339B has two extraterritorial jurisdiction provisions. One is general (there is extraterritorial jurisdiction over an offense under this section) and the other descriptive (there is extraterritorial jurisdiction over an offender under this section if the offender is a U.S. national, etc.). Section 2339A has no such provisions, but is likely applicable at a minimum when an offender or victim is a U.S. national; the offense has an impact in the United States; the offense is committed against U.S. national interests; or the offense is universally condemned.

INTRODUCTION

The two federal material support statutes have been at the heart of the Justice Department's terrorist prosecution efforts.[1] One provision outlaws providing material support for the commission of certain designated offenses that might be committed by terrorists, 18 U.S.C. 2339A.[2] The other outlaws providing material support to certain designated terrorist organizations, 18 U.S.C. 2339B. They share a common definition of the term "material support," some aspects of which have recently come under constitutional attack.

BACKGROUND

Since their inception in the mid-1990s, Congress has periodically expanded and sought to clarify the scope of sections 2339A and 2339B. It enacted Section 2339A with little fanfare as part of a wide-ranging crime package, the Violent Crime Control and Law Enforcement Act of 1994.[3] Almost immediately thereafter, Congress amended Section 2339A and supplemented it with Section 2339B as part of the Antiterrorism and Effective Death Penalty Act of 1996 (AEDPA).[4] As the House committee report explained it, new Section 2339B reflects a recognition of

> the fungibility of financial resources and other types of material support. Allowing an individual to supply funds, goods, or services to an organization, or to any of its subgroups, that draw significant funding from the main organization's treasury, helps defray the costs to

the terrorist organization of running the ostensibly legitimate activities. This in turn frees an equal sum that can then be spent on terrorist activities.[5]

The USA PATRIOT Act amended both sections, increasing the maximum term of imprisonment from 10 to 15 years (and to life imprisonment when commission of the offense resulted in death); adding "expert advice or assistance" to forms of proscribed material support or resources; and subjecting attempts and conspiracies to violate Section 2339A to the same maximum penalties as the substantive violation of the section.[6]

The Intelligence Reform and Terrorism Prevention Act of 2004 amended the definition of "material support or resources" that applies to both sections.[7] The specific forms of support that had been used to define the term became examples of a more general definition which covers "any property, tangible or intangible, or service," 18 U.S.C. 2339A(b)(1). Clarifying definitions of the examples "training" and "expert advice or assistance," were added, as was a clarifying explanation of the term "personnel" as used in Section 2339B, 18 U.S.C. 2339A(b)(2), (3), 2339B(h). At the same time, the predicate offense list of Section 2339A was expanded to cover any of the federal crimes of terrorism, 18 U.S.C. 2339A(a).

Support of Designated Terrorist Organizations (18 U.S.C. 2339B)

In its present form, Section 2339B outlaws:

(1)(a) attempting to provide,
    (b) conspiring to provide, or
    (c) actually providing
(2) material support or resources
(3) to a foreign terrorist organization
(4) knowing that the organization
    (a) has been designated a foreign terrorist organization, or
    (b) engages, or has engaged, in "terrorism" or "terrorist activity."

Attempt, Conspiracy, Aiding and Abetting

Attempt is the unfulfilled commission of an underlying offense. If the attempt is successful, the offender cannot be prosecuted or punished for both the completed offense and the attempt to commit it.[8] Attempt has two elements: (1) an intent to commit the underlying offense; and (2) some substantial step towards its completion.[9] Mere preparation is not enough.[10] "To constitute a substantial step, a defendant's actions must cross the line between preparation and attempt by unequivocally demonstrating that the crime will take place unless interrupted by independent circumstances."[11] It is no defense that, unbeknownst to the defendant, commission of the underlying offense was impossible, as for example because he was dealing with government undercover agents rather than agents of a foreign terrorist organization.[12] An attempt to provide material support in violation of Section 2339B and actually providing such assistance are punished the same: imprisonment for not more than 15 years (for any term of years or life, if death results from the commission of the offense), and/or a fine of not more than $250,000 (not more than $500,000 for an organization)(or not more than twice the amount of gain or loss associated with the offense).[13]

Conspiracy to provide material support in violation of Section 2339B is the agreement to provide such support.[14] The offense is complete upon assent; the support need only be planned, not delivered.[15] Moreover, each of the conspirators is liable not only for the conspiracy, but for any other foreseeable offense committed by any of the conspirators in furtherance of the overall scheme.[16] Like attempt, conspiracy to provide material support carries the same penalties as the completed substantive offense: imprisonment for not more than 15 years (for any term of years or life, if death results from the commission of the offense), and/or a fine of not more than $250,000 (not more than $500,000 for an organization)(or not more than twice the amount of gain or loss associated with the offense).[17] Unlike attempt, conspirators may be punished for both conspiracy and for actually providing material support should their scheme succeed.[18]

Under the provisions of 18 U.S.C. 2, anyone who counsels, procures, aids, or abets a violation of Section 2339B or any other federal crime is punishable as though he had committed the offense himself. "In order to aid and abet another to commit a crime it is necessary that a defendant in some sort associate himself with the venture, that he participate in it as in something that he wishes to bring about, [and] that he seek by his action to make it succeed."[19] "Typically, the same evidence will support both a conspiracy and an aiding and abetting conviction."[20] Unlike conspiracy, however, liability under section 2 only attaches if someone else commits the substantive offense.[21]

Material Support

The precise scope of the term "material support or resources" for purposes of Section 2339B proved controversial almost from the beginning. The section uses the definition found in Section 2339A(b) and thus covers "any property, tangible or intangible, or service," 18 U.S.C. 2339B(g)(4). The term excludes medicine and religious materials, but includes

- currency or monetary instruments or financial securities,
- financial services,
- lodging,
- training (i.e., instruction or teaching designed to impart a specific skill, as opposed to general knowledge),
- expert advice or assistance (i.e., advice or assistance derived from scientific, technical, or other specialized knowledge),
- safehouses,
- false documentation or identification,
- communications equipment, facilities,
- weapons,
- lethal substances,
- explosives,
- personnel (one or more individuals who may be or include oneself), and
- transportation.[22]

Section 2339B also has a more explicit description of personnel covered by its proscription, which confines the term to those provided to a foreign terrorist organization to direct its activities or to work under its direction or control.[23]

Shortly after the creation of Section 2339B, groups seeking to support the nonviolent activities of two designated terrorist organizations sought to enjoin enforcement against them.[24] Among other things, they argued that prohibitions against providing "personnel" or "training" were unconstitutionally vague and might extend to things like advocating the organizations' interests before the U.N. Commission on Human Rights, petitioning Members of Congress on their behalf, seeking the release of political prisoners, or training the organizations' members on the use of international law to resolve political disputes peacefully.[25] The district court concluded that they demonstrated sufficient likelihood of the success on the merits to warrant issuance of a preliminary injunction.[26] The Court of Appeals for the Ninth Circuit agreed.[27]

When Congress amended the definition of material support in the USA PATRIOT Act to include the provision of "expert advice or assistance" to designated terrorist organizations,[28] the groups again sought to enjoin enforcement.[29] Again, the district court agreed the term was unconstitutionally vague, noting that "like the terms 'personnel' and 'training,' 'expert advice and assistance' could be construed to include unequivocally pure speech and advocacy protected by the First Amendment or to encompass First Amendment protected activities."[30]

Then Congress sought to clarify the definition in the Intelligence Reform and Terrorism Protection Act.[31] It recast the definition into its current form, with explanatory additions for the terms "personnel," "training," and "expert advice or assistance."[32] The Ninth Circuit vacated its earlier decisions and returned the case to the district court for further consideration in light of the amendments.[33]

The statute fared only slightly better on remand. The district court felt the amendments clarified the term "personnel" so that it was no longer unconstitutionally vague, but the amendments did not cure the defects it had previously seen in the terms "training" and "expert advice or assistance," a defect compounded by the introduction of the term "service" into the definition.[34]

The Ninth Circuit again agreed.[35] "[L]imiting the definition of the term 'training' to the 'imparting of skills' does not cure unconstitutional vagueness because, so defined, the term 'training' could still be read to encompass speech and advocacy protected by the First Amendment."[36] As for "expert advice or assistance," the Court noted that "[a]t oral argument, the government stated that filing an amicus brief in support of a foreign terrorist organization would violate AEDPA's prohibition against providing 'expert advice or assistance.' Because the 'other specialized knowledge' portion of the ban on providing 'expert advice or assistance' continues to cover constitutionally protected advocacy, we hold that it is void for vagueness."[37] Finally, like the district court, the Ninth Circuit found the term "service" unconstitutionally vague "because the statute defines 'service' to include 'training' or 'expert advice or assistance,' and because it is easy to imagine protected expression that falls within the bounds' of the term 'service.'"[38]

Vagueness challenges by defendants in other federal courts were largely unsuccessful, primarily either because the support involved clearly fell within the definition of proscribed personnel or expert advice or assistance,[39] or because the support involved money or some type of support other than personnel, training, or expert advice or assistance.[40] On September 30, 2009, the Supreme Court granted certiorari to review the Ninth Circuit's decision.[41]

On June 21, 2010, the Supreme Court reversed.[42] It found that the Ninth Circuit had inappropriately merged vagueness and First Amendment concerns.[43] Section 2339B survived scrutiny under each of those challenges when considered separately.[44] A statute is impermissibly vague when "it fails to provide a person of ordinary intelligence fair notice of what is prohibited, or is so standardless that it authorizes or encourages seriously discriminatory enforcement."[45] When a statute is clearly applicable to the conduct at issue, it is to no avail that its application may be unclear under other circumstances.[46]

The Court held that Section 2339B is not unconstitutionally vague as applied to the type of support at issue—coordinated advocacy on behalf of a terrorist organization and training such organization's members to use international law to resolve disputes and to petition the United Nations and other similar entities for relief.[47] A reasonable person would realize that such training constitutes providing "expert advice or assistance ... derived from ... specialized knowledge," and that such advocacy, when coordinated or directed by a terrorist organization, constitutes providing a service to such an organization.[48]

As for free speech, Congress may outlaw material support to a terrorist organization in the form of speech of the type at issue without offending the First Amendment. The government has a compelling interest in the suppression of terrorism. Training and coordinated support in the form of advocacy of a terrorist organization's lawful activities frees resources to service illicit activities; lends legitimacy to the organization; and may strain diplomatic relations with the countries against whom the organization's terrorist activities may be directed.[49] In the case at hand, "[a] foreign terrorist organization introduced to the structures of the international legal system might use the information to threaten, manipulate, and disrupt."[50] An organization guide to and through the avenues to international relief might secure relief in the form of fungible monetary aid.[51]

Finally, the Court confirmed rejection of the group's freedom of association argument; the section outlaws conduct, not membership.[52]

Other Constitutional Challenges

The constitutional challenges of Section 2339B on other grounds have been rejected in virtually every instance.

Overbreadth

At first glance, if various forms of "material support" are considered vague because they sweep in both protected and unprotected speech, then it would seem they should be considered overly broad for the same reason. It is true that a "showing that a law punishes a 'substantial' amount of protected free speech, judged in relation to the statute's plainly legitimate sweep, suffices to invalidate all enforcement of that law."[53] The Supreme Court emphasized in *Virginia v. Hicks*, however, that a challenged statute's "application to protected speech must be 'substantial' not only in an absolute sense, but also relative to the scope of the law's plainly legitimate applications, before applying the strong medicine of overbreadth invalidation."[54]

The Ninth Circuit and each of the other courts to consider the issue have agreed that the various forms of proscribed material support do not include a substantial amount of protected speech when compared to the amount of unprotected speech and conduct which the terms legitimately reach.[55]

Due Process

Closely related to the First Amendment freedom of association argument is a due process "absence of guilty intent" argument. The Supreme Court has said that due process restricts the extent to which the sins of an organization may be attributed to its members.[56] Due process, however, permits punishment "when the statute is found to reach only 'active' members having also a guilty knowledge and intent ... which therefore prevents a conviction on what otherwise might be regarded as merely an expression of sympathy with the alleged criminal enterprise, unaccompanied by any significant action in its support or any commitment to undertake such action."[57]

Some have argued that this means either that due process renders Section 2339B inoperable or that conviction is only possible when the accused knew and intended that his support would be used for the unlawful purposes of the designated terrorist organization.[58] By and large, the courts have found the argument unpersuasive. Some do so because Section 2339B punishes conduct, not mere membership.[59] Others do so because the section requires knowledge that the accused either knew the beneficiary was a designated terrorist organization or knew that it engaged in terrorism.

This, they believe, "satisfies the requirement of 'personal guilty' and eliminates any due process concerns."[60]

Finally, Section 2339B defendants suffer no due process deprivation simply because they may not challenge the terrorist designation of their beneficiary.[61]

Terrorist Organizations

Providing material support is only a crime under 2339B if the known beneficiary is a foreign terrorist organization. That is, the government must show either that (1) the defendant knows that the organization has been designated a foreign terrorist organization or (2) the defendant knows that the organization is or has engaged in "terrorism" or in "terrorist activities."

Designated Terrorist Organizations

The process under which the Secretary of State designates an entity a foreign terrorist organization is authorized in Section 219 of the Immigration and Nationality Act, 8 U.S.C. 1189. Under the procedure, an organization may challenge its designation, 8 U.S.C. 1189(a)(4)(B), and the Secretary may revoke the designation, 8 U.S.C. 1189(a)(6). The organization may appeal the Secretary's decision to the United States Court of Appeals for the District of Columbia, 8 U.S.C. 1189(c). A defendant, charged with providing material support to an organization, however, may not challenge the designation.[62]

Organizations Engaged in Terrorism or Terrorist Activities

Organizations that the accused knew engaged in "terrorism" or "engaged in terrorist activities" constitute a second class of banned beneficiaries. "Terrorism" for purposes of Section 2339B is simply "premeditated, politically motivated violence perpetrated against noncombatant targets by subnational groups or clandestine agents."[63]

The definition of an organization that "engages in terrorist activities" is more multi-faceted. For such purposes of Section 2339B, "the term 'engage in terrorist activity' means, in an individual capacity or as a member of an organization—(I) to commit or to incite to commit, under circumstances indicating an intention to cause death or serious bodily injury, a terrorist activity;

(II) to prepare or plan a terrorist activity;

(III) to gather information on potential targets for terrorist activity;

(IV) to solicit funds or other things of value for -

(aa) a terrorist activity;

(bb) a terrorist organization described in clause (vi)(I) or (vi)(II); or

(cc) a terrorist organization described in clause (vi)(III), unless the solicitor can demonstrate by clear and convincing evidence that he did not know, and should not reasonably have known, that the organization was a terrorist organization;

(V) to solicit any individual—

(aa) to engage in conduct otherwise described in this subsection;

(bb) for membership in a terrorist organization described in clause (vi)(I) or (vi)(II); or

(cc) for membership in a terrorist organization described in clause (vi)(III) unless the solicitor can demonstrate by clear and convincing evidence that he did not know, and should not reasonably have known, that the organization was a terrorist organization; or

(VI) to commit an act that the actor knows, or reasonably should know, affords material support, including a safe house, transportation, communications, funds, transfer of funds or other material financial benefit, false documentation or identification, weapons (including chemical, biological, or radiological weapons), explosives, or training—

(aa) for the commission of a terrorist activity;

(bb) to any individual who the actor knows, or reasonably should know, has committed or plans to commit a terrorist activity;

(cc) to a terrorist organization described in subclause (I) or (II) of clause (vi) or to any member of such an organization; or

(dd) to a terrorist organization described in clause (vi)(III), or to any member of such an organization, unless the actor can demonstrate by clear and convincing evidence that the actor did not know, and should not reasonably have known, that the organization was a terrorist organization."[64]

In the Immigration and Nationality Act, and thus for purposes of Section 2339B, "the term 'terrorist activity' means any activity which is unlawful under the laws of the place where it is committed (or which, if it had been committed in the United States, would be unlawful under the laws of the United States or any State) and which involves any of the following:

(I) The highjacking or sabotage of any conveyance (including an aircraft, vessel, or vehicle).
(II) The seizing or detaining, and threatening to kill, injure, or continue to detain, another individual in order to compel a third person (including a governmental organization) to do or abstain from doing any act as an explicit or implicit condition for the release of the individual seized or detained.
(III) A violent attack upon an internationally protected person (as defined in Section 1116(b)(4) of Title 18) or upon the liberty of such a person.
(IV) An assassination.
(V) The use of any—
(a) biological agent, chemical agent, or nuclear weapon or device, or
(b) explosive, firearm, or other weapon or dangerous device (other than for mere personal monetary gain), with intent to endanger, directly or indirectly, the safety of one or more individuals or to cause substantial damage to property.
(VI) A threat, attempt, or conspiracy to do any of the foregoing."[65]

Consequences of Charge or Conviction

Conviction for a violation of Section 2339B is punishable by imprisonment for not more than 15 years (for any period of years or for life if death results from commission of the offense) and/or a fine of not more than $250,000 (not more than $500,000 for an organizational defendant). Strictly speaking, the U.S. Sentencing Guidelines are not binding. Yet, they are an indispensible part any sentencing decision.[66] The Sentencing Guidelines contain a special terrorism enhancement that, if it applies, can have the effect of requiring a sentence at the statutory maximum, because it calls for a minimum sentencing range that exceeds the statutory maximum of 15 years. The terrorism enhancement Guideline, Section 3A1.4, establishes a minimum offense level of 32 with a criminal history category of VI for a felony offense that "involved, or was intended to promote, a federal crime of terrorism." The Guideline sentencing range of a crime with an offense level of 32 and a criminal history category of VI is 210 to 262 months (17.5 to 21.8 years) imprisonment.[67] Since the maximum term of imprisonment for violations of Section 2339B is 15 years and since a Sentencing Guideline sentence may not exceed the statutory maximum, the Guidelines call for a court to impose the statutory maximum.[68]

The application of the terrorism Guideline requires either that the offense of conviction constitutes a federal crime of terrorism or that the offense of conviction was intended to promote a federal crime of terrorism.[69] An offense qualifies as a federal crime of terrorism if it satisfies two conditions.[70] The crime must be one listed as a federal crime of terrorism in 18 U.S.C. 2332b(g)(5)(B). Section 2339B is listed. Second, the crime must be "calculated to influence or affect the conduct of government by intimidation or coercion, or to retaliate against government action," 18 U.S.C. 2332b(g)(5)(A).

Federal Crime of Terrorism

Classification as a federal crime of terrorism has several other consequences. Property derived from or used in the commission of such an offense is subject to confiscation, 18 U.S.C. 981(a)(1)(G). Federal crimes of terrorism are by definition predicate offenses for purposes of federal money laundering and RICO prosecutions.[71] Prosecution of a Section 2339B offense is subject to an eight-year statute of limitations, rather than the general five-year period.[72] An accused charged with a violation of a federal crime of terrorism faces an enhanced prospect of pre-trial detention.[73] A defendant convicted for violation of a federal crime of terrorism may be subject to a life-time term of supervised release, rather than the general five-year maximum term.[74]

Extraterritorial Jurisdiction

As a general rule, U.S criminal law is territorial, unless Congress indicates otherwise.[75] Congress has used one of two methods to signal overseas application of a criminal statute. In some instances, it states in general terms that a particular statute will have extraterritorial application.[76] In others, it describes the circumstances under which a criminal proscription will have extraterritorial application.[77]

A general declaration of overseas application relies upon the principles of international law under which a claim of extraterritorial jurisdiction might be recognized. Those principles are usually referred to as:

- the territorial principle (crimes that occur in or have an effect in a country's territory);
- the nationality principle (crimes committed by a country's nationals);
- the passive personality principle (crimes committed against a country's nationals);
- the protective principle (crimes that have an impact on a country's national interests); and
- the universal principle (crimes which are universally condemned).[78]

Section 2339B has both a descriptive and a general statement of extraterritorial jurisdiction. The general statement declares, "There is extraterritorial Federal jurisdiction over an offense under this section," 18 U.S.C. 2339B(d)(2). The descriptive statement provides, "There is jurisdiction over an offense under subsection (a) if—

A. an offender is a national of the United States ... or an alien lawfully admitted for permanent residence in the United States ... ;
B. an offender is a stateless person whose habitual residence is in the United States;
C. after the conduct required for the offense occurs an offender is brought into or found in the United States, even if the conduct required for the offense occurs outside the United States;
D. the offense occurs in whole or in part within the United States;
E. the offense occurs in or affects [U.S.] interstate or foreign commerce; or
F. an offender aids or abets any person over whom jurisdiction exists under this paragraph in committing an offense under subsection (a) or conspires with any

person over whom jurisdiction exists under this paragraph to commit an offense under subsection (a)," 18 U.S.C. 2339B(d)(1).

The general statement has been part of the section since its inception.[79] The descriptive statement appeared as part of the Intelligence Reform and Terrorism Prevention Act of 2004.[80] The legislative history of the 2004 act provides no explanation of why the apparently overlapping descriptive statement was thought necessary.[81] Had the general statement been dropped at the time, it would be clear Congress intended extraterritorial application to be confined to situations found in the descriptive statement. The inclusion of both suggests Congress intended extraterritorial application in any situation that falls within either provision.

Civil Actions

Section 2339B(c) authorizes the Attorney General or the Secretary of the Treasury to bring a civil suit in district court to enjoin violation of the section.

Although neither Section 2339B nor Section 2339A creates a private civil cause of action, 18 U.S.C. 2333 authorizes such suits for those injured in their person, property, or business by an act of international terrorism.[82] The courts have concluded that the violations of sections 2339A or 2339B may constitute "acts of international terrorism" for purposes of Section 2333.[83] They do so by construing violations of Section 2339A or 2339B as acts of "international terrorism" as defined in 18 U.S.C. 2331(1).[84]

Reporting Requirements

Section 2339B(a)(2) requires financial institutions to report assets held for a foreign terrorist organization to the Secretary of the Treasury. Failure to do so subjects the institution to a civil penalty of the greater of $50,000 or twice the value of the assets involved, 18 U.S.C. 2339B(b).

Protection of Classified Information

Section 2339B(f) establishes a procedure for the protection of classified information during the course of civil proceedings, complete with authority for interlocutory appeals by the government.

Support of Terrorism (18 U.S.C. 2339A)

Where Section 2339B outlaws support of terrorist organizations, Section 2339A outlaws support for the crimes a terrorist has committed or may be planning to commit. Section 2339B designates terrorist organizations; Section 2339A designates terrorist crimes. More precisely, Section 2339A outlaws:

(1)(a) attempting to,
    (b) conspiring to, or

(c) actually
(2)(a) providing material support or resources, or
(b) concealing or disguising
i. the nature,
ii. location,
iii. source, or
iv. ownership
of material support or resources
(3) knowing or intending that they be used
(a) in preparation for,
(b) in carrying out,
(c) in preparation for concealment of an escape from, or
(d) in carrying out the concealment of an escape from
(4) an offense identified as a federal crime of terrorism.[85]

Attempt, Conspiracy, and Aiding and Abetting

The law of attempt, conspiracy, and aiding and abetting is the same for sections 2339A and 2339B. As we said of Section 2339B, in the case of Section 2339A, attempt is the unfulfilled commission of an underlying offense. If the attempt is successful, the offender cannot be prosecuted or punished for both the completed offense and the attempt to commit it.[86] Attempt has two elements: (1) an intent to commit the underlying offense; and (2) some substantial step towards its completion.[87] Mere preparation is not enough.[88] "To constitute a substantial step, a defendant's actions must cross the line between preparation and attempt by unequivocally demonstrating that the crime will take place unless interrupted by independent circumstances."[89] It is no defense that, unbeknownst to the defendant, commission of the underlying offense was impossible, as for example because he was dealing with government undercover agents rather than agents of a foreign terrorist organization.[90] An attempt to provide material support in violation of Section 2339B and actually providing such assistance are punished the same: imprisonment for not more than 15 years (for any term of years or life, if death results from the commission of the offense), and/or a fine of not more than $250,000 (not more than $500,000 for an organization)(or not more than twice the amount of gain or loss associated with the offense).[91]

Conspiracy to provide material support in violation of Section 2339B is the agreement to provide such support.[92] The offense is complete upon assent; the support need only be planned, not delivered.[93] Moreover, each of the conspirators is liable not only for the conspiracy, but for any other foreseeable offense committed by any of the conspirators in furtherance of the overall scheme.[94] Like attempt, conspiracy to provide material support carries the same penalties as the completed substantive offense: imprisonment for not more than 15 years (for any term of years or life, if death results from the commission of the offense), and/or a fine of not more than $250,000 (not more than $500,000 for an organization)(or not more than twice the amount of gain or loss associated with the offense).[95] Unlike attempt, conspirators may be punished for both conspiracy and for actually providing material support should be their scheme succeed.[96]

Under the provisions of 18 U.S.C. 2, anyone who counsels, procures, aids, or abets a violation of Section 2339A or any other federal crime is punishable as though he had committed the offense himself. "In order to aid and abet another to commit a crime it is necessary that a defendant in some sort associate himself with the venture, that he participate in it as in something that he wishes to bring about, [and] that he seek by his action to make it succeed."[97] "Typically, the same evidence will support both a conspiracy and an aiding and abetting conviction."[98] Unlike conspiracy, however, liability under Section 2 only attaches if someone else commits the substantive offense.[99]

Material Support

Section 2339A uses roughly the same definition of "material support" as does Section 2339B, but to a somewhat different effect. Both use the definition found in 2339A(b) which covers "any property, tangible or intangible, or service."[100] The term excludes medicine and religious materials, but includes

- currency or monetary instruments or financial securities,
- financial services,
- lodging,
- training (i.e., instruction or teaching designed to impart a specific skill, as opposed to general knowledge),
- expert advice or assistance (i.e., advice or assistance derived from scientific, technical or other specialized knowledge),
- safehouses,
- false documentation or identification,
- communications equipment, facilities,
- weapons,
- lethal substances,
- explosives,
- personnel (one or more individuals who may be or include oneself), and
- transportation.[101]

Section 2339B alone has a more explicit description of "personnel" covered by its proscription, which confines the term to those provided to a foreign terrorist organization to direct its activities or to work under its direction or control.[102] The omission of a comparable provision from Section 2339A has led one court to include within the term those provided to work in a coordinated way for preparation or commission of a federal crime of terrorism.[103]

Because Section 2339A requires that the support be given while knowing or intending that it be used in preparation for or in the commission of a specific terrorist offense, the section has survived the vagueness challenges that have troubled Section 2339B.[104]

Concealing or Disguising Material Support

Section 2339A condemns either providing material support or concealing "the nature, location, source, or ownership" of such support. The provision has been part of Section 2339A from the beginning[105] and seems designed to reach the middle men or conduits between terrorists and their supporters. Expansion of the definition of material support to include services and the option of charging middle men with conspiracy or aiding and abetting may have rendered the provision redundant. In any event, concealment charges seem to have thus far been confined to those who have also been charged with providing support.[106]

Use in Relation to a Federal Crime of Terrorism

Section 2339A only outlaws activities related to one or more of the federal crimes of terrorism listed in 18 U.S.C. 2332b(g)(5)(B)(other than sections 2339A or 2339B). The crimes, mostly violent offenses, are those likely to be committed in a terrorist context. A few of the more than 40 crimes on the list, like 18 U.S.C. 1203 (hostage taking), have a specific terrorist element (e.g., committed to influence or retaliate for government action). Most, like 18 U.S.C. 81 (arson within a federal enclave), do not.[107]

The defendant must know or intend that the support will assist in the commission of a federal crime of terrorism. Since the section bans attempts, conspiracies, and support used in preparation for a federal crime of terrorism (as well as support for carrying out such a crime), a violation of Section 2339A may occur even if the anticipated federal crime of terrorism has not.[108] On the other hand, since the section also reaches support for concealment of an escape from a federal crime of terrorism, a violation of the section may occur even after the federal crime of terrorism.

Several of the federal crimes of terrorism statutes cover conspiracy to violate their provisions; for example, 18 U.S.C. 956 (conspiracy to commit certain violent crimes overseas). Although the law ordinarily does not permit prosecution of a conspiracy to conspire, the "[c]ourts have recognized that one conspiracy can serve as the predicate for another conspiracy when the '[overarching] conspiracy and the predicate conspiracy are distinct offenses with entirely different objectives.'"[109]

Consequences of Charge or Conviction

Conviction for a violation of Section 2339A is punishable by imprisonment for not more than 15 years (for any period of years or for life if death results from commission of the offense) and/or a fine of not more than $250,000 (not more than $500,000 for an organizational defendant). Although strictly speaking the U.S. Sentencing Guidelines are not binding, they weigh heavily in any sentencing decision.[110] The Sentencing Guidelines contain a special terrorism enhancement that, if it applies, can have the effect of requiring a sentence at the statutory maximum, because it calls for a minimum sentencing range that exceeds the statutory maximum of 15 years. The terrorism enhancement Guideline, Section 3A1.4, establishes a minimum offense level of 32 with a criminal history category of VI for a felony offense that "involved, or was intended to promote, a federal crime of terrorism." The

Guideline sentencing range of a crime with an offense level of 32 and a criminal history category of VI is imprisonment for from 210 to 262 months (17.5 to 21.8 years).[111] Since the maximum term of imprisonment for violations of Section 2339A is 15 years and since a Sentencing Guideline sentence may not exceed the statutory maximum, the Guidelines call for a court to impose the statutory maximum.[112]

The application of the terrorism Guideline requires either that the offense of conviction constitutes a federal crime of terrorism or that the offense of conviction was intended to promote a federal crime of terrorism.[113] An offense qualifies as a federal crime of terrorism if it satisfies two conditions.[114] The crime must be one listed as a federal crime of terrorism in 18 U.S.C. 2332b(g)(5)(B). Section 2339A is listed. Second, the crime must be "calculated to influence or affect the conduct of government by intimidation or coercion, or to retaliate against government action," 18 U.S.C. 2332b(g)(5)(A).

Federal Crime of Terrorism

Classification as a federal crime of terrorism has several other consequences. Property derived from or used in the commission of such an offense is subject to confiscation, 18 U.S.C. 981(a)(1)(G). Federal crimes of terrorism are by definition predicate offenses for purposes of federal money laundering and RICO prosecutions.[115] Prosecution of a Section 2339A offense is subject to an eight-year statute of limitations, rather than the general five-year period.[116] An accused charged with a violation of a federal crime of terrorism faces an enhanced prospect of pre-trial detention.[117] A defendant convicted for violation of a federal crime of terrorism may be subject to a life-time term of supervised release, rather than the general five-year maximum term.[118]

Extraterritorial Jurisdiction

Unlike Section 2339B, Section 2339A has neither a general nor a descriptive statement of extraterritorial jurisdiction. Nevertheless, it seems likely that the courts would find its provisions applicable overseas for any of several reasons. First, extraterritorial jurisdiction is thought to apply to overseas accomplices to crimes with extraterritorial application.[119] Second, to confine application to purely domestic violations would likely frustrate congressional intent and the purpose for its enactment.[120] Third, violations would most likely be prosecuted under circumstances evidencing one or more of the principles that justify the exercise of federal jurisdiction under international law, for example, the offense has an impact in the U.S. (territorial principle); the offender is a U.S. national (nationality principle); the victim is a U.S. national (passive personality principle); the offense has an impact on U.S. national interests (protective principle); or the offense is universally condemned (universal principle).[121]

Civil Actions

Repeating again the principles mutually applicable to sections 2339B and 2339A, we note that although neither Section 2339B nor Section 2339A creates a private civil cause of action, 18 U.S.C. 2333 authorizes such suits for those injured in their person, property, or business by an act of international terrorism.[122] The courts have concluded that the violations of sections 2339A or 2339B may constitute "acts of international terrorism" for purposes of Section 2333.[123] They do so by construing violations of Section 2339A or 2339B as acts of "international terrorism" as defined in 18 U.S.C. 2331(1).[124]

Venue

Section 2339A asserts that venue is proper in "any Federal judicial district in which the underlying offense was committed, or in any other Federal judicial district as provided by law," 18 U.S.C. 2339A(a). The reach of this provision may be limited by Supreme Court decisions suggesting that venue over offenses committed within the United States is only proper in those districts in which the conduct element of the offense occurs.[125]

APPENDIX A. 18 U.S.C. 2339A PREDICATE OFFENSES

18 U.S.C. 32 (destruction of aircraft)
18 U.S.C. 37 (violence at international airports)
18 U.S.C. 81 (arson within a federal enclave)
18 U.S.C. 175 (biological weapons offenses)
18 U.S.C. 175b (unlawful possession biological materials)
18 U.S.C. 175c (smallpox virus offenses)
18 U.S.C. 229 (chemical weapons offenses)
18 U.S.C. 351 (murder, kidnaping, or assault upon Members of Congress, etc.) 18 U.S.C. 831(nuclear material offenses)
18 U.S.C. 832 (material support of foreign nuclear weapons program) 18 U.S.C. 842(m) or (n) (plastic explosives offenses)
18 U.S.C. 844(f) or (i) (bombing federal property or property in or affecting commerce)
18 U.S.C. 930(c) (homicide with dangerous weapon in a federal facility)
18 U.S.C. 956 (conspiracy to commit certain violent crimes overseas)
18 U.S.C. 1030(a)(1), (5)(A)(i) (certain computer fraud and abuse offenses) 18 U.S.C. 1114 (murder of a federal officer or employees)
18 U.S.C. 1116 (murder of a foreign dignitary)
18 U.S.C. 1203 (hostage taking)
18 U.S.C. 1361 (destruction of federal property)
18 U.S.C. 1362 (destruction of communications property)
18 U.S.C. 1363 (destruction of property within a federal enclave) 18 U.S.C. 1366 (destruction of an energy facility)
18 U.S.C. 1751 (murder, kidnaping or assault of the President, inter alia) 18 U.S.C. 1992 (violent attacks on mass transit)
18 U.S.C. 2155 (destruction of national defense material)
18 U.S.C. 2156 (production of defective national defense material) 18 U.S.C. 2280 (violence against maritime navigation)

18 U.S.C. 2281 (violence against maritime fixed platforms) 18 U.S.C. 2332 (violence against Americans overseas)
18 U.S.C. 2332a (weapons of mass destruction offenses) 18 U.S.C. 2332b (multinational terrorism)
18 U.S.C. 2332f (bombing public places or facilities)
18 U.S.C. 2332g (anti-aircraft offenses)
18 U.S.C. 2332h (radiological dispersal device offenses) 18 U.S.C. 2339 (harboring terrorists)
18 U.S.C. 2339A (material support of terrorist offenses)
18 U.S.C. 2339B (material support of designated terrorist organizations) 18 U.S.C. 2339C (financing of terrorism)
18 U.S.C. 2339D (receipt of foreign terrorist organization training) 18 U.S.C. 2340A (torture)
21 U.S.C. 960a (narco-terrorism)
42 U.S.C. 2122 (atomic weapons offenses)
42 U.S.C. 2284 (atomic weapons offenses)
49 U.S.C. 46502 (air piracy)
49 U.S.C. 46504 (2d sentence) (assault on a flight crew with a dangerous weapon)
49 U.S.C. 46505(b)(3) or (c) (explosive or incendiary devices, or endangerment of human life by means of weapons, on an aircraft within U.S. jurisdiction)
49 U.S.C. 46506 (homicide or attempted homicide aboard an aircraft within U.S. jurisdiction) 49 U.S.C. 60123(b) (destruction of gas pipeline facilities)

Appendix B. 18 U.S.C. 2339A (text)

Providing Material Support to Terrorists

a) **Offense.** – Whoever provides material support or resources or conceals or disguises the nature, location, source, or ownership of material support or resources, knowing or intending that they are to be used in preparation for, or in carrying out, a violation of Section 32, 37, 81, 175, 229, 351, 831, 842(m) or (n), 844(f) or (i), 930(c), 956, 1091, 1114, 1116, 1203, 1361, 1362, 1363, 1366, 1751, 1992, 2155, 2156, 2280, 2281, 2332, 2332a, 2332b, 2332f, 2340A or 2442 of this title, Section 236 of the Atomic Energy Act of 1954 (42 U.S.C. 2284), Section 46502 or 60123(b) of Title 49, or any offense listed in Section 2332b(g)(5)(B) (except for sections 2339A and 2339B) or in preparation for, or in carrying out, the concealment of an escape from the commission of any such violation, or attempts or conspires to do such an act, shall be fined under this title, imprisoned not more than 15 years, or both, and, if the death of any person results, shall be imprisoned for any term of years or for life. A violation of this section may be prosecuted in any Federal judicial district in which the underlying offense was committed, or in any other Federal judicial district as provided by law.

(b) **Definitions.**– As used in this section –

1) the term "material support or resources" means any property, tangible or

intangible, or service, including currency or monetary instruments or financial securities, financial services, lodging, training, expert advice or assistance, safehouses, false documentation or identification, communications equipment, facilities, weapons, lethal substances, explosives, personnel (1 or more individuals who may be or include oneself), and transportation, except medicine or religious materials;

2) the term "training" means instruction or teaching designed to impart a specific skill, as opposed to general knowledge; and
3) the term "expert advice or assistance" means advice or assistance derived from scientific, technical or other specialized knowledge.

APPENDIX C. 18 U.S.C. 2339B (TEXT)

Providing Material Support or Resources to Designated Foreign Terrorist Organizations

(a) Prohibited activities. –

1) **Unlawful conduct.** – Whoever knowingly provides material support or resources to a foreign terrorist organization, or attempts or conspires to do so, shall be fined under this title or imprisoned not more than 15 years, or both, and, if the death of any person results, shall be imprisoned for any term of years or for life. To violate this paragraph, a person must have knowledge that the organization is a designated terrorist organization (as defined in subsection (g)(6)), that the organization has engaged or engages in terrorist activity (as defined in Section 212(a)(3)(B) of the Immigration and Nationality Act), or that the organization has engaged or engages in terrorism (as defined in Section 140(d) (2) of the Foreign Relations Authorization Act, Fiscal Years 1988 and 1989).
2) **Financial institutions.** – Except as authorized by the Secretary, any financial institution that becomes aware that it has possession of, or control over, any funds in which a foreign terrorist organization, or its agent, has an interest, shall –
   A. retain possession of, or maintain control over, such funds; and
   B. report to the Secretary the existence of such funds in accordance with regulations issued by the Secretary.

(b) Civil penalty. – Any financial institution that knowingly fails to comply with subsection
(a)(2) shall be subject to a civil penalty in an amount that is the greater of –

A. $50,000 per violation; or
B. twice the amount of which the financial institution was required under subsection (a)(2) to retain possession or control.

(c) Injunction. – Whenever it appears to the Secretary or the Attorney General that any person is engaged in, or is about to engage in, any act that constitutes, or would constitute, a violation of this section, the Attorney General may initiate civil action in a district court of the United States to enjoin such violation.

(d) Extraterritorial jurisdiction. –

(1) In general. – There is jurisdiction over an offense under subsection (a) if –

A. an offender is a national of the United States (as defined in Section 101(a)(22) of the Immigration and Nationality Act (8 U.S.C. 1101(a)(22)) or an alien lawfully admitted for permanent residence in the United States (as defined in Section 101(a)(20) of the Immigration and Nationality Act (8 U.S.C. 1101(a)(20));
B. an offender is a stateless person whose habitual residence is in the United States;
C. after the conduct required for the offense occurs an offender is brought into or found in the United States, even if the conduct required for the offense occurs outside the United States;
D. the offense occurs in whole or in part within the United States;
E. the offense occurs in or affects interstate or foreign commerce; or
F. an offender aids or abets any person over whom jurisdiction exists under this paragraph in committing an offense under subsection (a) or conspires with any person over whom jurisdiction exists under this paragraph to commit an offense under subsection (a).

(2) Extraterritorial jurisdiction. – There is extraterritorial Federal jurisdiction over an offense under this section.

(e) Investigations. –

(1) In general. – The Attorney General shall conduct any investigation of a possible violation of this section, or of any license, order, or regulation issued pursuant to this section.

(2) Coordination with the Department of the Treasury. – The Attorney General shall work in coordination with the Secretary in investigations relating to –

(A) the compliance or noncompliance by a financial institution with the requirements of subsection (a)(2); and
(B) civil penalty proceedings authorized under subsection (b).

(3) Referral. – Any evidence of a criminal violation of this section arising in the course of an investigation by the Secretary or any other Federal agency shall be referred immediately to the Attorney General for further investigation. The Attorney General shall timely notify the Secretary of any action taken on referrals from the Secretary, and may refer investigations to the Secretary for remedial licensing or civil penalty action.

(f) Classified information in civil proceedings brought by the United States. –

(1) Discovery of classified information by defendants. –

(A) Request by United States. – In any civil proceeding under this section, upon request made ex parte and in writing by the United States, a court, upon a sufficient showing, may authorize the United States to –

I. redact specified items of classified information from documents to be introduced into evidence or made available to the defendant through discovery under the Federal Rules of Civil Procedure;
II. substitute a summary of the information for such classified documents; or
III. substitute a statement admitting relevant facts that the classified information would tend to prove.

(B) Order granting request. – If the court enters an order granting a request under this paragraph, the entire text of the documents to which the request relates shall be sealed and preserved in the records of the court to be made available to the appellate court in the event of an appeal.

(C) Denial of request. – If the court enters an order denying a request of the United States under this paragraph, the United States may take an immediate, interlocutory appeal in accordance with paragraph (5). For purposes of such an appeal, the entire text of the documents to which the request relates, together with any transcripts of arguments made ex parte to the court in connection therewith, shall be maintained under seal and delivered to the appellate court.

(2) Introduction of classified information; precautions by court. –

(A) Exhibits. – To prevent unnecessary or inadvertent disclosure of classified information in a civil proceeding brought by the United States under this section, the United States may petition the court ex parte to admit, in lieu of classified writings, recordings, or photographs, one or more of the following:

I. Copies of items from which classified information has been redacted.
II. Stipulations admitting relevant facts that specific classified information would tend to prove.
III. A declassified summary of the specific classified information.

(B) Determination by court. – The court shall grant a request under this paragraph if the court finds that the redacted item, stipulation, or summary is sufficient to allow the defendant to prepare a defense.

(3) Taking of trial testimony. –

(A) Objection. – During the examination of a witness in any civil proceeding brought by the United States under this subsection, the United States may object to any question or line of inquiry that may require the witness to disclose classified information not previously found to be admissible.

(B) Action by court. – In determining whether a response is admissible, the court shall take precautions to guard against the compromise of any classified information, including –

I. permitting the United States to provide the court, ex parte, with a proffer of the witness's response to the question or line of inquiry; and
II. requiring the defendant to provide the court with a proffer of the nature of the information that the defendant seeks to elicit.

(C) Obligation of defendant. – In any civil proceeding under this section, it shall be the defendant's obligation to establish the relevance and materiality of any classified information sought to be introduced.
(4) Appeal. – If the court enters an order denying a request of the United States under this subsection, the United States may take an immediate interlocutory appeal in accordance with paragraph (5).
(5) Interlocutory appeal. –
(A) Subject of appeal. – An interlocutory appeal by the United States shall lie to a court of appeals from a decision or order of a district court –

I. authorizing the disclosure of classified information;
II. imposing sanctions for nondisclosure of classified information; or
III. refusing a protective order sought by the United States to prevent the disclosure of classified information.

(B) Expedited consideration. –

i. **In general.** – An appeal taken pursuant to this paragraph, either before or during trial, shall be expedited by the court of appeals.
ii. **Appeals prior to trial.** – If an appeal is of an order made prior to trial, an appeal shall be taken not later than 14 days after the decision or order appealed from, and the trial shall not commence until the appeal is resolved.
iii. **Appeals during trial.** – If an appeal is taken during trial, the trial court shall adjourn the trial until the appeal is resolved, and the court of appeals –

I. shall hear argument on such appeal not later than 4 days after the adjournment of the trial, excluding intermediate weekends and holidays;
II. may dispense with written briefs other than the supporting materials previously submitted to the trial court;
III. shall render its decision not later than 4 days after argument on appeal, excluding intermediate weekends and holidays; and
IV. may dispense with the issuance of a written opinion in rendering its decision.

(C) Effect of ruling. – An interlocutory appeal and decision shall not affect the right of the defendant, in a subsequent appeal from a final judgment, to claim as error reversal by the trial court on remand of a ruling appealed from during trial.
(6) Construction. – Nothing in this subsection shall prevent the United States from seeking protective orders or asserting privileges ordinarily available to the United States to protect against the disclosure of classified information, including the invocation of the military and State secrets privilege.
(g) Definitions. – As used in this section –

a. the term "classified information" has the meaning given that term in Section 1(a) of the Classified Information Procedures Act (18 U.S.C. App.);
2) the term "financial institution" has the same meaning as in Section 5312(a)(2) of Title 31, United States Code;

3) the term "funds" includes coin or currency of the United States or any other country, traveler's checks, personal checks, bank checks, money orders, stocks, bonds, debentures, drafts, letters of credit, any other negotiable instrument, and any electronic representation of any of the foregoing;
4) the term "material support or resources" has the same meaning given that term in Section 2339A (including the definitions of "training" and "expert advice or assistance" in that section);
5) the term "Secretary" means the Secretary of the Treasury; and
6) the term "terrorist organization" means an organization designated as a terrorist organization under Section 219 of the Immigration and Nationality Act.

(h) Provision of personnel. – No person may be prosecuted under this section in connection with the term "personnel" unless that person has knowingly provided, attempted to provide, or conspired to provide a foreign terrorist organization with 1 or more individuals (who may be or include himself) to work under that terrorist organization's direction or control or to organize, manage, supervise, or otherwise direct the operation of that organization. Individuals who act entirely independently of the foreign terrorist organization to advance its goals or objectives shall not be considered to be working under the foreign terrorist organization's direction and control.

(i) Rule of construction. – Nothing in this section shall be construed or applied so as to abridge the exercise of rights guaranteed under the First Amendment to the Constitution of the United States.

(j) Exception. – No person may be prosecuted under this section in connection with the term "personnel", "training", or "expert advice or assistance" if the provision of that material support or resources to a foreign terrorist organization was approved by the Secretary of State with the concurrence of the Attorney General. The Secretary of State may not approve the provision of any material support that may be used to carry out terrorist activity (as defined in Section 212(a)(3)(B)(iii) of the Immigration and Nationality Act).

End Notes

[1] A Review of the Material Support to Terrorism Prohibition Improvements Act: Hearing Before the Subcomm. On Terrorism, Technology and Homeland Security, 109th Cong., 1st Sess. 45 (2005)(statement of Barry Sabin, Chief, Counterterrorism Section, U.S. Dept. of Justice); Implementation of the USA PATRIOT Act: Prohibition of Material Support Under Sections 805 of the USA PATRIOT Act and 6603 of the Intelligence Reform and Terrorism Prevention Act of 2004, 109th Cong., 1st Sess. 18 (2005)(statement of Barry Sabin, Chief, Counterterrorism Section, U.S. Dept. of Justice); Cole, Out of the Shadows: Preventive Detention, Suspected Terrorists, and War, 97 CALIFORNIA LAW REVIEW 693, 723 (2009)("The most important of these statutes is 18 U.S.C. §2339B.... [R]arely enforced before 9/11, it has since become a principal tool in the Justice Department's 'terrorism' prosecutions").

[2] The text of 18 U.S.C. 2339A and 2339B is appended.

[3] P.L. 103-322, §120005, 108 Stat. 2022 (1994). The Violent Crime Control Act was a three hundred and fifty-five page amalgam of legislative proposals consisting of thirty-three separate titles which included Cop on the Beat grants, the Violence Against Women Act, revival of the death penalty as a federal sentencing alternative, a ban on assault weapons, DNA identification, and crime victims rights. Its various components had been the subject of two dozen House committee reports, listed in 1994 U.S.C.C.A.N. 1801 (1994), none which appear to have addressed Section 2339A. The section, however, had been included in much the same language in separate

legislative proposals offered by members of both parties in both Houses, see e.g., H.R. 1301, §110 (Representative Schumer); H.R. 2847, §702 (Representative Sensenbrenner); H.R. 2872, §421 (Representative McCullom); H.R. 1313 (Representative Brooks); S. 8, §702 (Senator Hatch); S. 1488, §726 (Senator Biden).

[4] P.L. 104-132, §§323, 303, 110 Stat. 1255, 1250, respectively. The Section 323 amendments to Section 2339A enlarged its predicate offense list to include 18 U.S.C. 37 (violence at international airports), 81 (arson), 175 (biological weapons), 831 (nuclear weapons), 842(m) and (n) (plastic explosives), 1362 (destruction of communications facilities), 2155 and 2156 (destruction, or defective production, of war materials), 2332 (terrorist violence against Americans overseas), 2332a (weapons of mass destruction), and 2332b(multi-national terrorism). Later in the year, Congress added three other crimes to Section 2339A's predicate offense list: 18 U.S.C. 930(c) (use of a firearm during a murderous attack on a federal facility), 1992 (train wrecking), and 2332c (chemical weapons), P.L. 104-294, §601(b)(2), (s)(2), (s)(3), 110 Stat. 3502, 3506 (1996).

[5] H.Rept. 104-383, 81 (1995). AEDPA also eliminated a restriction on Section 2339A investigations which the report characterized as "effectively negat[ing] the efficacy of 2339A," id. at 82.

[6] P.L. 107-56, §§810(c), (d), 811(d), 115 Stat. 380, 381 (2001). At the time, attempts and conspiracies to violate Section 2339B were already subject to the same maximum penalty as the underlying substantive offense, 18 U.S.C. 2339B (2000 ed.).

[7] P.L. 108-458, §6603, 118 Stat. 3762 (2004). The amendments, initially temporary, were made permanent in the USA PATRIOT Act Improvement and Reauthorization Act, P.L. 109-177, §104, 120 Stat. 195 (2006).

[8] United States v. Rivera-Relle, 333 F.3d 914, 921 n.11 (9th Cir. 2003).

[9] Braxton v. United States, 500 U.S. 344, 349 (1991); United States v. Bristol-Martir, 570 F.3d 29, 39 (1st Cir. 2009).

[10] United States v. Barlow, 568 F.3d 215, 219 (5th Cir. 2009); United States v. DeMarce, 564 F.3d 989, 998 (8th Cir. 2009).

[11] United States v. Mincoff, 574 F.3d 1186, 1195 (9th Cir. 2009); United States v. Morris, 549 F.3d 548, 550 (7th Cir. 2008).

[12] United States v. Rehak, 589 F.3d 965, 970-71 (8th Cir. 2009); United States v. Cot , 504 F.3d 682, (7th Cir. 2007); cf., United States v. Lakhani, 480 F.3d 171, 174-77 (3d Cir. 2007).

[13] 18 U.S.C. 2339B(a), 3571.

[14] United States v. Jimenez Recio, 537 U.S. 270, 274 (2003)("the essence of a conspiracy is an agreement to commit an unlawful act")(here and hereafter internal citations and quotation marks have been omitted unless otherwise indicated); United States v. Lockett, 601 F.3d 837, (8th Cir. 2010)("In order to convict a defendant of conspiracy, the government must prove (1) the existence of an agreement to achieve an illegal purpose, (2) the defendant's knowledge of the agreement, and (3) the defendant's knowing participation in the agreement. The agreement does not have to be a formal, explicit agreement; a tacit understanding will suffice"); United States v. Boria, 592 F.3d 476, 481 (3d Cir. 2010); see generally CRS Report R41223, Federal Conspiracy Law: A Brief Overview, by Charles Doyle.

[15] United States v. Rehak, 589 F.3d 965, 971 (8th Cir. 2009); United States v. Schaffer, 586 F.3d 414, 422 (6th Cir. 2009).

[16] Pinkerton v. United States, 328 U.S. 640, 647 (1946); United States v, Nerkubi, 592 F.3d 22, 29 (1st Cir. 2010); United States v. Wardell, 591 F.3d 1279, 1291 (10th Cir. 2009).

[17] 18 U.S.C. 2339B(a), 3571.

[18] Iannelli v. United States, 420 U.S. 770, 777-78 (1975); United States v. Chandia, 514 F.3d 365, 372 (4th Cir. 2008)("We also disagree with Chandia's argument that Congress did not intend to authorize multiple punishments for a conspiracy and a substantive violation under §2339B. Chandia's argument is based on the language of the statute, which prohibits the conspiracy and the actual provision of material support in the same section. See 18 U.S.C. §2339B(a)(1). ("Whoever knowingly provides material support ... or attempts or conspires to do so ..."). But, as the Supreme Court has held, the "settled principle" that "the commission of the substantive offense and a conspiracy to commit it are separate and distinct offenses" does not give way simply because the statute describing the substantive offense also specifically prohibits conspiracies. Callanan v. United States, 364 U.S. 587, 593 (1961)").

[19] Nye & Nissen v. United States, 336 U.S. 613, 619 (1949); United States v. Turner, 583 F.3d 1062, 1067 (8th Cir. 2009).

[20] United States v. Rodriguez, 553 F.3d 380, 391 (5th Cir. 2008).

[21] United States v. Liera, 585 F.3d 1237, 1246 (9th Cir. 2009)("the aiding and abetting theory required the jury to find that: (1) someone committed the underlying offense; and (2) that Liera aided and abetted its commission"); United States v. Tagg, 572 F.3d 1320, 1324 (11th Cir. 2009)("To prove guilty under a theory of

aiding and abetting, the Government must prove: (1) the substantive offense was committed by someone; (2) the defendant committed an act which contributed to and furthered the offense; and (3) the defendant intended to aid in its commission"); United States v. Gonzalez, 570 F.3d 16, 28-9 (1st Cir. 2009).

[22] 18 U.S.C. 2339A(b)(2) and (b)(3) supply respectively the precise definitions of "training" and "expert advice or assistance" noted above.

[23] 18 U.S.C. 2339B(h)("No person may be prosecuted under this section in connection with the term "personnel" unless that person has knowingly provided, attempted to provide, or conspired to provide a foreign terrorist organization with 1 or more individuals (who may be or include himself) to work under that terrorist organization's direction or control or to organize, manage, supervise, or otherwise direct the operation of that organization. Individuals who act entirely independently of the foreign terrorist organization to advance its goals or objectives shall not be considered to be working under the foreign terrorist organization's direction and control").

[24] Humanitarian Law Project v. Reno, 9 F.Supp.2d 1176 (C.D.Cal. 1998).

[25] Id. at 1203-204.

[26] Id. at 1204-205.

[27] Humanitarian Law Project v. Reno, 205 F.3d 1130 (9th Cir. 2000).

[28] P.L. 107-56, §805(a)(2), 115 Stat. 377 (2001).

[29] Humanitarian Law Project v. Ashcroft, 309 F.Supp.2d 1185 (C.D.Cal. 2004).

[30] Id. at 1200-201.

[31] P.L. 108-458, §6603, 118 Stat. 3762 (2004).

[32] 18 U.S.C. 2339B(h), 2339A(b)(2), (3).

[33] Humanitarian Law Project v. United States Department of Justice, 393 F.3d 902 (9th Cir. 2004).

[34] Humanitarian Law Project v. Gonzales, 380 F.Supp.2d 1134, 1150-153 (C.D.Cal. 2005)(emphasis of the court) ("[T]he Court finds that 'training' fails to satisfy the enhanced requirement of clarity for statutes touching upon protected activities under the First Amendment.... The IRTPA amendments define 'expert advice or assistance' as 'scientific, technical, or other specialized knowledge Similar to the Court's discussion of 'training' above, 'expert advice or assistance' remains impermissibly vague because 'specialized knowledge' includes the same protected activities that 'training' covers, such as teaching international law for peacemaking resolutions or how to petition the United Nations to seek redress for human rights violations.... The Court finds that the undefined term 'service' in the IRTPA is impermissibly vague, as the statute defines 'service' to include 'training' or 'expert advice or assistance,' terms the Court has already ruled are vague. Like 'training' and 'expert advice or assistance,' it is easy to imagine protected expression that falls within the bounds of the term 'service'").

[35] Humanitarian Law Project v. Mukasey, 552 F.3d 916 (9th Cir. 2009), cert. granted sub nom., Humanitarian Law Project v. Holder, 130 S.Ct. 48 (2009).

[36] Id. at 929.

[37] Id. at 930.

[38] Id.

[39] United States v. Taleb-Jedi, 566 F.Supp.2d 157, 181-82 (E.D.N.Y. 2008)(defendant who worked in the terrorist organization's political department provided personnel within the meaning of Section 2339B); United States v. Warsame, 537 F.Supp.2d 1005, 1018 (D.Minn. 2008)(defendant participated in al Qaeda training camp provided personnel); United States v. Shah, 474 F.Supp.2d 492, 497 n.5 (S.D.N.Y. 2007)(the doctor who treated al Qaeda wounded jihardists provided personnel and expert assistance); United States v. Marzook, 383 F.Supp.2d 1056, 1066 (N.D.Ill. 2005)(defendant directed another to perform several tasks for the benefit of terrorist organization including scouting targets for possible attacks).

[40] United States v. Assi, 414 F.Supp.2d 707, 718 (E.D.Mich. 2006)(defendant provided equipment, i.e., "weapons" and "other physical assets"); United States v. Hammoud, 381 F.3d 316, 331 (4th Cir. 2004)("There is nothing at all vague about the term ' currency' [which is what the defendant provided the terrorist organization]"); see also United States v. Lindh, 212 F.Supp.2d 541, 574 (E.D.Va. 2002)("The Ninth Circuit's vagueness holding in Humanitarian Law Project [prior to the 2004 amendments] is neither persuasive nor controlling").

[41] Holder v. Humanitarian Law Project, 130 S.Ct. 48 (2009).

[42] Holder v. Humanitarian Law Project, 78 U.S.L.W. 4625(U.S. June 21, 2010)

[43] Id. at 4630.

[44] As a threshold matter, the Court rejected the suggestion that it avoid the constitutional issues by construing the section to outlaw only that support provided with the intent to further an organization's terrorist aims, id. at 4629. The language of the section simply precluded any such construction, id.

[45] Id., quoting United States v. Williams, 553 U.S. 285, 304 (2008).

[46] Id. citing Hoffman Estates v. Flipside, Hoffman Estates, Inc., 455 U.S. 489, 495 (1982).

[47] Id. at 4631.

[48] Id.

[49] Id. at 4632-634.

[50] Id. at 4635-636.

[51] Id.

[52] Id. at 4636.

[53] Virginia v. Hicks, 539 U.S. 113, 118-19 (2003).

[54] Id. at 119-20.

[55] Humanitarian Law Project v. Mukasey, 552 F.3d 916, 931-32 (9th Cir. 2009); United States v. Hammoud, 381 F.3d 316, 329-30 (4th Cir. 2004); United States v. Taleb-Jedi, 566 F.Supp.2d 157, 184-85 (E.D.N.Y. 2008); United States v. Warsame, 537 F.Supp.2d 1005, 1016 (D. Minn. 2008); United States v. Assi, 414 F.Supp.2d 707, 716 (E.D.Mich. 2006).

[56] Scales v. United States, 367 U.S. 203, 224-25 (1961)("In our jurisprudence guilt is personal, and when the imposition of punishment on a status or on conduct can only be justified by reference to the relationship of that status or conduct to other concededly criminal activity (here advocacy of violent overthrow [of the U.S. government]), that relationship must be sufficiently substantial to satisfy the concept of personal guilty in order to withstand attack under the Due Process Clause of the Fifth Amendment. Membership, without more, in an organization engaged in illegal advocacy, it is now said, has not heretofore been recognized by this Court to be such a relationship").

[57] Id. at 228.

[58] United States v. Kassar, 582 F.Supp.2d 488, 498 (S.D.N.Y. 2008)("Defendants contend that because Section 2339B does not require a showing of specific intent to further the illegal activities of a foreign terrorist organization, it violates the due process clause of the Fifth Amendment").

[59] Id.; United States v. Warsame, 537 F.Supp.2d 1005, 1015 (D.Minn. 2008); United States v. Marzook, 383 F.Supp.2d 1056, 1067 (N.D.Ill. 2005)

[60] Humanitarian Law Project v. Mukasey, 552 F.3d 916, 926 (9th Cir. 2009); United States v. Taleb-Jedi, 566 F.Supp.2d 157, 179 (E.D.N.Y. 2008). Prior to the 2004 amendment which added the knowledge requirement to Section 2339B, one court, in order to avoid the section constitutionally suspect on due process grounds, construed it to require proof that the defendant knew "the recipient could or would utilize the support to further the illegal activities of the entity," United States v. Al-Arian, 329 F.Supp.2d 1294, 1298-1300 (M.D.Fla. 2004).

[61] United States v. Afshari, 426 F.3d 1150, 1155-159 (D.C.Cir. 2005); United States v. Hammoud, 381 F.3d 316, 331 (4th Cir. 2004); United States v. Warsame, 537 F.Supp.2d at 1023; United States v. Marzook, 383 F.Supp.2d 1056, 1071-72 (N.D.Ill. 2005); United States v. Al-Arian, 329 F.Supp.2d at 1343-346.

[62] 8 U.S.C. 1189(a)(8); United States v. Afshari, 426 F.3d 1150, 1155-159 (9th Cir. 2005); United States v. Hammoud, 381 F.3d 316, 331 (4th Cir. 2004).

[63] "Terrorism" is defined by cross reference to section 140(d)(2) of the Foreign Relations Authorization Act, Fiscal Years 1988 and 1989, P.L. 100-204, 101 Stat. 1349 (1987), 22 U.S.C. 2656(f)(d)(2).

[64] "Engage in terrorist activity" is defined by cross reference to section 212(a)(3)(B), 8 U.S.C. 1182(a)(3)(B), of the Immigration and Nationality Act, which defines the term in subparagraph (iv).

[65] "Terrorist activity" is defined by cross reference to section 212(a)(3)(B), 8 U.S.C. 1182(a)(3)(B), of the Immigration and Nationality Act, which defines the term in subparagraph (iii).

[66] A sentencing must begin by correctly calculating the applicable sentencing range under the Sentencing Guidelines; should it elect to impose a sentence outside the Guideline range, it must demonstrate why it is reasonable for it to do so, United States v. Stewart, 590 F.3d 93, 134 (2d Cir. 2009).

[67] U.S.S.G. Sentencing Table.

[68] U.S.S.G. §5G1.1(a)("Where the statutorily authorized maximum sentence is less than the minimum of the applicable guideline range, the statutorily required minimum sentence shall be the guideline sentence"); United States v. Warsame, 651 F.Supp.2d 978, 981 (D. Minn. 2009)("The parties agreed, however, to the application a twelve-level enhancement pursuant to U.S.S.G. §3A1.4.... In light of these determinations, Warsame's guidelines sentencing range was 292 to 365 months. U.S.S.G. Ch.5, Pt.A. Because his single count of conviction carries a statutory maximum of 180 months [15 years], however, see 18 U.S.C. 2339B(a)(1), 180 months became his advisory guideline sentence").

[69] United States v. Stewart, 590 F.3d at 137 ("The enhancement is not limited, however, to offenses that are themselves federal crimes of terrorism. By including the "intended to promote" language, the drafters of the guidelines unambiguously cast a broad net. The criminal conduct at issue need not itself meet the statutory definition of a federal crime of terrorism if a goal or purpose of the defendant's act was to bring or help bring into being a crime listed in 18 U.S.C. 2332b(g)(5)(B)"); United States v. Arnaout, 431 F.3d 994, 1000-1001 (7th Cir. 2005)("The district court found §3A1.4 did not apply because Arnaout was not convicted of a federal crime of terrorism as defined by 18 U.S.C. 2332b(g)(5)(B). We disagree.... We find that a defendant need not be convicted of a federal crime of terrorism as defined by 18 U.S.C. 2332b(g)(5)(B) for the district court to apply §3A1.4. Instead, the terrorism enhancement is applicable where a defendant is convicted of a federal crime of terrorism as defined by 18 U.S.C. 2332b(g)(5)(B) or where the district court finds that the purpose or intent of the defendant's substantive offense of conviction or relevant conduct was to promote a federal crime of terrorism as defined by 18 U.S.C. 2332b9g)(5)(B)").

[70] U.S.S.G. §3A1.4, cmt. 1 ("For purposes of this guideline, 'federal crime of terrorism' has the meaning given that term in 18 U.S.C. §2332b(g)(5)"); United States v. Stewart, 590 F.3d at 137; United States v. Chandia, 514 F.3d 365, 375-76 (4th Cir. 2008).

[71] 18 U.S.C. 1956(c)(7)(D), 1961(1)(G). Among other things, the federal racketeering statute prohibits conducting, through the patterned commission of more than one predicate offense, the affairs of an enterprise whose activities affect interstate or foreign commerce, 18 U.S.C. 1962, 1961. Among other things, the principal federal money laundering statute prohibits engaging in a financial transaction involving the proceeds of a predicate offense that is designed to launder the proceeds or to use them promote further predicate offenses, 18 U.S.C. 1956(a)(1), (c)(7).

[72] 18 U.S.C. 3286(a), 3282. Prosecution of a federal crime of terrorism may be brought at any time if the offenses involve the risk of serious bodily injury, 18 U.S.C. 3286(b).

[73] 18 U.S.C. 3142(f)((1)(A), (g)(1).

[74] 18 U.S.C. 3583(j), (b).

[75] Smith v. United States, 507 U.S. 197, 203 (1993); Small v. United States, 544 U.S. 385, 388-89 (2005); see generally Extraterritorial Application of American Criminal Law, CRS Rept. 94-166.

[76] 18 U.S.C. 351(i) (crimes committed against Members of Congress)("There is extraterritorial jurisdiction over the conduct prohibited by this section"); 18 U.S.C. 2381 (treason)("Whoever ... within the United States or elsewhere... ").

[77] 18 U.S.C. 175(a)(biological weapon offenses)("There is extraterritorial Federal jurisdiction over an offense under this section committed by or against a national of the United States"); 18 U.S.C. 1203(b) (hostage taking)("It is not an offense under this section if the conduct required for the offense occurred outside the United States unless – (A) the offender or the person seized or detained is a national of the United States; (B) the offender is found in the United States; or (C) the governmental organization sought to be compelled is the Government of the United States").

[78] United States v. Corey, 232 F.3d 1166, 1179 (9th Cir. 2000); United States v. Bin Laden, 92 F.Supp.2d 189, 195-96 (S.D.N.Y. 2000).

[79] P.L. 104-132, §303, 110 Stat. 1250 (1996), 18 U.S.C. 2339B(d)(2000 ed.).

[80] P.L. 108-458, §6603(d), 118 Stat. 3763 (2004).

[81] H.Rept. 108-724, Pt. V, at 172-73; Pt. VI, at 173-74 (2004).

[82] 18 U.S.C. 2332(a)("Any national of the United States injured in his or her person, property, or business by reason of an act of international terrorism, or his or her estate, survivors, or heirs, may sue therefor in any appropriate district court of the United States and shall recover threefold the damages he or she sustains and the cost of the suit, including attorneys fees").

[83] Boim v. Quranic Literacy Institute, 291 F.3d 1000, 1015 (7th Cir. 2002)("If the plaintiffs could show that [the defendants] violated either Section 2339A or 2339B, that conduct would certainly be sufficient to meet the definition of 'international terrorism' under sections 2333 and 2331.... Congress has made clear, though, through the criminal liability imposed in sections 2339A and 2339B, that even small donations made knowingly and intentionally in support of terrorism may meet the standard for civil liability in section 2333"); Goldberg v. UBS AG, 609 F.Supp.2d 92, 114 (E.D. N.Y. Mar. 5, 2010)("Following the Seventh Circuit's lead, numerous authorities have similarly interpreted section 2331(1), citing inter alia, Weiss v. National Westminster Bank PLC, 453 F.Supp.2d 609, 613 (E.D.N.Y. 2006); Almog v. Arab Bank, PLC, 471 F.Supp.2d 257, 268 (E.D.N.Y. 2007); see also Abecassis v. Wyatt, F.Supp.2d ___, ___ (S.D.Tex. Mar. 31, 2010); In re Chiquita Brands International, Inc., 690 F.Supp.2d 1296, 1309 (S.D.Fla. 2010); In re Terrorist Attacks, 392 F.Supp.2d 539, 564-65(S.D.N.Y. 2005).

[84] Boim v. Holy Land Foundation, 549 F.3d 685, 690 (7th Cir. 2008)(en banc)("The first panel opinion discussed approvingly an alternative and more promising ground for bringing donors to terrorist organizations within the grasp of section 2333. The ground involves a chain of explicit statutory incorporations by reference. The fist link in the chain is the statutory definition of 'international terrorism' as 'activities that ... involve violent acts or acts dangerous to human life that are a violation of the criminal laws of the United States,' that 'appear to be intended ... to intimidate or coerce a civil population' or 'affect the conduct of a government by ... assassination, and that 'transcend national boundaries in terms of the means by which they are accomplished' or persons they appear intended to intimidate or coerce.' 18 U.S.C. §2331(1). Section 2331...includes not only violent acts but also 'acts dangerous to human life that are violation of the criminal laws of the United States. Giving money to Hamas, like giving a loaded gun to a child (which also is not a violent act), is an 'act dangerous to human life.' And it violates ... 18 U.S.C. §2339A(a), which provides that 'whoever provides material support or resources ... knowing or intending that they are to be used in preparation for, or in carrying out, of a violation of [e.g.,][18 U.S.C. 2332],' shall be guilty of a federal crime. So we go to 18 U.S.C. §2332 and discover that it criminalizes the killing [of] ... any American citizen outside the United States. By this chain of incorporations by reference (section 2332(as) to section 2331(1) to Section 2339A to section 2332), we see that a donation to a terrorist group that targets Americans outside the United States may violate section 2333"); Goldberg v. UBS AG, 690 F.Supp.2d at 113 ("[S]ections 2339A and 2339B make clear Congress' intent that the intentional (or reckless) provision of material support to a terrorist organization fulfills each prong of section 2331(1)'s definition of 'international terrorism,' and therefore suffice to establish liability under section 2333(a)").

[85] More exactly, Section 2339A(a) declares, "Whoever provides material support or resources or conceals or disguises the nature, location, source, or ownership of material support or resources, knowing or intending that they are to be used in preparation for, or in carrying out, a violation of section 32, 37, 81, 175, 229, 351, 831, 842(m) or (n), 844(f) or (i), 930(c), 956, 1114, 1116, 1203, 1361, 1362, 1363, 1366, 1751, 1992, 2155, 2156, 2280, 2281, 2332, 2332a, 2332b, 2332f, or 2340A of this title, section 236 of the Atomic Energy Act of 1954 (42 U.S.C. 2284), section 46502 or 60123(b) of Title 49, or any offense listed in section 2332b(g)(5)(B) (except for sections 2339A and 2339B) or in preparation for, or in carrying out, the concealment of an escape from the commission of any such violation, or attempts or conspires to do such an act, shall be fined under this title, imprisoned not more than 15 years, or both, and, if the death of any person results, shall be imprisoned for any term of years or for life...." Each of the individually listed sections, such as 18 U.S.C. 32, is also among the listed federal crimes of terrorism. A full list of the federal crimes of terrorism, with identifying captions, is appended.

[86] United States v. Rivera-Relle, 333 F3d. 914, 921 n.11 (9th Cir. 2003).

[87] Braxton v. United States, 500 U.S. 344, 349 (1991); United States v. Bristol-Martir, 570 F.3d 29, 39 (1st Cir. 2009).

[88] United States v. Barlow, 568 F.3d 215, 219 (5th Cir. 2009); United States v. DeMarce, 564 F.3d 989, 998 (8th Cir. 2009).

[89] United States v. Mincoff, 574 F.3d 1186, 1195 (9th Cir. 2009); United States v. Morris, 549 F.3d 548, 550 (7th Cir. 2008).

[90] United States v. Rehak, 589 F.3d 965, 970-71 (8th Cir. 2009); United States v. Cot , 504 F.3d 682, (7th Cir. 2007); cf., United States v. Lakhani, 480 F.3d 171, 174-77 (3d Cir. 2007).

[91] 18 U.S.C. 2339B(a), 3571.

[92] United States v. Jimenez Recio, 537 U.S. 270, 274 (2003)("the essence of a conspiracy is an agreement to commit an unlawful act"); United States v. Lockett, 601 F.3d 837, (8th Cir. 2010)("In order to convict a defendant of conspiracy, the government must prove (1) the existence of an agreement to achieve an illegal purpose, (2) the defendant's knowledge of the agreement, and (3) the defendant's knowing participation in the agreement. The agreement does not have to be a formal, explicit agreement; a tacit understanding will suffice"); United States v. Boria, 592 F.3d 476, 481 (3d Cir. 2010); see generally CRS Report R41223, Federal Conspiracy Law: A Brief Overview, by Charles Doyle.

[93] United States v. Rehak, 589 F.3d 965, 971 (8th Cir. 2009); United States v. Schaffer, 586 F.3d 414, 422 (6th Cir. 2009).

[94] Pinkerton v. United States, 328 U.S. 640, 647 (1946); United States v, Nerkubi, 592 F.3d 22, 29 (1st Cir. 2010); United States v. Wardell, 591 F.3d 1279, 1291 (10th Cir. 2009).

[95] 18 U.S.C. 2339B(a), 3571.

[96] Iannelli v. United States, 420 U.S. 770, 777-78 (1975); United States v. Chandia, 514 F.3d 365, 372 (4th Cir. 2008)("We also disagree with Chandia's argument that Congress did not intend to authorize multiple

punishments for a conspiracy and a substantive violation under §2339B. Chandia's argument is based on the language of the statute, which prohibits the conspiracy and the actual provision of material support in the same section. See 18 U.S.C. §2339B(a)(1). ('Whoever knowingly provides material support ... or attempts or conspires to do so ...'). But, as the Supreme Court has held, the 'settled principle' that 'the commission of the substantive offense and a conspiracy to commit it are separate and distinct offenses' does not give way simply because the statute describing the substantive offense also specifically prohibits conspiracies. Callanan v. United States, 364 U.S. 587, 593 (1961)").

97 Nye & Nissen v. United States, 336 U.S. 613, 619 (1949); United States v. Turner, 583 F.3d 1062, 1067 (8th Cir. 2009).

98 United States v. Rodriguez, 553 F.3d 380, 391 (5th Cir. 2008).

99 United States v. Liera, 585 F.3d 1237, 1246 (9th Cir. 2009)("the aiding and abetting theory required the jury to find that: (1) someone committed the underlying offense; and (2) that Liera aided and abetted its commission"); United States v. Tagg, 572 F.3d 1320, 1324 (11th Cir. 2009)("To prove guilty under a theory of aiding and abetting, the Government must prove: (1) the substantive offense was committed by someone; (2) the defendant committed an act which contributed to and furthered the offense; and (3) the defendant intended to aid in its commission"); United States v. Gonzalez, 570 F.3d 16, 28-9 (1st Cir. 2009).

100 18 U.S.C. 2339A(b); 18 U.S.C. 2339B(g)(4).

101 18 U.S.C. 2339A(b)(2) and (b)(3) supply respectively the precise definitions of "training" and "expert advice or assistance" noted above.

102 18 U.S.C. 2339B(h)("No person may be prosecuted under this section in connection with the term 'personnel' unless that person has knowingly provided, attempted to provide, or conspired to provide a foreign terrorist organization with 1 or more individuals (who may be or include himself) to work under that terrorist organization's direction or control or to organize, manage, supervise, or otherwise direct the operation of that organization. Individuals who act entirely independently of the foreign terrorist organization to advance its goals or objectives shall not be considered to be working under the foreign terrorist organization's direction and control").

103 United States v. Abu-Jihaad, 600 F.Supp.2d 362, 400 (D. Conn. 2009).

104 United States v. Stewart, 590 F.3d 93, 117 (2d Cir. 2009); United States v. Amawi, 545 F.Supp.2d 681, 684 (N.D. Ohio 2008); United States v. Abdi, 498 F.Supp.2d 1048, 1058 (S.D. Ohio 2007).

105 P.L. 103-322, §120005(a), 108 Stat. 2022 (1994), 18 U.S.C. 2339A (1994 ed.).

106 United States v. Stewart, 590 F.3d at 114 ("The government charged that the defendants provided 'material support or resources' in the form of 'personnel'.... The government further asserted that Stewart and Yousry 'conceal[ed] and disguise[d] the nature, location, and source' of their material support by means of the defendants' covert conduct"); United States v. Hassoun, 476 F.3d 1181, 1183-184 (11th Cir. 2007)("Count Three charges the defendants with violating 18 U.S.C. §2339A(a) by providing material support and resources, and concealing and disguising the nature thereof, all with the knowledge and intent that the material support and resources be used in preparation for and carrying out a violation of §956").

107 18 U.S.C. 2332b(g)(5) consists of two parts. One, section 2332b(g)(5)(A), includes within the definition of federal crimes of terrorism those offenses that are "calculated to influence or affect the conduct of government by intimidation or coercion, or to retaliate against government conduct." The second, section 2332b(g)(5)(B) includes within the definition any offense proscribed by one of the statutes listed there. The definition of federal crimes of terrorism for purposes of Section 2339A by cross reference to 2332b(g)(5)(B) suggests that a violation of Section 2339A need not involve the terrorism-related circumstances of (5)(A) except when a prosecution involves a (5)(B) offense that has such a requirement.

108 United States v. Hassoun, 476 F.3d 1181, 1188 (11th Cir. 2007)(emphasis in the original)("[T]he Government need not prove all the elements of §956 [conspiracy to commit certain violent crimes overseas], the object offense, in order to satisfy the elements of the substantive § 2339A charge. By its elements, §2339A criminalizes material support given 'in preparation for' the object offense – clearly, the object offense need not even have been completed yet, let alone proven as an element of the material support offense. To meet its burden under §2339A, the Government must at least prove that the defendants provided material support or resources knowing that they be used in preparation for the § 956 conspiracy ").

109 United States v. Khan, 461 F.3d 477, 493 (4th Cir. 2006).

110 A sentencing must begin by correctly calculating the applicable sentencing range under the Sentencing Guidelines; should it elect to impose a sentence outside the Guideline range, it must demonstrate why it is reasonable for it to do so, United States v. Stewart, 590 F.3d 93, 134 (2d Cir. 2009).

111 U.S.S.G. Sentencing Table.

112 U.S.S.G. §5G1.1(a)("Where the statutorily authorized maximum sentence is less than the minimum of the applicable guideline range, the statutorily required minimum sentence shall be the guideline sentence"); United States v. Warsame, 651 F.Supp.2d 978, 981 (D. Minn. 2009)("The parties agreed, however, to the application a twelve-level enhancement pursuant to U.S.S.G. §3A1.4.... In light of these determinations, Warsame's guidelines sentencing range was 292 to 365 months. U.S.S.G. Ch.5, Pt.A. Because his single count of conviction carries a statutory maximum of 180 months [15 years], however, ... 180 months became his advisory guideline sentence").

113 United States v. Stewart, 590 F.3d at 137 ("The enhancement is not limited, however, to offenses that are themselves federal crimes of terrorism. By including the "intended to promote" language, the drafters of the guidelines unambiguously cast a broad net. The criminal conduct at issue need not itself meet the statutory definition of a federal crime of terrorism if a goal or purpose of the defendant's act was to bring or help bring into being a crime listed in 18 U.S.C. 2332b(g)(5)(B)"); United States v. Arnaout, 431 F.3d 994, 1000-1001 (7th Cir. 2005)("The district court found §3A1.4 did not apply because Arnaout was not convicted of a federal crime of terrorism as defined by 18 U.S.C. 2332b(g)(5)(B). We disagree.... We find that a defendant need not be convicted of a federal crime of terrorism as defined by 18 U.S.C. 2332b(g)(5)(B) for the district court to apply §3A1.4. Instead, the terrorism enhancement is applicable where a defendant is convicted of a federal crime of terrorism as defined by 18 U.S.C. 2332b(g)(5)(B) or where the district court finds that the purpose or intent of the defendant's substantive offense of conviction or relevant conduct was to promote a federal crime of terrorism as defined by 18 U.S.C. 2332b9g)(5)(B)").

114 U.S.S.G. §3A1.4, cmt. 1 ("For purposes of this guideline, 'federal crime of terrorism' has the meaning given that term in 18 U.S.C. §2332b(g)(5)"); United States v. Stewart, 590 F.3d at 137; United States v. Chandia, 514 F.3d 365, 375-76 (4th Cir. 2008).

115 18 U.S.C. 1956(c)(7)(D), 1961(1)(G). Among other things, the federal racketeering statute prohibits conducting, through the patterned commission of more than one predicate offense, the affairs of an enterprise whose activities affect interstate or foreign commerce, 18 U.S.C. 1962, 1961. Among other things, the principal federal money laundering statute prohibits engaging in a financial transaction involving the proceeds of a predicate offense when the transaction is designed to launder the proceeds or to use them to promote further predicate offenses, 18 U.S.C. 1956(a)(1), (c)(7).

116 18 U.S.C. 3286(a), 3282. Prosecution of a federal crime of terrorism may be brought at any time if the offense involves the risk of serious bodily injury, 18 U.S.C. 3286(b).

117 18 U.S.C. 3142(f)((1)(A), (g)(1).

118 18 U.S.C. 3583(j), (b).

119 United States v. Felix-Guiterrez, 940 F.2d 1200, 1205 (9th Cir. 1991)("We conclude that the crime of "accessory after the fact" gives rise to extraterritorial jurisdiction to the same extent as the underlying offense. That is, if the underlying substantive statute applies extraterritorially, the statute making it unlawful to assist another in avoiding apprehension, trial or punishment also applies extraterritorially when invoked in connection with an extraterritorial violation of the underlying statute.... We have inferred extraterritorial application of conspiracy statutes on the basis of a finding that the underlying substantive statutes reach extraterritorial offenses. We see no reason why a different rule should apply in accessory after the fact cases").

120 United States v. Bowman, 260 U.S. 94, 98 (1922)(Some offenses "are such that to limit their locus to the strictly territorial jurisdiction would be greatly to curtail the scope and usefulness of the statue and leave open a large immunity for frauds as easily committed by citizens on the high seas and in foreign countries as at home. In such cases, Congress has not thought it necessary to make specific provision in the law that the locus shall include the high seas and foreign countries, but allows it to be inferred from the nature of the offense").

121 United States v. Clark, 435 F.3d 1100, 1106 (9th Cir. 2006); United States v. Yousef, 327 F.3d 56, 90-1 (2d Cir. 2003); United States v. McAllister, 160 F.3d 1304, 1308 (11th Cir. 1998).

122 18 U.S.C. 2332(a)("Any national of the United States injured in his or her person, property, or business by reason of an act of international terrorism, or his or her estate, survivors, or heirs, may sue therefor in any appropriate district court of the United States and shall recover threefold the damages he or she sustains and the cost of the suit, including attorneys fees").

123 Boim v. Quranic Literacy Institute, 291 F.3d 1000, 1015 (7th Cir. 2002)("If the plaintiffs could show that [the defendants] violated either Section 2339A or 2339B, that conduct would certainly be sufficient to meet the definition of 'international terrorism' under sections 2333 and 2331.... Congress has made clear, though, through the criminal liability imposed in sections 2339A and 2339B, that even small donations made knowingly and intentionally in support of terrorism may meet the standard for civil liability in section 2333"); Goldberg v. UBS AG, 690 F.Supp.2d 92, 114 (E.D. N.Y. 2010)("Following the Seventh Circuit's lead,

numerous authorities have similarly interpreted section 2331(1), citing inter alia, Weiss v. National Westminster Bank PLC, 453 F.Supp.2d 609, 613 (E.D.N.Y. 2006); Almog v. Arab Bank, PLC, 471 F.Supp.2d 257, 268 (E.D.N.Y. 2007); see also Abecassis v. Wyatt, F.Supp.2d ___, ___ (S.D.Tex. Mar. 31, 2010); In re Chiquita Brands International, Inc., 690 F.Supp.2d 1296, 1309 (S.D.Fla. 2010); In re Terrorist Attacks, 392 F.Supp.2d 539, 564-65(S.D.N.Y. 2005).

[124] Boim v. Holy Land Foundation, 549 F.3d 685, 690 (7th Cir. 2008)(en banc)("The first panel opinion discussed approvingly an alternative and more promising ground for bringing donors to terrorist organizations within the grasp of section 2333. The ground involves a chain of explicit statutory incorporations by reference. The fist link in the chain is the statutory definition of 'international terrorism' as 'activities that ... involve violent acts or acts dangerous to human life that are a violation of the criminal laws of the United States,' that 'appear to be intended ... to intimidate or coerce a civil population' or 'affect the conduct of a government by ... assassination, and that 'transcend national boundaries in terms of the means by which they are accomplished' or persons they appear intended to intimidate or coerce.' 18 U.S.C. §2331(1). Section 2331...includes not only violent acts but also 'acts dangerous to human life that are a violation of the criminal laws of the United States. Giving money to Hamas, like giving a loaded gun to a child (which also is not a violent act), is an 'act dangerous to human life.' And it violates ... 18 U.S.C. §2339A(a), which provides that 'whoever provides material support or resources ... knowing or intending that they are to be used in preparation for, or in carrying out, of a violation of [e.g.,][18 U.S.C. 2332],' shall be guilty of a federal crime. So we go to 18 U.S.C. §2332 and discover that it criminalizes the killing [of] ... any American citizen outside the United States. By this chain of incorporations by reference (section 2332(as) to section 2331(1) to Section 2339A to section 2332), we see that a donation to a terrorist group that targets Americans outside the United States may violate section 2333"); Goldberg v. UBS AG, 690 F.Supp.2d at 113 (E.D.N.Y. 2010)("[S]ections 2339A and 2339B make clear Congress' intent that the intentional (or reckless) provision of material support to a terrorist organization fulfills each prong of section 2331(1)'s definition of 'international terrorism,' and therefore suffice to establish liability under section 2333(a)").

[125] United States v. Rodriguez-Moreno, 526 U.S. 275, 279 (1999); United States v. Cabrales, 524 U.S. 1, 6-7 (1998).

In: Terrorists, Enemy Combatant Detainees …
Editors: Jian Sun and Miguel Masipag

ISBN: 978-1-61470-391-4

Chapter 4

TERRORIST ATTACKS ON COMMERCIAL AIRLINES: FEDERAL CRIMINAL PROHIBITIONS[*]

Charles Doyle

SUMMARY

Federal authorities can and have prosecuted terrorist attacks on commercial airlines under a wide variety of federal statutes. Some of those statutes outlaw crimes committed aboard a commercial airliner; some, crimes committed against the aircraft itself; others, crimes involving the use of firearms or explosives; still others, crimes committed for terrorist purposes. Within each category, the law reaches co-conspirators and other accomplices. Moreover, although most apply when committed within the United States, many apply to terrorist attacks overseas, particularly but necessarily, when the victims are Americans or U.S. airlines.

INTRODUCTION

A handful of terrorists have been prosecuted in federal court for attacks on commercial airlines or their passengers. Most often they have been charged with several crimes. Prosecution for some crimes depends upon where they were committed; some on the nationality of the airline, of the victim, or of the offender; some on whether the crimes has been planned, attempted, or completed; some on the nature of the attack; and some without regard to any of these factors. For instance, Umar Farouk Abdulmutallab, the alleged so-called Christmas bomber, has been charged with attempted use of a weapon of mass destruction; attempted murder within the special aircraft jurisdiction of the United States; attempt to destroy an aircraft within such jurisdiction; placing an endangering destructive device upon an aircraft there; and possession of a destructive device in furtherance of a crime of violence.[1] The offenses with which terrorists may be charged fall within one or more of

[*] This is an edited, reformatted and augmented version of a Congressional Research Service publication, CRS Report for Congress R41035, from www.crs.gov, dated January 22, 2010.

several categories: crimes committed aboard an aircraft; crimes committed against an aircraft; crimes committed using dangerous instrumentalities, such as a bomb; crimes of terrorism; crimes committed by or against certain classes of individuals; and crimes for which accomplices may be liable. This is a brief description of those offenses, and an outline of the penalties to which they may be subject and of the jurisdictional circumstances under which offenses they may be federally prosecuted regardless of whether they are committed within the United States or overseas. Perhaps because of the range of existing criminal proscriptions, there have been no legislative proposals to enlarge upon them as of yet.[2]

Crimes Aboard an Aircraft

Chapter 465 of title 49 of the United States Code prohibits, among other offenses, murder, manslaughter, attempted murder or manslaughter, and assault, when committed within the special aircraft jurisdiction of the United States.[3] It defines the special aircraft jurisdiction of the United States to include any aircraft in flight (from when the doors are closed after boarding until when they are opened after landing) in the United States.[4] It includes any aircraft of an America carrier, or any U.S. military craft, in flight anywhere else in the world.[5] It also includes any aircraft of a foreign carrier in flight and destined for, or departing from, the United States, as well as any foreign aircraft which in a case of air piracy lands in the United States with the hijacker aboard.[6]

In addition to outlawing murder, manslaughter, attempted murder or manslaughter, assault and a few other common law crimes committed within the special aircraft jurisdiction of the United States,[7] chapter 465 outlaws:

- aircraft piracy within the special aircraft jurisdiction of the U.S. (violently taking over an aircraft in flight or the attempt or conspiracy to do so);[8]
- aircraft piracy outside the special aircraft jurisdiction of the U.S. (violently taking over an aircraft in flight or the attempt or conspiracy to do so where an American was aboard, the offender is an American, or where the offender is later found in the U.S.);[9]
- interfering with (assaulting) security screening personnel in the United States;[10]
- interfering with (assaulting, intimidating, or attempting or conspiring to assault or intimidate) a flight crew member or attendant in the special aircraft jurisdiction of the United States;[11]
- placing, causing to be placed, or possessing a loaded firearm, explosive, or incendiary device aboard an aircraft in intrastate, interstate, or foreign air transportation (or attempting to do so);[12] and
- threatening to commit, or provide false information concerning the commission of, one of these offenses. [13]

Terrorists who have attacked commercial aircraft have most often been prosecuted under chapter 465 or its air piracy predecessor 49 U.S.C. App. 1472 (1988 ed.). This is a because of the number of individual offenses in the chapter and because the air piracy statute was one of the first federal laws that addressed directly terrorism aboard commercial airlines.

The early air piracy statute was used to convict Omar Mohammed Ali Rezaq. Rezaq was one of several terrorists who hijacked an Air Egypt flight after it took off from Athens and who subsequently murdered or attempted to murder several passengers including three Americans.[14] The statute was also used to prosecute Fawaz Yunis who participated in the seizure of a Jordanian airliner in flight from Beirut to Cyprus.[15]

Over the years, Congress added other on board crimes to the section before it broke them out into the separate sections of chapter 465. For instance, the expanded statute was used to convict Mohammed Rashed for placing a bomb on a Pan Am flight from Tokyo to Honolulu that killed a Japanese passenger and injured several others.[16]

Since the components of the original air piracy statute have been divided into the various sections of chapter 465, they have been used to prosecute Richard Reid, the shoe bomber;[17] Umar Farouk Abdulmutallab, the alleged Christmas bomber;[18] Zacarias Moussaoui, the co-conspirator of the 9/11 terrorists;[19] and Ahmed Omar Abu Ali, convicted in connection with the activities of an al Qeada cell in Saudi Arabia.[20]

CRIMES AGAINST AN AIRCRAFT

Although there is some overlap with chapter 465, crimes committed against aircraft are the province of chapter 2 of title 18 of the United States Code, principally 18 U.S.C. 32.[21] Among other things, section 32 outlaws damaging or destroying an aircraft in the special aircraft jurisdiction of the United States by fire or destructive device (or attempting or conspiring to do so).[22] It provides similar protection for foreign flagged aircraft, when the offender is an American, when an American is aboard the aircraft which is the subject of the attack, or when the offender later comes or is brought to the United States.[23]

The inventory of section 32 crimes includes:

- damaging or destroying an aircraft in the special aircraft jurisdiction of the United States or one used in interstate, overseas, or foreign air commerce;[24]
- endangering the safety of such aircraft by placing a destructive device or substance on or near it (causing such advice or substance to be so placed);[25]
- endangering the safety of such aircraft by damaging, destroying, or violently interfering with the operation of air navigation facilities;[26]
- intending to damage, destroy, or disable such aircraft by damaging or destroying nearby or closely related equipment, material or facilities;[27]
- interfering with those operating such aircraft or related navigation facilities with the intent to injury or reckless disregard of the risk of injuring such individuals;[28]
- assaulting or incapacitating another aboard such aircraft when likely to endanger its safety;[29]
- endangering the safety of such aircraft in flight by communicating a hoax;[30]
- attempting or conspiring to commit any such offense;[31]

and with respect to foreign flagged aircraft (those registered outside the U.S.)

- assaulting another aboard such aircraft when likely to endanger its safety;[32]
- incapacitating, destroying, or inflicting endangering damage to such aircraft;[33]
- placing aboard such aircraft (or causing to be placed) a device or substance likely to incapacitate it, destroy it, or inflict endangering damage upon it;[34]
- attempting or conspiring to commit any such offense.[35]

Since terrorist attacks upon airline passengers and crew will often involve damage to the plane as well, it is not surprising that most prosecutions have involve charges under both section 32 and chapter 465. One exception is the case of Ramzi Ahmed Yousef. Yousef, who had participated in the first attack on the World Trade Center, then proceeded to devise a scheme to place explosive devices on a dozen American airliners operating in Asia. As a test, he planted a bomb on a Philippine Airlines flight from Manila to Japan. The bomb exploded in flight killing a Japanese passenger and injuring several others. The plot was discovered, however, before he could plant explosives on the planes he had targeted.[36] Yousef was convicted for complicity in the first World Trade Center bombing and for the airline offenses. He was sentenced to 240 years imprisonment for the World Trade Center bombing and life imprisonment for the airline bombing offenses.[37]

In addition to the proscriptions in chapter 465 and section 32, prosecutors originally charged Reid under 18 U.S.C. 1993 (2000 ed. Supp. I), which prohibited terrorist attacks on mass transit systems. The court dismissed, however, the charge on the grounds that the section's proscriptions did not protect air travel.[38] Congress amended the proscription so that as section 1992 it now protects commercial air travel in terms reminiscent of section 32. It condemns:

- wrecking or disabling a mass transportation vehicle (which includes any vehicle "used . . . as a means of transportation . . . through the air");[39]
- endangering personal safety on a mass transportation vehicle by placing a destructive device or dangerous substance on or near it;[40]
- endangering personal safety on a mass transportation vehicle by placing a destructive device or dangerous substance on or near equipment, material, or facilities relating to its operation; [41]
- damaging or contaminating equipment, material, or facilities relating to the operation of a mass transportation vehicle;[42]
- interfering with those operating or controlling a mass transportation vehicle with the intent to injury or reckless disregard of the risk of personal injury;[43]
- use of a dangerous weapon with the intent to cause serious injury to a person on a facility used to operate or facilitate the operation of a mass transportation vehicle;[44]
- collecting information to facilitate the commission of one of these offenses;[45]
- communication false information relating to a purported commission of an offense under the section;[46] and
- attempting or conspiring to commit one of these offenses.[47]

CRIMES INVOLVING DESTRUCTIVE DEVICES

Federal prohibitions relating to the use of destructive devices are implicated whenever terrorists use (or conspire to use or attempt to use) explosives in their attacks on commercial air carriers. The shoe bomber, the alleged Christmas bomber, Yousef, Moussaoui, and Rashed have each been prosecuted for violation of the bans on the criminal use of explosives found 18 U.S.C. 844, 924 and 2332a.[48]

Section 2332a outlaws, among other things, the use (or attempts, conspiracies, or threats to use) a weapon of mass destruction by or against an American overseas or against property in this country used in interstate or foreign commerce.[49] It defines destructive devices by cross reference to include explosive and incendiary devices.[50] Section 844 outlaws, among other things, damage or destruction of property used in, or whose use affects, interstate or foreign commerce, or conspiracy to do so.[51] Section 924 outlaws, among other things, using or carrying an explosive or incendiary device during and in relation to a federal crime of violence.[52]

Finally, 18 U.S.C. 2332f outlaws, among other things, placing or detonating explosives on foreign flagged airlines in the United States or on U.S. flagged airlines overseas (or attempting or conspiring to do so).

OTHER TERRORIST CRIMES

There is no single federal terrorist offense, but Congress has created a number of federal offenses with terrorists in mind. Some have already been mentioned. Most of the crimes associated with violence committed aboard and against commercial airlines and found in section 32, section 1992, and chapter 465 certainly fit this description. So do the weapons of mass destruction offenses of section 2332a and the bombing of public facilities offenses of section 2332f.

Other statutes focus on the offenses which a terrorist might commit against an American. For instance, both Reid and Yousef were convicted for violating 18 U.S.C. 2332 which outlaws killing or attempting to kill an American overseas for terrorist purposes.[53] Moussaoui was convicted under 18 U.S.C. 2332b for conspiracy to commit murder in the United States having travelled from overseas, and Yunis under 18 U.S.C. 1203 for taking an American hostage overseas.[54]

CRIMES AGAINST PROTECTED INDIVIDUALS

A number of federal statutes protect various groups of individuals, some without regard to the means used to harm them, the location of the offense, or the character of the offender. Beyond section 2332 which protects Americans from overseas terrorist attacks and other sections already mentioned, federal law outlaws killing or assaulting federal employees and officers and members of the U.S. armed forces during or because of the performance of their duties,[55] anywhere in the world.[56] Under separate legislation, it protects the President and high executive branch officials,[57] Members of Congress and the Supreme Court, and foreign dignitaries.[58] Each would apply to killings and assaults by terrorists aboard an aircraft no matter the registry of the aircraft or where it was located when the crime occurred.[59] Each proscription applies to attempts and conspiracies as well.[60]

ACCOMPLICE LIABILITY

The accomplices who facilitate a terrorist attack on a commercial airline or help the terrorist avoid apprehension may be subject to federal criminal liability as well. Regardless of the offense, anyone who aids or abets in the commission of a federal crime is punishable as if he had committed the act himself.[61] To aid and abet in the commission of a federal crime, an accused must have contributed, and intended to contribute, to the success of the criminal endeavor of another.[62]

Aiding and abetting occurs prior to or during the commission of an offense. Criminal liability as an accessory after the fact flows from conduct committed after another has committed an offense. Under federal law, an accessory after the fact is one who knowing a federal offense has been committed "receives, relieves, comforts or assists the offender in order to hinder or prevent his apprehension, trial or punishment," 18 U.S.C. 3. The elements of the offense are "(1) commission of a specified offense by some person, (2) the defendant's knowledge of the crime's commission and the principal's participation in it, and (3) the defendant's assistance to the principal with the specific purpose or plan to hinder or prevent the principal's apprehension, trial, or punishment."[63]

The aiding and abetting statute also treats as a principal one who commands the commission of a completed federal offense;[64] 18 U.S.C. 373 imposes criminal liability upon one who recruits another to commit a federal crime of violence even if the crime is in fact never committed. Conviction requires that the prosecution establish that the defendant "(1) had the intent for another to commit a crime of violence and (2) solicited, commanded, induced or otherwise endeavored to persuade such other person to commit the crime of violence under circumstances that strongly corroborate evidence of that intent."[65]

There is also a general conspiracy statute, 18 U.S.C. 371. It outlaws conspiracies to commit any other substantive federal criminal offense. Because offenses under section 371 are only punishable by imprisonment for not more than five years, Congress has often made conspiracy to commit more serious offenses, including several of the offenses already discussed, punishable to the same extent as the underlying substantive offense. Thus, for example, conspiracy to violate any of the proscriptions of sections 32(a) or 32(b) is punished just as severely as the underlying substantive offense.[66]

In addition to these generally applicable provisions, Congress has enacted others more specifically directed at those complicit in any terrorist attack which include:

- *18 U.S.C. 956* which outlaws conspiracy within the U.S. to kill, maim, or destroy property overseas;
- *18 U.S.C. 2339A* which outlaws material support for a violation of: 18 U.S.C. 844(i)(bombing that affects interstate or foreign commerce), 1203 (hostage taking), 1992 (terrorist attacks on airlines), 2332 (killing Americans overseas), 2332a (use of weapons of mass destruction), 2332b(multi-national crimes of terrorism), 2332f

(bombing certain airlines), 49 U.S.C. 46502 (air piracy), or of federal crime of terrorism, e.g., 18 U.S.C. 32 (violence against aircraft), 49 U.S.C. 46504 (assaulting a flight crew member with a dangerous weapon), 46505(b)(3), (c)(bombs on aircraft), 46506 (murder, manslaughter or attempted murder or manslaughter within the special aircraft jurisdiction);

- *18 U.S.C. 2339* which outlaws harboring a terrorist who has or is about to violate, among others, 18 U.S.C. 32 (violence against aircraft), 2332a (use of weapons of mass destruction), 2332b (multi-national crimes of terrorism), or 49 U.S.C. 46502 (air piracy); and
- *18 U.S.C. 2284* which outlaws providing maritime transportation for a terrorist who has or is about to violate a federal crime of terrorism, e.g., 18 U.S.C. 32 (violence against aircraft), 844(i) (bombing that affects interstate or foreign commerce), 1992 (terrorist attacks on airlines), 2332 (killing Americans overseas), 2332a (use of weapons of mass destruction), 2332b (multi-national crimes of terrorism), 2332f (bombing certain airlines), 49 U.S.C. 46502 (air piracy), or of federal crime of terrorism, e.g., 49 U.S.C. 46504 (assaulting a flight crew member with a dangerous weapon), 46505(b)(3), (c) (bombs on aircraft), 46506 (murder, manslaughter or attempted murder or manslaughter within the special aircraft jurisdiction).

Selected Procedural Aspects

Special procedures often apply to those accused or convicted of terrorists attacks on commercial airlines. Other than murder, for which there is no statute of limitations,[67] most federal crimes must be prosecuted within five years of their commission.[68] The statute of limitations for federal crimes of terrorism, however, is eight years, unless the offense involves a risk of serious physical injury in which case there is no statute of limitations.[69] Moreover, any applicable statute of limitations is tolled while the offender is a fugitive.[70]

When a suspect is arrested for violation of a federal crime of terrorism, he is subject to the preventive detention provisions of the federal bail laws.[71] Upon conviction, federal crimes of terrorism are subject to an escalated sentencing guideline,[72] and to the possibility of a life-time period of supervised release rather than the five year maximum that applies to convictions for most crimes.[73]

Pertinent Penalties and Territorial Jurisdictional Factors

Although federal law punishes severely most of crimes discussed above, the maximum terms of imprisonment vary considerably among them. Even greater diversity marks the jurisdictional circumstances under which federal law permits the prosecution of such offenses especially when committed overseas.[74] A rough outline of the pertinent terms of imprisonment and jurisdictional factors follows:

Crimes Aboard Aircraft

49 U.S.C. 46502 (air piracy)(imprisonment for not less than 20 years; if death results, death or life imprisonment)

Jurisdictional factors:

in flight within the special aircraft jurisdiction of the United States

- U.S. aircraft;
- other aircraft within the U.S.; or
- other aircraft outside the U.S.
  - - the last point of departure or next point of arrival is U.S. or
  - - the pirated aircraft lands in the U.S. with the pirate aboard

in flight outside the special aircraft jurisdiction of the United States

- a U.S. national is aboard;
- the offender is U.S. national; or
- the offender is later found in the U.S.

49 U.S.C. 46503 (interfering with securing screening personnel in the U.S.) (imprisonment for not more than 10 years; imprisonment for any term of years or for life, if a dangerous weapon is used)

49 U.S.C. 46504 (assaulting or intimidating a flight crew member within the special aircraft jurisdiction of the United States) (imprisonment for not more than 20 years; imprisonment for any term of years or for life, if a dangerous weapon is used)

Jurisdictional factors:

in flight within the special aircraft jurisdiction of the United States

- U.S. aircraft;
- other aircraft within the U.S.; or
- other aircraft outside the U.S.
  - - the last point of departure or next point of arrival is U.S. or
  - - the pirated aircraft lands in the U.S. with the pirate aboard

49 U.S.C. 46505 (placing (or causing to be placed) an explosive or incendiary device, or an accessible dangerous weapon or loaded firearm, aboard an aircraft in U.S. air transportation (or attempted or conspiring to do so) (imprisonment for not more than 10 years; not more than 20 years, if done without regard for, or in reckless disregard for, human safety; imprisonment for any terms of years or for life, if death results))

Jurisdictional factors

- intrastate air transportation;
- common carrier interstate air transportation; or
- common carrier air transportation between the U.S. and elsewhere

49 U.S.C.46506 (murder, manslaughter, attempted murder or manslaughter, assault, or maiming within the special aircraft jurisdiction of the United States)

- murder: death or life imprisonment (1st degree); imprisonment for any term of years or for life (2d degree);
- manslaughter: imprisonment for not more than 15 years (voluntary); imprisonment for not more than 8 years (involuntary);
- attempted murder: imprisonment for not more than 20 years; attempted manslaughter, imprisonment for not more than 7 years;

- assault: imprisonment for not more than 20 years, if committed with the intent to murder; imprisonment for not more than 10 years, if committed with the intent to commit any other felony, or if assault with a dangerous weapon, or if resulting in serious bodily injury; imprisonment for not more than 5 years, if resulting in substantial bodily injury; imprisonment for not more than 6 months, if simple assault; or imprisonment for not more than 1 year, if the victim is under 16 years of age;
- maiming: imprisonment for not more than 20 years

Jurisdictional factors:
in flight within the special aircraft jurisdiction of the United States

- U.S. aircraft;
- other aircraft within the U.S.; or
- other aircraft outside the U.S.
  - - the last point of departure or next point of arrival is U.S.; or
  - - the pirated aircraft lands in the U.S. with the pirate aboard

Crimes Against Aircraft

18 U.S.C. 32 (crimes against aircraft punishable by imprisonment for not more than 20 years; 18 U.S.C. 34: punishable by death or imprisonment for life, if death results)
Offenses within the special aircraft jurisdiction of the U.S.

- damaging or destroy aircraft or endangering its safety by placing (or causing the placement of) a destructive device or substance on or near an aircraft;
- endangering safety of an aircraft by damaging, destroying, or violently interfering with the operation of air navigation facilities;
- intending to damage, destroy or disable aircraft by damaging or destroying nearby or closely related equipment, material, or facilities;
- interfering with those operating aircraft or related navigation facilities with the intent to injury or recklessly disregarding the risk of injury such individuals
- assaulting or incapacitating another aboard an aircraft when likely to endanger its safety;
- attempting or conspiring to commit any of these offenses

Jurisdictional factors:
In flight within the special aircraft jurisdiction of the United States

- U.S. aircraft;
- other aircraft within the U.S.; or
- other aircraft outside the U.S.
  - - the last point of departure or next point of arrival is U.S. or
  - - the pirated aircraft lands in the U.S. with the pirate aboard

Offenses relating to aircraft not registered in the U.S.

- assaulting another aboard an aircraft when likely to endanger its safety;
- incapacitating, destroying or inflicting endangering damage to an aircraft;
- placing aboard aircraft (or causing placement of) a device or substance likely to incapacitate it, destroy it, or inflict endangering damage upon it;
- attempting or conspiring to commit such an offense

Jurisdictional factors:

- the aircraft is in the special aircraft jurisdiction of the United States; - the victim or offender is a United States national; or
- the offender is found in the United States

18 U.S.C. 1992 (terrorist attack on mass transit; punishable by imprisonment for not more than 20 years; by death or imprisonment for any term of years or for life if death results)
- wrecking or disabling a mass transportation vehicle (which includes any vehicle "used . . . as a means of transportation . . . through the air;"
- endangering personal safety on a mass transportation vehicle by placing a destructive device or dangerous device or substance on or near it;
- endangering personal safety on a mass transportation vehicle by placing a destructive device or dangerous or substance on or near equipment, material, or facilities relating to its operation;
- damaging or contaminating equipment, material, or facilities relating to the operation of a mass transportation vehicle;
- interfering with those operating or controlling a mass transportation vehicle with the intent to injury or reckless disregard of the risk of personal injury;
- use of a dangerous weapon with intent to cause serious injury to a person on a facility used to operate or to facilitate the operation of a mass transportation vehicle;
- collecting information to facilitate the commission of one of these offenses' and - attempting or conspiring to commit one of these offenses

Jurisdictional factors

offense is committed against the vehicle of a provider of transportation services in the interstate or foreign commerce of the United States

Crimes Involving Destructive Devices

18 U.S.C. 2332a (use of weapons of mass destruction)(or attempts or conspiracy to do so) (imprisonment for any term of years or life; by death or imprisonment for any term or years or for life, if death results)

Jurisdictional factors:
- within the U.S: property or conduct affects interstate or foreign commerce or involves property owned or leased by a foreign government
- outside the U.S.: offender or victim is an American

18 U.S.C. 2332f (bombing of public transportation a system)(or attempts or conspiracy to do so) (imprisonment for any term of years or life; by death or imprisonment for any term or years or for life, if death results)

Jurisdictional factors:

within the U.S.:
- committed against a foreign government;
- committed to compel U.S. or foreign government action; - committed aboard an aircraft of foreign registry;
- the victim or offender is a foreign national; or - the offender is found outside the U.S.

(but not if, the victim and offender are U.S. nationals and the offender is found in the U.S.) outside the U.S.:

- the victim or offender is an American;
- committed aboard an aircraft of U.S. registry; - the offender is found in the U.S.; or
- committed to compel U.S. government action

18 U.S.C. 844(i) (bombing property)(or attempting or conspiring to do so)(imprisonment for not less than 5 nor more than 20 years; if personal injury results, not less than 7 nor more than 40 years; if death results, death or imprisonment for any term of years or for life)

Jurisdictional factor:

property used in or used in an activity which affects U.S. interstate or foreign commerce attempt and conspiracy are included

18 U.S.C 924(c) (possession of a firearm or other destructive device during and in furtherance of a federal crime of violence)

- imprisonment for not less than 5 years;
- if the firearm or destructive device is brandished, imprisonment for not less than 7 years;
- if the firearm is discharged (and perhaps if the destructive device detonated or ignited), imprisonment for not less than 10 years;
- if the offender has a prior conviction, imprisonment for not less than 25 years;
- if the firearm has a silencer or is a machine gun or a destructive device, imprisonment for less than 30 years;
- if the offender has a prior conviction and the firearm has a silencer or is a machine gun or a destructive device, imprisonment for life)

Jurisdictional factor: same as the underlying offense

Other Terrorist Offenses

18 U.S.C. 2332 (killing, attempting to kill, conspiring to kill, or assaulting an American overseas) - murder: death or imprisonment for any term of years or for life;

- manslaughter: imprisonment for not more than 10 years (voluntary); imprisonment for not more than 3 years (involuntary);
- attempted murder: imprisonment for not more than 20 years;
- conspiracy to murder: imprisonment for any term of years or for life;
- assault with intent to, or with resulting in, serious bodily injury: imprisonment for not more than 10 years;

Jurisdictional factor: the victim is an American overseas (but the Attorney General must certify the offense was committed for terrorist purposes)

18 U.S.C. 2332b (acts of transnational terrorism committed within the U.S.) (killing, maiming, serious assaults, or damaging or destroy property or attempting to do so at the risk of serious bodily injury to others)

- killing: death or imprisonment for any term of years or for life;
- maiming: imprisonment for not more than 35 years;
- assault with a dangerous weapon or resulting in serious bodily injury: imprisonment for not more than 30 years;
- property damage or destruction: imprisonment for not more than 25 years;

- attempt or conspiracy to commit such an offense: imprisonment for not more than the term authorized for the underlying offense;

Jurisdictional factor:

- the offense affects interstate or foreign commerce of the U.S.;
- the victim of a federal official, employee or member of the U.S. armed forces; or
- the offense occurs aboard an aircraft of American registry outside the jurisdiction of any other nation victim is an American overseas (but the Attorney General must certify the offense was committed for terrorist purposes)

18 U.S.C. 1203 (hostage taking)(or attempting or conspiring to do so)(imprisonment for any term of years or for life; if death results, death or life imprisonment)

Jurisdictional factors

within the U.S.

- the offender or one of victims is a foreign national; - the offender is found outside the U.S. or
- the offense is committed to compel U.S. government action

outside the U.S.:

- the offender or the victim is an American;
- the offender is later found in the U.S.; or
- the offense is committed to compel U.S. government action'

Crimes Against Protected Individuals

18 U.S.C. 1751 (killing, attempting to kill, conspiring to kill, or assaulting the President or other senior executive branch official)

- murder: death or life imprisonment (1st degree); imprisonment for any term of years or for life (2d degree);
- manslaughter: imprisonment for not more than 15 years (voluntary); imprisonment for not more than 8 years (involuntary);
- attempt to kill: imprisonment for any term of years or for life;
- conspiracy to kill: imprisonment for any term of year or for life; if death results, by death or imprisonment for any term of years or for life;
- assault: imprisonment for not more than 10 years, if committed against the President or Vice President, or with dangerous weapon, or resulting in bodily injury; imprisonment for not more than 1 year in all other cases

Jurisdictional factor: the victim is a federal official or employee

18 U.S.C. 351 (killing, attempting to kill, conspiring to kill, or assaulting a Member of Congress, a Justice of the Supreme Court or senior executive branch official)

- murder: death or life imprisonment (1st degree); imprisonment for any term of years or for life (2d degree);
- manslaughter: imprisonment for not more than 15 years (voluntary); imprisonment for not more than 8 years (involuntary);
- attempt to kill: imprisonment for any term of years or for life;
- conspiracy to kill: imprisonment for any term of year or for life; if death results, by death or imprisonment for any term of years or for life;

- assault: imprisonment for not more than 10 years, if committed with dangerous weapon or resulting in bodily injury; imprisonment for not more than 1 year in all other cases

Jurisdictional factor: the victim is a federal official or employee

18 U.S.C. 1116 (killing foreign dignitaries or members of their families)

- murder: death or life imprisonment (1st degree); imprisonment for any term of years or for life (2d degree);
- manslaughter: imprisonment for not more than 15 years (voluntary); imprisonment for not more than 8 years (involuntary);
- attempt to kill: imprisonment for not more than 20 years (murder) or not more than 7 years (manslaughter);
- conspiracy to murder: imprisonment for any term of year or for life (18 U.S.C. 1117)

Jurisdictional factor:

- in the U.S. or
- outside the U.S.
  - - the victim is U.S. officer or employee;
  - - the offender is an American; or
  - - the offender is later found in the U.S.

18 U.S.C. 112 (assault on foreign dignitaries)

- using a deadly or dangerous weapon or inflicting bodily injury: imprisonment for not more than 10 years;
- in other cases: imprisonment for not more than 3 years

Jurisdictional factor:

- in the U.S. or
- outside the U.S.
  - - the victim U.S. officer or employee;
  - - the offender is an American; or
  - - the offender is later found in the U.S.

Accomplice Liability

18 U.S.C. 2 (aiding, abetting, commanding the commission of a federal offense)(punishment & jurisdiction: same as the underlying offense)[75]

18 U.S.C. 3 (accessory after the fact to the commission of a federal offense)(imprisonment for not more than one half the maximum of the underlying offense; imprisonment for not more than 15 years, if the underlying offense is punishable by death or by life imprisonment)

Jurisdictional factor: same as the underlying offense[76]

18 U.S.C. 371 (conspiracy to violate a federal criminal statute)(imprisonment for not more than 5 years)

Jurisdictional factors: same as the underlying offense[77]

18 U.S.C. 373 (solicitation to commit a federal crime of violence) (imprisonment for not more than one half the maximum of the underlying offense; imprisonment for not more than 20 years, if the underlying offense is punishable by death or by life imprisonment)

Jurisdictional factors: same as the underlying offense[78]

18 U.S.C. 956 (conspiracy within the U.S. to kill, maim, or damage property overseas) - killing: imprisonment for any term of years or for life;

- maiming: imprisonment for not more than 35 years;
- property damage: imprisonment for not more than 25 years

Jurisdictional factor: scheme is hatched within the U.S. and underlying offenses are to be committed overseas

18 U.S.C. 2284 (maritime transportation of a terrorist who has or is about to violate a federal law of terrorism)(imprisonment for any term of years or for life)

Jurisdictional factors:

- in the U.S. or
- aboard a vessel of U.S. registry

18 U.S.C. 2339 (harboring a terrorist who has or is about to commit various federal terrorist offenses) (imprisonment for not more than 10 years)

Jurisdictional factors: same as the underlying offense[79]

18 U.S.C. 2339A (providing material support for the commission of various federal terrorist offenses) (imprisonment for not more than 15 years; imprisonment for any term of years or for life, if death results)

Jurisdictional factors: same as the underlying offense[80]

End Notes

1 INDICTMENT, *United States v. Abdulmutallab*, 2:10-cr-2005 (E.D. Mich. (S.D) Jan. 6, 2010).

2 For a general discussion of proposals concerning aviation security see CRS Report RL33512, *Transportation Security: Issues for the 111th Congress*, by David Randall Peterman, Bart Elias, and John Frittelli and CRS Report RL33645, *Terrorist Watchlist Checks and Air Passenger Prescreening*, by William J. Krouse and Bart Elias.

3 49 U.S.C. ch. 465; 49 U.S.C. 46501, 46506.

4 49 U.S.C. 46501.

5 *Id.*

6 *Id.*

7 49 U.S.C. 46506 prohibits by cross reference crimes described in 18 U.S.C. 113 (assault), 114 (maiming), 661 (theft), (continued...)

(...continued)

662 (receipt of stolen property), 1111 (murder), 1112 (manslaughter), 1113 (attempted murder or manslaughter), 2111 (robbery), and ch. 109A (sexual abuse) – when committed in the special aircraft jurisdiction of the United States.

8 49 U.S.C. 46502(a).

9 49 U.S.C. 4605(2)(b).

10 49 U.S.C. 46503.

11 49 U.S.C. 46504.

12 49 U.S.C. 46505.

13 49 U.S.C. 46507.

14 *United States v. Rezaq*, 134 F.3d 1121, 1126 (D.C.Cir. 1998). Rezaq was sentenced to life imprisonment following

his conviction, id. at 1127.

15 *United States v. Yunis*, 924 F.2d 1086, 1089-90 (D.C.Cir. 1991). Yunis was charged with conspiracy (18 U.S.C. 371); hostage taking (18 U.S.C. 1203); air piracy (49 U.S.C. App. 1472(n)(1988 ed.)); violence aboard an aircraft (18 U.S.C. 32(b)(1)); damaging an aircraft (18 U.S.C. 32(b)(2)); and placing a destructive device on an aircraft (18 U.S.C. 32(b)(3)). He was convicted of all but the section 32 offenses and sentenced to concurrent sentences of imprisonment for 30 years (hostage taking), 20 years (air piracy), and 5 years (conspiracy).

[16] *United States v. Rashed,* 83 F.Supp.2d 96, 100 (D.D.C. 1999). Rashed was initially charged with conspiracy to commit murder (18 U.S.C. 1117); murder (18 U.S.C. 1111); damaging an aircraft (18 U.S.C. 32); destroying property with an explosive (18 U.S.C. 844(i)); placing a bomb on an aircraft intended for foreign transportation (49 U.S.C. 1472(l)(2)1988 ed.)); and assault (18 U.S.C. 113), *id.* He subsequently pleaded guilty to the conspiracy and murder charges under a plea agreement which called for him to serve 25 years in prison, Department of Justice, *Press Release* (Mar. 24, 2006), available at http://www.justice.gov/opa/pr/2006/March/06_crm_172.html.

[17] *United States v. Reid,* 369 F.3d 619, 619-20 (1st Cir. 2004). Reid attempted to destroy an American Airline aircraft in flight between Paris and Miami, using explosives hidden in his shoes. He was charged with an attack on mass transit (18 U.S.C. 1993 (2000 ed.); attempted use of a weapon of mass destruction (18 U.S.C. 2332a(a)(1)); attempted homicide (18 U.S.C. 2332(b)(1)); placing an explosive device on board an aircraft (49 U.S.C. 46505); attempted murder (49 U.S.C. 456506(1) and 18 U.S.C. 1113); interfering with an airline flight crew and attendants (49 U.S.C. 46504); attempted destruction of an aircraft (18 U.S.C. 32(a)); and using a destructive device during and in relation to a crime of violence(18 U.S.C. 924(c)). He pleaded guilty to and was sentenced to life imprisonment for each of the offenses with which he was charged other than alleged violation of 18 U.S.C. 1993 which was only later amended to include attacks on air transportation (now amended as 18 U.S.C. 1992).

[18] Abdulmutallab was charged with attempting to destroy a Northwest Airline aircraft in flight between Amsterdam and Detroit, using explosives hidden in his underwear. More specifically, the indictment charged him with attempted use of a weapon of mass destruction (18 U.S.C. 2332a(a)(2)); attempted murder (49 U.S.C. 456506(1) and 18 U.S.C. 1113); attempted destruction of an aircraft (18 U.S.C. 32(a)(1), (2), (8)); and using a destructive device during and in relation
to a crime of violence, (18 U.S.C. 924(c)(1)(A), (c)(1)(B)(ii)), INDICTMENT, *United States v. Abdulmutallab*, 2:10-cr-
2005 (E.D. Mich. (S.D) Jan. 6, 2010).

[19] Moussaoui pleaded guilty to being a co-conspirator in the 9/11 terrorist attacks and was sentenced to six terms of life imprisonment. His plea covered charges for conspiracy to commit acts of terrorism transcending national boundaries (18 U.S.C. 2332b(a)(2) and (6)); conspiracy to commit air piracy (18 U.S.C. 46502(a)(1)(A) and (a)(2)(B)); conspiracy to destroy aircraft (18 U.S.C. 32(a)(7) and 34); conspiracy to use weapons of mass destruction (18 U.S.C. 2332a(a)); conspiracy to murder federal employees (18 U.S.C. 1114, 1117); and conspiracy to use explosives to destroy property used in or whose use affects the interstate or foreign commerce of the United States (18 U.S.C. 844(f), (i), (n)), *United States v. Moussaoui,* ___ F.3d ____, ____ (4th Cir. Jan. 4, 2010).

[20] *United States v. Abu Ali,* 528 F.3d 210, 225 (4th Cir. 2008). Abu Ali, an American, was charged with, convicted of,
and sentenced to imprisonment for 30 years, for violation of: 18 U.S.C. 49 U.S.C. 46502(a)(2)(conspiracy to commit air piracy); 18 U.S.C. 32(b)(4) (conspiracy to destroy aircraft); and several unrelated terrorism offenses, *id.*

[21] Other related chapter 2 offenses include imparting or conveying false information (18 U.S.C. 35), violence at international airports (18 U.S.C. 37), and fraud involving aircraft parts (18 U.S.C. 38).

[22] 18 U.S.C. 32(a)(1), (8).

[23] 18 U.S.C. 32(b).

[24] 18 U.S.C. 31(a)(1).

[25] 18 U.S.C. 31(a)(2).

[26] 18 U.S.C. 31(a)(3).

[27] 18 U.S.C. 31(a)(4).

[28] 18 U.S.C. 31(a)(5).

[29] 18 U.S.C. 31(a)(6).

[30] 18 U.S.C. 31(a)(7).

[31] 18 U.S.C. 31(a)(8).

[32] 18 U.S.C. 32(b)(1).

[33] 18 U.S.C. 32(b)(2).

[34] 18 U.S.C. 32(b)(3).

[35] 18 U.S.C. 32(b)(4).

[36] *United States v. Yousef,* 327 F.3d 56, 80-1 (2d Cir. 2003).

[37] *Id.* at 80. Charges in the airline bombing case included violations of 18 U.S.C. 32(a)(1), (7)[now (8)](attempting to destroy an aircraft within the special aircraft jurisdiction of the United States); 18 U.S.C. 32(a)(2), (7)[now (8)](attempting to place a bomb on such aircraft); 18 U.S.C. 32(b)(3) (placing a bomb on a foreign flagged aircraft); 18 U.S.C. 2332(b), (d)(conspiring to kill Americans outside the U.S.); 18 U.S.C. 2332a (conspiracy to use a weapon of mass destruction against Americans outside the U.S.); 18 U.S.C. 924(c), 2 (aiding, abetting, or commanding another's using and carrying a bomb during and in connection with a crime of violence), *id.* at 83-4.

[38] *United States v. Reid*, 206 F.Supp.2d 132, 142 (D.Mass. 2002).

[39] 18 U.S.C. 1992(a)(1), (d)(16).

[40] 18 U.S.C. 1992(a)(2).

[41] 18 U.S.C. 1992(a)(3).

[42] 18 U.S.C. 1992(a)(4).

[43] 18 U.S.C. 1992(a)(6).

[44] 18 U.S.C. 1992(a)(7).

[45] 18 U.S.C. 1992(a)(8).

[46] 18 U.S.C. 1992(a)(9).

[47] 18 U.S.C. 1992(a)(10).

[48] *United States v. Reid*, 369 F.3d 619, 619-20 (1st Cir. 2004)(18 U.S.C. 924(c), 2332a); INDICTMENT, *United States v. Abdulmutallab*, 2:10-cr-2005 (E.D. Mich. (S.D) Jan. 6, 2010)(18 U.S.C. 924(c), 2332a); *United States v. Yousef*, 327 F.3d 56, 80 (2d Cir. 2003)(18 U.S.C. 924(c), 2332a); *United States v. Moussaoui*, ___ F.3d ____, ____ (4th Cir. Jan. 4, 2010)(18 U.S.C. 844, 2332a); *United States v. Rashed,* 83 F.Supp.2d 96, 100 (D.D.C. 1999)(18 U.S.C. 844).

[49] 18 U.S.C. 2332a(a), (b).

[50] 18 U.S.C. 2332a(c)(2)(A), 921(4)(A).

[51] 18 U.S.C. 844(i), (n).

[52] 18 U.S.C. 924(c), 921(3), (4).

[53] *United States v. Reid*, 369 F.3d 619, 619-20 (1st Cir. 2004); *United States v. Yousef*, 327 F.3d 56, 80 (2d Cir. 2003).

Section 2332 also condemns manslaughter, conspiracy to kill, or other crimes of physical violence when committed against an American overseas for terrorist purposes.

[54] *United States v. Moussaoui*, ___ F.3d ____, ____ (4th Cir. Jan. 4, 2010); *United States v. Yunis*, 924 F.2d 1086, 1089-

90 (D.C.Cir. 1991). Section 2332b prohibits acts of terrorism transcending national boundaries when they involving killing, kidnapping, maiming, seriously assaulting someone in the United States; or dangerously damaging or destroy property here (on attempting or conspiring to do so).

[55] 18 U.S.C. 1114, 111. 18 U.S.C. 115 also protects the families of such individuals, former federal officers and employees, and members of their families from murder, manslaughter, and assault – during or because of the performance of official duties.

[56] *United States v. Felix-Guiterrez*, 940 F.2d 1200, 1204-206 (9th Cir. 1991); *United States v. Benitez*, 741 F.2d 1312,

1316-317, (11th Cir. 1984).

[57] 18 U.S.C. 1751.

[58] 18 U.S.C. 351, 1116, 112.

[59] 18 U.S.C. 1751(k), 351(i), 1116(c).

[60] Other than attempt to commit an assault; 18 U.S.C. 1114(3); 1117 (conspiracy to violation sections 1114 or 1116); 1751(c), (d); 351(c), (d); 115(a), (b)(3); 371 (conspiracy to commit any federal offense).

[61] 18 U.S.C. 2.

[62] *Nye & Nissen v. United States*, 336 U.S. 613, 619 (1949); *United States v. Tagg*, 572 F.3d 1320, 1324(11th Cir.

2009); *United States v. Carbo*, 572 F.3d 112, 118 (3d Cir. 2009).

[63] *United States v. Snype*, 441 F.3d 119, 142 (2d Cir. 2006); see also *United States v. Montgomery*, 384 F.3d 1050, 1059

(9th Cir. 2004).

[64] 18 U.S.C. 2.

[65] *United States v. Caldwell*, 433 F.3d 378, 390 (4th Cir. 2005); see also *United States v. Hale*, 448 F.3d 971, 982 (7th

Cir. 2006).

[66] 18 U.S.C. 32(a)(8), 32(b)(4).
[67] 18 U.S.C. 3281.
[68] 18 U.S.C. 3282.
[69] 18 U.S.C. 3286, 3281
[70] 18 U.S.C. 3290.
[71] 18 U.S.C. 3142(e), (f).
[72] U.S.S.G. §3A1.4.
[73] 18 U.S.C. 3583(j), (b).
[74] For a general discussion of federal extraterritorial criminal jurisdiction see *Extraterritorial Application of American Criminal Law*, CRS Rept. 94-166.
[75] 18 U.S.C. 2; cf., *United States v. Yousef*, 327 F.3d 56, 84-8 (2d Cir. 2003).
[76] *United States v. Felix-Gutierrez*, 940 F.2d 1200, 1205 (9th Cir. 1991).
[77] *United States v. Yousef*, 327 F.3d at 87-8; *Brulay v. United States*, 383 F.2d 345, 349-50 (9th Cir. 19967).
[78] Cf., *United States v. Felix-Gutierrez*, 940 F.2d at 1205.
[79] *Id.*
[80] *id.*

In: Terrorists, Enemy Combatant Detainees …
Editors: Jian Sun and Miguel Masipag

ISBN: 978-1-61470-391-4

Chapter 5

TERRORISM, *MIRANDA*, AND RELATED MATTERS*

Charles Doyle

SUMMARY

The Fifth Amendment to the United States Constitution provides in part that "No person ... shall be compelled in any criminal case to be a witness against himself, nor be deprived of life, liberty, or property, without due process of law." In *Miranda v. Arizona*, the Supreme Court declared that statements of an accused, given during a custodial interrogation, could not be introduced in evidence in criminal proceedings against him, unless he were first advised of his rights and waived them. In *Dickerson v. United States*, the Court held that the *Miranda* exclusionary rule was constitutionally grounded and could not be replaced by a statutory provision making all voluntary confessions admissible. In *New York v. Quarles*, the Court recognized a "limited" "public safety" exception to *Miranda*, but has not defined the exception further. The lower federal courts have construed the exception narrowly in cases involving unwarned statements concerning the location of a weapon possibly at hand at the time of an arrest.

The Supreme Court has yet to decide to what extent *Miranda* applies to custodial interrogations conducted overseas. The lower federal courts have held that the failure of foreign law enforcement officials to provide *Miranda* warnings prior to interrogation does not preclude use of any resulting statement in a subsequent U.S. criminal trial, unless interrogation was a joint venture of U.S. and foreign officials or unless the circumstances shock the conscience of the court. They suggest that warnings are a prerequisite for admissibility in U.S. courts following overseas interrogation by U.S. officials.

Miranda applies to courts-martial that are subject to a requirement for an additional warning under the Uniform Code of Military Justice. The statutory provisions governing military commissions call for the admission of some unwarned, involuntary custodial statements. At least one tribunal operating under those provisions has concluded that the Fifth Amendment protections do not apply in the commission trial at Guantanamo Bay of an unprivileged foreign belligerent.

Rule 5 of the Federal Rules of Criminal Procedure requires that federal arrestees be brought before a committing magistrate without unnecessary delay. In the *McNabb v.*

* This is an edited, reformatted and augmented version of a Congressional Research Service publication, CRS Report for Congress R41252, from www.crs.gov, dated May 24, 2010.

United States and *Mallory v. United States* cases, the Court declared inadmissible confessions extracted during a period of unnecessary delay. The cases were decided under the Court's supervisory authority over the lower federal courts, and in *Corley v. United States,* the Court held that *McNabb-Mallory* had been statutorily supplemented with a provision that made admissible voluntary confession given within six hours of presentment.

Neither *Miranda* nor *McNabb-Mallory* violations preclude the subsequent prosecution of the accused; they simply preclude the uninvited use of any unwarned, unwaived statements in such prosecutions.

Related legislative proposals have been introduced in the 111th Congress. P.L. 111-84 (H.R. 2647) prohibits members of the military from providing *Miranda* warnings to foreign nationals captured, or held in Defense Department custody, outside the United States as enemy belligerents. Among the legislative proposals yet to secure enactment, one would prohibit the use of funds to provide such warnings (H.R. 2701); others would restrict their use in the interrogation of high-value detainees overseas (S. 3081 and H.R. 4892); and still others would call upon the Administration to provide Congress with information related to the use of *Miranda* warnings in such circumstances (H.R. 3170, H.Res. 537, H.Res. 570, H.Res. 602).

INTRODUCTION

In *Miranda v. Arizona*, the Supreme Court held that no statement made by an individual during a custodial interrogation may be admitted into evidence against him at his criminal trial, unless he was first warned of his relevant constitutional rights and waived them.[1] In *New York v. Quarles*, the Court later held that the *Miranda* rule was subject to a "public safety" exception.[2] Throughout this period, federal law stated that following arrest a suspect should be presented to a magistrate and advised of his rights without "unnecessary delay."[3] Confessions made during the course of any unnecessary delay are generally inadmissible at the suspect's subsequent criminal trial.[4] The realities of contemporary terrorism are such that some have questioned whether these general rules can be, and should be, re-examined and adjusted.

BACKGROUND

Miranda

Before *Miranda*, the Supreme Court relied on the Fifth Amendment in federal cases, but had largely relied upon due process guarantees to exclude a defendant's involuntary confession from his criminal trial in cases that came to it from the states.[5] Then, as now, the due process inquiry asks "whether a defendant's will was overborne by the circumstances surrounding the giving of a confession."[6] Recourse to due process was no longer necessary in state cases once it became clear that the Fifth Amendment right was itself binding on the states through the Fourteenth Amendment.[7]

In *Miranda*, the Court provided a more specific standard than the "voluntary under the circumstances" due process test. Convinced that the coercive atmosphere of a law enforcement custodial interrogation could undermine the protection against self-incrimination,[8] the Court declared that confessions that followed such interrogations could only be admitted in evidence against a defendant if he had been given explicit warnings beforehand.[9] That is, the defendant must be warned that he "has the right to remain silent, that anything he says can be used against him in a court of law, that he has the right to the presence of an attorney, and that if he cannot afford an attorney one will be appointed for him prior to any questioning if he so desires."[10]

The warnings having been given, the defendant may explicitly waive them.[11] When a defendant requests the presence of an attorney, questioning must stop until one is made available or until the defendant himself initiates the colloquy.[12] Authorities may not avoid *Miranda* demands by extracting an unwarned confession, providing the *Miranda* warnings, and then eliciting the same confession, this time "for the record."[13] Nor may authorities persistently return to questioning after an interrogation has been stopped by a defendant's claim of privilege—except upon the arrival of requested defense counsel, at the defendant's invitation, or following a break in interrogation-related custody of at least 14 days.[14]

The Court has recognized exceptions to the rule. One, discussed below in greater detail, permits admission into evidence of unwarned statements elicited in the interest of an officer's safety and that of the public.[15] Another permits use of unwarned statements for impeachment purposes.[16] Moreover, on a number of occasions, the Court has declined to recognize a *Miranda* equivalent of the Fourth Amendment's "fruit of the poisonous tree" doctrine.[17]

Shortly after *Miranda* was handed down, Congress sought to overturn it by statute, 18 U.S.C. 3501.[18] For three decades, however, the provision lay dormant, for the Justice Department considered the provision constitutionally suspect, and would not assert it.[19] Thus, when *Dickerson v. United States* arose in the Fourth Circuit, the Justice Department declined to defend the section's constitutionality.[20] In spite of Justice Department reservations, the Fourth Circuit decided that section "3501, rather than *Miranda*, governs the admissibility of confessions in federal court."[21] The Supreme Court disagreed.[22] "*Miranda* announced a constitutional rule," which the Court declined to overrule and which "Congress may not supersede legislatively."[23]

Public Safety Exception

In *Quarles*, police officers pursued a rape suspect into a supermarket, frisked him, discovered he was wearing an empty holster, and handcuffed him.[24] They asked him where the gun was; he told them, "the gun is over there" (nodding to some empty cartons); they arrested him, and then read him his *Miranda* warnings.[25] The Supreme Court recognized that the "case presents a situation where concern for public safety must be paramount to adherence to the literal language of the prophylactic rules enumerated in *Miranda*."[26]

It contrasted the *Miranda* concerns with the exigencies of the case before it. On one hand, "[t]he *Miranda* decision was based in large part on this Court's view that the warnings which it required police to give to suspects in custody would reduce the likelihood that the suspects would fall victim to constitutionally impermissible practices of police interrogation in the presumptively coercive environment of the station house."[27] On the other hand, "[t]he police in this case ... were confronted with the immediate necessity of ascertaining the whereabouts of a gun which they had every reason to believe the suspect had just removed from his empty holster and discarded in the supermarket. So long as the gun was concealed somewhere in the supermarket, with its actual whereabouts unknown, it obviously posed more than one danger to the public safety."[28] The Court perceived the exception as a "narrow" one, and believed police would have no difficulty distinguishing "between questions necessary to secure their own safety or the safety of the public and questions designed solely to elicit testimonial evidence from a suspect."[29]

The Court has yet to further refine the exception, but the lower federal appellate courts have construed it narrowly—some more narrowly than others.[30] It has been applied in cases immediately following an arrest when officers have asked an unwarned suspect whether or where a weapon might be found in the immediate area, under circumstances when officers might reasonably believe such a weapon exists and if not secured would pose a danger to themselves or the public.[31]

Although the public safety exception, as currently understood, may only be available in limited circumstances in a terrorist context, its existence suggests that the Court might expand its application under compelling circumstances or might recognize other policy-based exceptions to *Miranda*.[32]

Miranda Overseas

The Supreme Court has thus far not indicated to what extent, if at all, *Miranda* applies overseas. In fact, it has spoken only infrequently about the extent to which the Fifth Amendment applies outside the United States. Its most recent discussion occurred in *Verdugo-Urquidez* when it contrasted the difference between the extraterritorial application of the Fourth and Fifth Amendments.[33] There, it noted a violation of the Fifth Amendment privilege against self-incrimination can only occur at trial; a violation of the Fourth Amendment occurs upon the performance of an unreasonable search or seizure—regardless of whether the fruits of the violation are ever offered at trial.[34] For Fifth Amendment purposes, the point of violation is not the place where a statement was coerced, but the place of the criminal proceedings where the statement is offered against the defendant.[35] The Court went on to point out that it previously "rejected the claim that aliens are entitled to Fifth Amendment rights outside the sovereign territory of the United States."[36] Moreover, even where it had recognized that American civilians, subject to U.S. overseas court-martial proceedings, were entitled to some Fifth and Sixth Amendment protections, a majority of the Court had been unwilling to define the precise scope of such entitlement.[37]

The lower federal courts, however, have held that the *Miranda* warnings ordinarily do not apply to overseas custodial interrogations conducted by foreign officials. Such unwarned statements may be introduced against the defendant, if voluntary and otherwise admissible.[38] They often identify, but rarely find, two exceptions to this general rule of admissibility—where the interrogation is a joint venture in which U.S. officials are joint participants, or where the circumstances shock the conscience of the court.[39]

Implicit in the first exception is that the privilege against self-incrimination—and the attendant *Miranda* requirements—apply to the admissibility in criminal proceedings in this country of statements taken overseas by U.S. law enforcement officers.[40] A few courts have suggested that this may be said of the statements of U.S. citizens and foreign nationals alike.[41] They have indicated, however, that "where *Miranda* has been applied to overseas interrogations by U.S. agents, it has been so applied in a flexible fashion to accommodate the exigencies of the local conditions."[42]

In a case in which overseas statements were offered before an overseas tribunal, a military commission tribunal has concluded that the question of the application of the Fifth Amendment extraterritorially requires a case-by-case consideration.[43]

Miranda and the Military

As a general rule, *Miranda* applies to custodial interrogations conducted in the course of a military criminal investigation. Both by constitutional imperative and statutory command, unwarned statements are inadmissible against the defendant in any subsequent military prosecution.[44]

The statutory provisions applicable to military commissions, however, declare that the Article 831(a), (b), and (d) of the Code of Military Justice (10 U.S.C. 831(a), (b), and (d), relating to compulsory self-incrimination) shall not apply in commission trials.[45] No one may be required to testify against himself in such proceedings.[46] Nor may statements secured by torture or by cruel, inhuman, or degrading treatment be admitted there.[47] Otherwise, statements of the accused may be admitted in evidence, if they are reliable, probative, and either voluntary or were "made incident to lawful conduct during military operations at the point of capture or during closely related active combat engagement, and the interests of justice would best be served by admission of the statement into evidence."[48]

One of the Guantanamo detainees, tried by military commission for the offense of providing material support for terrorism, moved to suppress statements which he contended were secured in violation of the Fifth Amendment.[49] Based on its reading of *Boumediene*,[50] the tribunal determined that

> when analyzing the extraterritorial application of the Constitution in Guantanamo Bay, the Commission concludes that it should consider (1) the citizenship and status of the detainee and the adequacy of the process through which the status determination was made; (2) the nature of the sites where apprehension and then detention took place; (3) whether practical considerations and exigent circumstances counsel against application of the constitutional right; (4) whether the Executive has provided the accused an adequate substitute for the Constitutional right being sought; (5) whether there is "necessity for the Constitution to apply to prevent injustice; and (6) whether application of the Constitutional right would be "impractical and anomalous."[51]

It further concluded that "[t]he preponderance of these factors analyzed weighs against application of the 5th Amendment in Guantanamo Bay."[52]

McNabb-Mallory

"[T]he rule known simply as *McNabb-Mallory* generally renders inadmissible confessions made during periods of detention that violate the prompt presentment requirement of Rule 5(a)."[53] In *McNabb v. United States*, the Supreme Court was faced with a case in which federal officers had disregarded statutory obligations to promptly present arrested defendants to a committing magistrate.[54] The officers had instead detained and interrogated the suspects over the course of several days, until the confessions upon which the defendants' convictions were based had been extracted.[55] The Court found it "unnecessary to reach the Constitutional issues pressed upon" it.[56] Based instead on its supervisory authority over the federal courts, the Court announced that henceforth such confessions, voluntary or involuntary, secured without regard to prompt presentation requirements could not be admitted in evidence against a defendant.[57]

When the various statutory presentation requirements were later superseded by rule 5(a) of the Federal Rules of Criminal Procedure (requiring presentation "without unnecessary delay"), no explicit mention was made of either the *McNabb* exclusionary rule or any other means of enforcement.[58] The Court, however, quickly affirmed the continued vitality of *McNabb* when following the promulgation of rule 5; it reiterated that *McNabb* applied to both voluntary and involuntary confessions.[59] In *Mallory*, it made clear that any "delay must not be of as a nature to give opportunity for the extraction of confession."[60]

A second provision within section 3501 addresses the *McNabb-Mallory* rule, 18 U.S.C. 3501(c). It states that a presentation delay of less than six hours does not by itself render a voluntary confession inadmissible. Recently, the question arose whether, as with *Miranda*, section 3501 was intended to abrogate the *McNabb-Mallory*, rather than to simply limit its application to voluntary confessions made within six hours of detention.[61] The Court held that Congress intended to modify, not repudiate, *McNabb-Mallory*.[62] Thus, "[u]nder the rule as revised by §3501(c), a district court with a suppression claim must find whether the defendant confessed within six hours of arrest (unless a longer delay was reasonable considering the means of transportation and the distance to be traveled to the nearest available magistrate)."[63] If so, the confession is admissible as section 3501(c) provides, "so long as it was made voluntarily and the weight to be given it is left to the jury."[64] If not, "the court must decide whether delaying that long was unreasonable or unnecessary under the *McNabb-Mallory* cases, and if it was, the confession is to be suppressed."[65]

Legislative Proposals

A number of related legislative proposals have been introduced thus far in the 111th Congress. They include:

P.L. 111-84

Section 1040 of the National Defense Authorization Act for Fiscal Year 2010, P.L. 111-84 (H.R. 2647), 123 Stat. 2454 (2009), prohibits members of the Armed Forces as well as Defense Department officers and employees from providing *Miranda* warnings to foreign nationals captured, or held in Defense Department custody, outside the United States as enemy belligerents. The prohibition does not apply to the Justice Department. The section also directs the Secretary of Defense to report to the Armed Services Committees within 90 days on the impact of providing the warnings to detainees in Afghanistan.

H.R. 2701

Section 504 of the Intelligence Authorization Act for Fiscal Year 2010 (H.R. 2701), as reported out of the House Select Committee on Intelligence (H.Rept. 111-186), would prohibit the use of funds authorized for appropriation under the bill to provide *Miranda* warnings to foreign nationals outside the United States who are either in the custody of the Armed Forces or believed to have terrorist-related information. The House passed H.R. 2701, as amended, on February 26, 2010, 156 *Cong. Rec.* H946 (daily ed. February 26, 2010).

H.R. 3170

Section 744 of Financial Services and General Government Appropriations Act, 2010 (H.R. 3170), as reported out of the House Appropriations Committee (H.Rept. 111-202), would call upon the Administration to supply Congress with information relating to *Miranda* warnings provided by the Justice Department to foreign nationals who are either in the custody of the Armed Forces or suspected of terrorism. The Consolidated Appropriations Act, 2010, P.L. 111- 117, 123 Stat. 3034 (2009), which absorbed many of the provisions of H.R. 3170, has no comparable provision.

S. 3081

Section 3(b)(3) of the Enemy Belligerent Interrogation, Detention, and Prosecution Act of 2010 (S. 3081), as introduced, would direct that an unprivileged belligerent, interrogated under the bill's procedures relating to high-value detainees, not be given *Miranda* or comparable warnings.

H.R. 4892

Section 3(a)(1)(D) of the Enemy Belligerent Interrogation, Detention, and Prosecution Act of 2010 (H.R. 4892), as introduced, would require the approval of the Director of National Intelligence before *Miranda* warnings could be provided to high-value detainees believed to have terrorism-related information and captured, held, or questioned by an entity with an intelligence community element.

H.Res. 537

H.Res. 537, as adversely reported by the House Judiciary Committee (H.Rept. 111-189), would call upon the Administration to supply Congress with information relating to *Miranda* warnings provided by the Justice Department to foreign nationals who are in the custody of the Armed Forces in Afghanistan and suspected of terrorism.

H.Res. 570

H.Res. 570 would direct the Secretary of Homeland Security to provide the House with information relating to the immigration status of any foreign national captured in Afghanistan who was given *Miranda* warnings by the Justice Department, is in the Defense Department's custody, may be suspected of terrorism, and may be subject to a transfer or release into the United States for civilian or military proceedings.

H.Res. 602

H.Res. 602 would call upon the Administration to provide the House with information, generated on or after January 1, 2005, and relating to the impact of providing *Miranda* warnings to Defense Department detainees in Afghanistan suspected of terrorism.

End Notes

[1] 384 U.S. 436, 468 (1966).
[2] 467 U.S. 649, 655-56 (1984).
[3] F.R.Crim.P. 5(a).
[4] *Mallory v. United States*, 354 U.S. 449, 455 (1957); see also, *McNabb v. United States*, 318 U.S. 332, 345 (1943); *Corley v. United States*, 129 S.Ct. 1558, 1566 (2009); 18 U.S.C. 3501(c).
[5] *Dickerson v. United States*, 530 U.S. 428, 433(2000), citing inter alia *Bram v. United States*, 168 U.S. 532, 542 (1897) and *Brown v. Mississippi*, 297 U.S. 278 (1936), and noting that "Over time, our cases recognized two constitutional bases for the requirement that a confession be voluntary to be admitted into evidence: the Fifth Amendment right against self-incrimination and the Due Process Clause of the Fourteenth Amendment."
[6] *Dickerson v. United States*, 530 U.S. at 434, citing *Schneckloth v. Bustamonte*, 412 U.S. 218, 226 (1973); see also, *Brown v. Mississippi*, 297 U.S. at 287 ("Coercing the supposed state's criminals into confessions and using such confession so coerced from them against them in trials has been the curse of all countries. It was the chief inequity, the crowning infamy of the Star Chamber, and the Inquisition, and other similar institutions. The constitution recognized the evils that lay behind these practices and prohibited them in this country.... In the instance case, the trial court was fully advised by the undisputed evidence of the way in which the confessions had been procured.... The conviction and sentence were void for want of the essential elements of due process").
[7] *Dickerson v. United States*, 530 U.S. at 434 (parallel citations omitted) ("We have never abandoned this due process jurisprudence, and thus continue to exclude confessions that were obtained involuntarily. But our decisions in *Malloy v. Hogan*, 378 U.S. 1 (1964), and *Miranda* changed the focus of much of the inquiry in determining the admissibility of suspects' incriminating statements. In *Malloy*, we held that the Fifth Amendment's Self-Incrimination Clause is incorporated in the Due Process Clause of the Fourteenth Amendment and thus applies to the States. 378 U.S. at 6-11. We decided *Miranda* on the heels of *Malloy*.").
[8] *Miranda v. Arizona*, 384 U.S. 436, 445-58 (1966).
[9] *Id.* at 467.
[10] *Id.* at 479.
[11] *Id.* at 475.
[12] *Edwards v. Arizona*, 451 U.S. 436, 477-78 (1981).
[13] *Missouri v. Seibert*, 542 U.S. 600, 617 (2004).
[14] *Maryland v. Shatzer*, 130 S.Ct. 1213, 1219-224 (2010).
[15] *New York v. Quarles*, 467 U.S. 649 (1984).
[16] *Harris v. New York*, 401 U.S. 222 (1971).
[17] *United States v. Patane*, 542 U.S. 630, 631-33 (2004); *Oregon v. Elstad*, 470 U.S. 298, 318 (1985); *Michigan v. Tucker*, 417 U.S. 433, 451-52 (1974).

[18] S.Rept. 90-1097, at 51 (1968) ("The committee feels that it is obvious from the opinion of Justice Harlan and other dissenting Justices ... that the overwhelming weight of judicial opinion in this country is that the voluntariness test does not offend the Constitution.... [T]he *Miranda* decision itself was by a bare majority of one, and with increasing frequency the Supreme Court has reversed itself. The committee feels that by the time the issue of constitutionality would reach the Supreme Court, the probability rather is that his legislation would be upheld....The need for a revision of the *Miranda* decision has been well documented in the proceeding section of this report.").

[19] *Davis v. United States*, 512 U.S. 452, 463-64 (Scalia, J., concurring) ("In fact, with limited exceptions the provision [18 U.S.C. 3501(a)] has been studiously avoided by every Administration, not only in this Court but in the lower courts, since its enactment more than 25 years ago. See Office of Legal Policy, U.S. Dept. of Justice, Report to Attorney General on Law of Pre-Trial Interrogation 72-73 (1986) (discussing '[t]he abortive implementation of §3501' after its passage in 1968)."); *United States v. Dickerson*, 166 F.3d 667, 682 (4th Cir. 1999) ("The Department of Justice has taken the position that unless the Supreme Court overrules *Miranda*, 'the United States is not free to urge the lower courts' to 'rely on Section 3501.' See Letter from John C. Keeney, Acting Assistant Attorney General, to all United States Attorneys and all Criminal Division Section Chiefs (Nov. 6, 1997).").

[20] *Id.* at 680-82.

[21] *Id.* at 692.

[22] *Dickerson v. United States*, 530 U.S. 428, 438 (2000).

[23] *Id.* at 444.

[24] 467 U.S. 649, 651-52 (1984).

[25] *Id.* at 652.

[26] *Id.* at 653.

[27] *id.* at 656.

[28] *Id.* at 657.

[29] *Id.*

[30] *Matters of Public Safety and the Current Quarrel Over the Scope of the* Quarles *Exception to* Miranda, 78 FORDHAM LAW REVIEW 1931, 1931 (2010) ("However, latent ambiguity arising from the *Quarles* decision authored by [then] Justice William Rehnquist has resulted in a split among the federal courts of appeals as to what constitutes a 'public safety threat.' Some courts broadly extend the *Quarles* exception to inherently dangerous situations, including the threat of an officer mishandling an undiscovered weapon. Other courts narrowly apply *Quarles* to exigent circumstances where there is actual evidence that a suspect or other third party could inflict immediate harm to officers or the public.").

[31] *United States v. Are*, 590 F.3d 499, 506 (7th Cir. 2009) ("We, too, have concluded that questioning a suspect about whether he has a gun may fall within *Quarles*' public safety exception.... The FBI agent's question to Daniels about the presence of a weapon in the house falls within the public safety exception to *Miranda*. The question seemed reasonably prompted by a concern for the public safety. Though Daniels was cuffed and the officers and agents had conducted a brief protective sweep, they knew ... he had several prior drug and weapons offenses. But they did not know the location of any weapon that he may have had in the house. A weapon might have been hidden near the place where the officers placed Daniels before taking him outside and thus would have been within his reach.... Furthermore, the presence of Daniels' wife and children bolsters the conclusion that the question about the weapon falls within the public safety exception."); *United States v. Jackson*, 544 F.3d 351, 360 n.9 (1st Cir. 2008) ("The government also argues that the statements at the apartment are admissible, even if they were the product of custodial interrogation, under the public safety exception to *Miranda*'s suppression requirement. The government's contention is without merit. The gun, stuffed inside a cereal box in the refrigerator, was clearly outside of the reach of Jackson, who was not even in the apartment and, in any event, was surrounded by a number of police officers."); *United States v. Liddell*, 517 F.3d 1007, 1011-12 (8th Cir. 2008) ("As I read *Quarles*, the public safety exception to *Miranda* applies only when (1) an immediate danger to the police officers or the public exists, or (2) when the public may later come upon a weapon and thereby create an immediately dangerous situation."); *United States v. Williams*, 483 F.3d 425, 429 (6th Cir. 2007) ("An officer may rely on the public safety exception only if he has a[n] objectively reasonable belief that he is in danger."); *United States v. DeJear*, 552 F.3d 1196, 1201 (10th 2009) (citing *Williams* with approval); see also *United States v. Spoerke*, 568 F.3d 1236, 1249 (11th Cir. 2009); *United States v. Jones*, 567 F.3d 712, 714-17 (D.C.Cir. 2009); *United States v. Reyes*, 353 F.3d 148, 152-55 (2d Cir. 2003).

[32] Cf., *In re Terrorist Bombings of U.S. Embassies in East Africa*, 552 F.3d 177, 203 (2d Cir. 2008)("*Miranda*'s public
safety exception would likely apply overseas with no less force than it does domestically. When exigent circumstances compel an un-warned interrogation in order to protect the public, *Miranda* would not impair the government's ability to obtain that information. Second, we emphasize that the *Miranda* framework governs only the admission of custodial statements at U.S. trials. In so far as U.S. agents do not seek to introduce statements obtained through overseas custodial interrogations at U.S. trials").

[33] *United States v. Verdugo-Urquidez*, 494 U.S. 259, 264-74 (1990).

[34] *Id.* at 264.

[35] *Id.* ("The privilege against self-incrimination guaranteed by the Fifth Amendment is a fundamental trial right to criminal defendants. Although conduct by law enforcement officials prior to trial may ultimately impair that right, a constitutional violation occurs only at trial.")

[36] *Id.* at 269, citing *Johnson v. Eisentrager*, 339 U.S. 763 (1950).

[37] *Id.* at 269-70, citing *Reid v. Covert*, 354 U.S. 1, 75 (1957) (Harlan, J., concurring in the result).

[38] *United States v. Frank*, 599 F.3d 1221, 1228 (11th Cir. 2010); *United States v. Abu Ali*, 528 F.3d 210, 227 (4th Cir. 2008); *United States v. Yousef*, 327 F.3d 56, 145 (2d Cir. 2003); *United States v. Heller*, 625 F.2d 594, 599 (5th Cir. 1980); *United States v. Mundt*, 508 F.2d 904, 906 (10th Cir. 1974); *United States v. Chavarria*, 443 F.2d 904, 905 (9th Cir. 1971); *United States v. Mendes-Mesquita*, 541 F.Supp.2d 30, 34 (D.D.C. 2008); *United States v. Marzook*, 435 F.Supp.2d 708, 743 (N.D. Ill. 2006); *United States v. Ravine*, 11 M.J. 325, 329 (C.M.A. 1981).

[39] *United States v. Frank*, 599 F.3d at 1228-229; *United States v. Abu Ali*, 528 F.3d at 227-28; *United States v. Yousef*, 327 F.3d at 145-46; *United States v. Heller*, 625 F.2d at 599; *United States v. Mundt*, 508 F.2d at 906-907; *United States v. Karake*, 443 F.Supp.2d 8, 49 (D.D.C. 2006); *United States v. Marzook*, 435 F.Supp.2d at 743-44; *United States v. Jones*, 6 M.J. 226, 229 (C.M.A. 1979).

[40] Cf., *In re Terrorist Bombings*, 552 F.3d 177, 203 (2d Cir. 2008) ("Other circuits have explicitly recognized the applicability of *Miranda* to custodial statements elicited overseas through the active participation of U.S. agents. In light of these precedents, we are proceeding on the assumption that the *Miranda* 'warning/waiver' framework generally governs the admissibility in our domestic courts of custodial statements obtained by U.S. officials from individuals during their detention under the authority of foreign governments."), citing *United States v. Heller*, 625 F.2d 594, 599 (5th Cir. 1980) and *Pfeifer v. U.S. Bureau of Prisons*, 615 F.2d 873, 877 (9th Cir. 1980).

[41] *United States v. Clarke*, 611 F.Supp.2d 12, 29-30 (D.D.C. 2009) ("It is by now well-established that the Fifth Amendment privilege against self-incrimination protects nonresident aliens facing a criminal trial in the United States even where the questioning by United States authorities takes place abroad."), citing *In re Terrorist Bombings*, 552 F.3d at 198-201; *United States v. Yousef*, 327 F.3d at 145-46; *United States v. Straker*, 596 F.Supp.2d 80, 90 (D.D.C. 2009).

[42] *United States v. Clarke*, 611 F.Supp.2d at 30 (D.D.C. 2009), citing *In re Terrorist Bombings*, 552 F.3d at 204-205; *United States v. Dopf*, 434 F.2d 205, 207 (5th Cir. 1970); *Cranford v. Rodriguez*, 512 F.2d 860, 862-63 (10th Cir. 1975).

[43] *United States v. Hamdan*, 1 M.C.Rept. 121 (M.C. 2008), available at http://www.wcl.american.edu/nimj/military_commission.cfm.

[44] *United States v. Tempia*, 16 C.M.A. 629, 635-37 (1967); *United States v. DeLaRosa*, 67 M.J. 318, 320 (C.A.A.F. 2009) ("Prior to initiating interrogation, law enforcement officials must provide rights warnings to a person in custody. Military officials and civilians acting on their behalf are required to provide rights warnings prior to interrogating a member of the armed forces if that service member is a suspect, irrespective of custody."), citing *Miranda v. Arizona,* 384 U.S. 436, 445 (1966); *United States v. Tempia*, 16 C.M.A. 629, 637 (1967); U.S. Const. Amend. V; Article 31(b), USMJ (10 U.S.C. 831(b)), and Military Rules of Evidence 305(b)(1), 305(c).

[45] 10 U.S.C. 948b(d)(1)(B).

[46] 10 U.S.C. 948(b).

[47] 10 U.S.C. 948r(a) ("except against a person accused of torture or such treatment as evidence that the statement was made").

[48] 10 U.S.C. 948r(c), (d).

[49] *United States v. Hamdan*, 1 M.C.Rept. at 121. Hamdan sought to enjoin his trial by military commission. Without going to the merits, the court refused the injunction, but noted with regard to an earlier version of the admissibility of involuntary statements: "Another departure [from the standards that would apply in either U.S.

criminal trials or courts-martial], and a startling one, is that under 10 U.S.C. §948r(c), evidence obtained by 'coercion' may be used against the defendant so long as the military judge decides that its admission is in the interest of justice and that it has 'sufficient' probative value. *Compare Chambers v. Florida*, 309 U.S. 227 (1940) (reversing conviction and excluding evidence obtained through five days of coercive interrogation)," *Hamdan v. Gates*, 565 F.Supp.2d 130, 132 (D.D.C. 2008).

[50] *Boumediene v. Bush*, 128 S.Ct. 2229 (2008).

[51] *United States v. Hamdan*, 1 M.C.Rept. at 131.

[52] *Id.* at 134. A second military commission tribunal appears to have concluded as well that suppression issues should be resolved under commission rules—instructed, but not governed, by Fifth Amendment principles, *United States v. Jaward*, 1 M.C.Rept. 349, 350 n.5 (M.C. 2008) ("The Supreme Court's opinion in *Elstad* was based, in part, on the Fifth Amendment self-incrimination and warning requirements that were put in place in *Miranda v. Arizona*, 451 U.S. 471 (1966) as a practical reinforcement of those rights. While, in the case at bar, the accused's self-incrimination protections are set forth in M.C.R.E. 301 and M.C.R.E. 304, a reasonably similar *Elsad* analysis is appropriate with regard to the admissibility of confessions allegedly the product of coercion.").

[53] *Corley v. United States*, 129 S.Ct. 1558, 1563 (2009).

[54] 318 U.S. 332, 342-44 (1943), citing 18 U.S.C. 595, 593; and 5 U.S.C. 300a (1940 ed.).

[55] *Id.* at 334-38.

[56] *Id.* at 340.

[57] *Id.* at 349.

[58] F.R.Crim.P. 5(a), 18 U.S.C. App. (1946 ed.).

[59] *Upshaw v. United States*, 335 U.S. 410, 412 (1948).

[60] *Mallory v. United States*, 354 U.S. 449, 455 (1957); see also *Corley v. United States*, 129 S.Ct. 1558, 1563 (2009) ("delay for the purpose of interrogation is the epitome of 'unnecessary delay'"); *County of Riverside v. McLaughlin*, 500 U.S. 44, 61 (1991) (Scalia, J., dissenting) ("the only element bearing upon the reasonableness of delay was not such circumstances as the pressing need to conduct further investigation, but the arresting officer's ability, once the prisoner had been secured, to reach a magistrate.").

[61] *Corley v. United States*, 129 S.Ct. 1558 (2009).

[62] *Id.* at 1571.

[63] *Id.*

[64] *Id.*

[65] *Id.*

INDEX

#

A

B

C

D

E

F

G

H

I

J

K

L

M

N

O

P

Q

R

S

Y